狗的自述

马克·吐温短篇小说精选

名家导读有声版

英汉对照·插图版

[美] 马克·吐温 著
朱振武 主编
高静 张惠英 副主编

華東理工大學出版社
EAST CHINA UNIVERSITY OF SCIENCE AND TECHNOLOGY PRESS

图书在版编目(CIP)数据

狗的自述：马克·吐温短篇小说精选：英汉对照·名家导读有声版 / 朱振武主编. —上海：华东理工大学出版社, 2019.2
（经典短篇双语阅读）
ISBN 978-7-5628-5471-5

Ⅰ. ①狗…　Ⅱ. ①朱…　Ⅲ. ①英语-汉语-对照读物 ②短篇小说-小说集-美国-近代　Ⅳ. ①H319.4：Ⅰ

中国版本图书馆CIP数据核字(2018)第098523号

策划编辑 / 信　艳
责任编辑 / 赵楚月
装帧设计 / 风信子
插　　画 / 李　丹
出版发行 / 华东理工大学出版社有限公司
地址：上海市梅陇路130号，200237
电话：021-64250306
网址：www.ecustpress.cn
邮箱：zongbianban@ecustpress.cn
印　　刷 / 上海盛通时代印刷有限公司
开　　本 / 890mm × 1240mm　1/32
印　　张 / 10.5
字　　数 / 291千字
版　　次 / 2019年2月第1版
印　　次 / 2019年2月第1次
定　　价 / 39.80元

走进上海师范大学

博士生导师朱振武教授的

文学课堂

扫一扫，听有声导读

聆听该音频，你可以获知：

1. 马克 · 吐温的国际影响力及传奇人生。
2. 《狗的自述》精彩导读。
3. 经典阅读的当下意义。

经典阅读的当下意义

朱振武

有个学生要考我的研究生，我回信给她说，考我的研究生，要能够静下心来读书，不枉过三年，不要只顾蝇头微利，不要陷入琐碎，不要流于肤浅，立足在眼前，但立志要高远，至少要做一个文化人，而不是个只顾眼前利益的小市民，渐次达到人生较高的境界。这个学生很坚决，她回信说，读研的目的不仅是学习更多的知识，更重要的是充实人生，完善人格，提高自己的精神境界。回答得很好，正是我要的答案，后来她得偿所愿，心无旁骛地读起书来，再后来表现出很强的后劲。

要否读书，读书重要与否，重要到什么程度，这些在不久前被看作是只有白痴才会问的问题在当下还真成了问题。我们的孔老夫子曾说，不读诗，无以言。十七世纪英国哲人弗朗西斯·培根说得好，读书使人充实，不常读书者须欺世有术，始能无知而显有知。人之才智但有滞碍，无不可读适当之书使之顺畅。读书，首要的是读什么书呢？当然是读经典著作。什么是经典？常念为经，常数为典，是为经典。经典就是经得起反复重复的文本，其之所以得以如此就在于其丰厚的文化蕴含，就在于我们每次对之重温都能从中开掘出熏染和涤荡我们灵魂的东西。

同样一篇文章或一个理论，能经得起人反复咀嚼。经典还具有不可超越性，更不是我们眼前这些急功近利的东西所能替代的。著名电视导演张纪中说："经典是不能超越的。你可以在他旁边再垒一座山，却无法超越这座山。"经典就是这样的一些作品，常读常新，且不会过时或落伍。历史文化学者易中天说得好，经典就是最有价值、最有意义的著作。他还引用中国那句老话教育大家，"取法其上，得乎其中。取法其中，得乎其下。""取法其上"，对于我们读书人来说，当然就是阅读经典。

有个读者在网上留帖子说，没有读意大利的伊塔洛·卡尔维诺的《为什么读经典》，那是旷世奇憾。旷世不旷世不敢说，遗憾是肯定有的。卡尔维诺对经典的阐发确实深刻，他认为，经典作品是一些产生某种特殊影响的书，他们要么本身以难忘的方式给我们的想象力打下印记，要么乔装成个人或集体的无意识隐藏在深层记忆中，经典作品是一本不会耗尽它要向你说的一切东西的书。他还认为，经典作品是这样的一些书，它们带着先前解释的气息走向我们，背后拖着它们经过文化或多种文化（或只是多种语言和风俗）时留下的足迹。这些话说得真是深刻，我曾经在一次关于经典阅读的讲座上稍事夸张地说：经典文学是这样的书：

> 它是使没有头脑的人变得有头脑，没有文化的人变得有文化的书，是使肤浅之徒变得稳重、呆板之人变得诙谐、迟滞之人变得睿智、短视之人变得远见、丑陋之人变得俊拔、狭隘之人变得宽容、妒忌变得羡慕、贪婪变得节制、吝啬变得慷慨、苛刻变得宽容、卑微变得高贵、猥琐变得雍容、空虚变得充实、奢靡变得简朴、情调低俗变得品位高雅、百无聊赖变得丰富多彩的书，是那些让你得到调整、使

你得到憩息、能够与你沟通、可以帮你排遣郁闷的书，是能够为你提供生活坐标的书，是可以让你放松身心、宣泄激愤的书，是使你保持坦荡荡免于常戚戚的书，是使你高出只掌握某种一般技能的人的书，是使你摆脱生存尴尬、尽享人生乐趣的书，是使你懂得一个人为什么要活着的书，是使高级动物有别于其他动物的书。

有个听众问我什么时候读经典，我戏谑地回答说："当你神情抑郁、兴趣寡淡的时候，当你情场失意、官场失落的时候，当你挫败连连、股市大跌的时候，当你参透人生、看破红尘的时候，当你失业下岗的时候，当你屡试不中的时候，当你穷得只剩下钱的时候，当你辗转反侧、夜不成寐、茶饭无思、百无聊赖的时候，当你不知道人为什么而活着的时候，当你不知道你到底有什么用处的时候，当你在充满喧哗与骚动的都市里无处逃逸的时候，不要想入非非，不要萌生他想，尽情享受经典阅读带给你的乐趣吧！"

为什么要读经典？

易中天说得好，就是因为能从经典中读人生，读智慧，读社会。我颇以为然，所以，每天没有不看书的时候，没有不接触经典的时候，否则就觉得怅然若失，缺少了根基，没了底气，丢了自信。

这套四卷本的"美国名家短篇小说精选"所收作家作品就是前面所说的那样的经典之作，很具代表性，基本上让我们看到了美国短篇小说的整体面貌，而且这些作品仍与当下有着很强的意义关联，因此，其读者群也比较宽广。画龙点睛般的导读、简练严谨的注释和紧扣源语的译文为读者体会作品主旨意蕴、创作技巧和学习、欣赏原文文本提供了很大便利。

这套书的撰译者都是在高校里专门从事英美文学教学和研究的人员，主编是上海师范大学的朱振武，副主编是上海师范大学的冯德河、蓝云春，山东大学的高静，三峡大学的陈月红、杨鸿雁、黎智林、任慧芝以及上海大学外国语学院的张惠英。大家在多年的教研实践中达成一个共识：一个不读经典作品的人是不完整的人，没有一定的英美文学经典作品的阅读量，一个人的英语水平是不可能达到较高层次的，他在这个方面的整体文化素养肯定是有缺陷的。因此，我们向各位读者奉上这套“美国名家短篇小说精选”。

关于马克·吐温

李　丹

不论是在西方还是在中国，马克·吐温（Mark Twain, 1835—1910）都是个如雷贯耳的名字。他一生著作颇丰，创作体裁多样，有小说、游记、随笔、传记、小品、文论和戏剧等，其中以小说最为出色。但大多数人都只知《汤姆·索亚历险记》和《哈克贝里·费恩历险记》，对他同样优秀的短篇小说却知之甚少。

初读此书，你一定会被马克·吐温亦庄亦谐的幽默文风和荒诞不经的奇趣故事逗得捧腹大笑。《卡拉维拉斯县有名的跳蛙》《寓言一则》《加利福尼亚人的故事》《火车上的食人族》《狗的自述》《一张百万英镑的钞票》《他是生是死？》……每个故事都充满了幽默笑料。但马克·吐温绝不是为了娱乐而逗笑。鲁迅先生曾说过，这位讲笑话的好手是“含着哀怨而在嬉笑”。可见这位外表风趣幽默的文学家心中实则隐藏着极为深刻严肃的情感思想。

马克·吐温，原名赛缪尔·兰霍恩·克莱门斯（Samuel Langhorne Clemens），1835 年 11 月 30 日出生在美国中西部密苏里州的佛罗里达村，马克·吐温是其笔名。

马克·吐温一生遍游世界各地、尝尽人世冷暖。他的父亲曾做过律师和商人，母亲是一位基督教长老会教徒。家中共有六个孩子，马克·吐温排行第五。十二岁时，他父亲因肺炎去世，于是他辍学当印刷学徒，并开始在报刊上陆续发表幽默短文。十八岁时，马克·吐温离开家乡，开始游历生涯。他在各地当排字工，也发表了一些旅行见闻。二十二岁时，马克·吐温搭乘汽船沿密西西比河南下，开始学做领航员。河上的岁月让他接触到各色人物，为日后的文学创作积累了众多鲜活素材。1861年，美国南北战争爆发，河上航运中断，马克·吐温也结束了领航员生涯。他加入了南方军，但只待了三个星期；后来与人合伙投资采矿，却赔得血本无归。穷困之际，他当起记者，开始使用“马克·吐温”这个笔名。“马克·吐温”原是领航术语，意即“两英寻”（英寻是测量水深单位，1英寻约等于1.8米），是可以安全航行的深度。

1867年，马克·吐温搭乘“贵格会城”号轮船前往欧洲和巴勒斯坦观光，并为报纸写旅行报道以抵销旅费。在船上，马克·吐温与一位十八岁少年查尔斯·兰登相谈甚欢，随后结成亲密友伴，并对其姐姐奥莉维亚·兰登一见倾心。1870年，马克·吐温与奥莉维亚在纽约结婚，并在哈特福德精心建造了一座漂亮的豪华宅邸，开始了他人生中的黄金时代。马克·吐温在那里住了近二十年，不仅创作出了他大部分重要的文学作品，还养育了三个宝贝女儿：苏茜、克拉拉和琼。

在笔耕不辍的同时，马克·吐温也并未停止一直以来热心的商业投资和科技发明，但大部分都不成功。1893年，美国经济危机爆发，马克·吐温也因此变得负债累累。为了偿还债务，他携妻子及次女克拉拉，开始了全球巡回演讲之旅，听众场场爆满。一年后，演讲旅行结束，本应团聚的一家却等来大女儿苏茜病逝的消息。之后，其兄、妻、挚友和小女儿相继离他而去。马克·吐温仍在不停地写作，既是为了还清债务，也为了逃避家庭不幸所带来的忧伤。1910年4月21日，马克·吐温因心脏病溘然辞世。

马克·吐温开始创作的年代正是美国现实主义文学兴起的时期，乡土文学的繁盛和西部幽默的传承滋润了美国文学贫瘠的土地，也促成了这位伟大文豪的诞生。他大胆采用口语和方言进行创作，为后来的美国文学家们提供了更加鲜活、更具本土特色和更富表达力的文学用语。而这样大范围地运用方言口语来进行文学创作的情况，在当时的美国也是绝无仅有的。当时的美国文学仍旧遵循着英国维多利亚时期的文学传统，崇尚的是得体规范的语言和高雅的文学趣味。马克·吐温的《跳蛙》正如一场清新的春雨，不仅扫去了旧日的陈腐文风，还为美国文学的茁壮成长注入了新的活力。此后，马克·吐温也一直不忘提炼加工美国的民间口语，使自己的语言始终保持简洁朴实、生动幽默的特色。美国著名文学家、诺贝尔奖获得者海明威说“所有的美国作品都发源于《哈克贝里·费恩历险记》”，指的也正是马克·吐温自《跳蛙》以来所凝练而成的独具一格的语言特色。马克·吐温的另一特色便是其复杂多变的幽默文风。早期的轻松活泼，中期的辛辣嘲讽以及晚期的悲凉荒诞，都融合在了日常生活里种种复杂的欢笑和喜乐之中。马克·吐温是现实主义作家，对生活有着深刻细致的观察和思考。他对社会各方面的关怀不仅仅在他那史诗般的长篇小说中得到了体现，还更多地散落在了其诸多短篇小说之中。

我们精心挑选了九篇马克·吐温的短篇小说，力图从语言特色、叙述技巧和主题思想等各方面来向读者展示这位伟大作家的艺术风貌。马克·吐温的文学用语极富地方特色，口语和方言使用极多，因此疏漏纰缪之处在所难免，望广大读者不吝指正！

目　　录

Samuel Langhorne Clemens

1835 – 1910

Samuel Langhorne Clemens

(November 30, 1835 – April 21, 1910), better known

by his pen name Mark Twain,

was an American writer, humorist, entrepreneur,

publisher, and lecturer.

The Notorious Jumping Frog of Calaveras County

卡拉维拉斯县有名的跳蛙[1]

① 马克·吐温的成名之作，最初发表在1865年11月18日的《星期六新闻报》(Saturday Press)上，当时的名字为《吉姆·斯迈利和他的跳蛙》(Jim Smiley and His Jumping Frog)，后经马克·吐温多次润色修改，又更名为 The Celebrated Jumping Frog of Calaveras County 或 The Notorious Jumping Frog of Calaveras County。

《卡拉维拉斯县有名的跳蛙》（The Notorious Jumping Frog of Calaveras County，1865）是马克·吐温的成名之作，讲述的是美国西部矿区里一个嗜赌成性的矿工吉姆·斯迈利的故事。“我”受好友之托，要向西蒙·惠勒老人打听一个叫利奥尼达斯·W. 斯迈利的人的消息。可西蒙·惠勒却滔滔不绝地讲起了吉姆·斯迈利的赌博史来。小说以“我”的叙述作为开场白和结束语，中间则全是西蒙·惠勒在讲故事。西蒙·惠勒有着浓重的地方口音，他在讲述吉姆·斯迈利那荒诞无稽的赌博趣闻时总是“不露笑脸，不皱眉头”，表情严肃得似乎都不知道他所讲故事中的可笑之处，他那冷淡的叙事口吻和滑稽的故事内容形成鲜明对比。“我”一开始就像被逮住的猎物般让西蒙·惠勒用椅子给堵在了角落，被迫听他那“令人恼火”和“乏味冗长”的往事；“我”被这些没完没了、一连串的赌博故事烦得要死，而西蒙讲述时却始终怀着“一股感人至深的热诚和真挚”；最后“我”找了个机会溜走，而西蒙讲的故事似乎才刚开头。

“我”正如东部新英格兰地区那些秉承英国传统斯文文风的绅士，所用的是极为规范的书面语；而西蒙·惠勒则代表着粗犷豪迈的西部拓荒者，用的是方言口语。整个故事也正是因为有了西蒙·惠勒这个西部矿区老头的角色才带有了西部民间口头文学的浓厚色彩，从而呈现出了一种轻松诙谐的幽默语境。

In compliance with the request of a friend of mine, who wrote me from the East, I called on good-natured, garrulous old Simon Wheeler, and inquired after my friend's friend, Leonidas W. Smiley, as requested to do, and I hereunto append the result. I have a lurking suspicion that Leonidas W. Smiley is a myth; that my friend never knew such a personage; and that he only conjectured that if I asked old Wheeler about him, it would remind him of his infamous Jim Smiley, and he would go to work and bore me to death with some exasperating① reminiscence of him as long and as tedious as it should be useless to me. If that was the design, it succeeded.

I found Simon Wheeler dozing comfortably by the bar-room stove of the dilapidated② tavern in the decayed mining camp of Angel's, and I noticed that he was fat and bald-headed, and had an expression of winning gentleness and simplicity upon his tranquil countenance. He roused up, and gave me good day. I told him that a friend of mine had commissioned me to make some inquiries about a cherished companion of his boyhood named Leonidas W. Smiley—Rev.③ Leonidas W. Smiley, a young minister of the Gospel, who he had heard was at one time a resident of Angel's Camp. I added that if Mr. Wheeler could tell me anything about this Rev. Leonidas W. Smiley, I would feel under many obligations to him.

Simon Wheeler backed me into a corner and blockaded me there with his chair, and then sat down and reeled off the

① exasperating *adj.* 使人恼怒的 ② dilapidated *adj.* 破旧的，破烂的
③ Rev. *adj.* (Reverend 的缩写）尊敬的

一位朋友从东部来信，受他所托，我拜访了性情温和、爱扯闲话的西蒙·惠勒老人。应这位朋友的请求，我向他打听我朋友的朋友利奥尼达斯·W.斯迈利的情况，现附上此事的探查结果。我心底有些怀疑那位利奥尼达斯·W.斯迈利是个捏造出来的人物，我的朋友压根儿就不认识这么一个人，朋友只是猜测，要是我向老惠勒问起此人，就会让他想起臭名昭著的吉姆·斯迈利，于是他就会开始来劲儿，搬出他那些令人恼火的往事把我烦死，因为那些往事乏味冗长，对我却毫无用处。如果这就是我那朋友的意图的话，那他确实达到了目的。

安吉尔镇衰败的矿区营地里有一家破落酒馆，我在酒馆里找到了西蒙·惠勒，他正在酒吧间的炉边舒舒服服地打盹，我发现他身材肥胖，还秃了顶，安详的脸上露出一副讨人喜欢的亲切和质朴的神情。他醒了过来，向我问好。我告诉他，受朋友所托，我要询问一些有关朋友少年时代的挚友利奥尼达斯·W.斯迈利的情况——利奥尼达斯·W.斯迈利牧师，是福音会里的一位年轻牧师，听说曾在安吉尔矿区住过。接着我补充道，要是惠勒先生能告诉我任何有关这位利奥尼达斯·W.斯迈利牧师的情况，我将感激万分。

西蒙·惠勒把我逼退到一个角落，用他的椅子把我堵在那儿，然后坐下来，滔滔不绝地讲出了下面这一段单调乏味的故事。他不

monotonous narrative which follows this paragraph. He never smiled, he never frowned, he never changed his voice from the gentle-flowing key to which he tuned his initial sentence, he never betrayed the slightest suspicion of enthusiasm; but all through the interminable narrative there ran a vein of impressive earnestness and sincerity, which showed me plainly that, so far from his imagining that there was anything ridiculous or funny about his story, he regarded it as a really important matter, and admired its two heroes as men of transcendent genius in finesse. I let him go on in his own way, and never interrupted him once.

"Rev. Leonidas W. H'm, Reverend Le—well, there was a feller [①] here once by the name of Jim Smiley, in the winter of '49—or maybe it was the spring of '50—I don't recollect exactly, somehow, though what makes me think it was one or the other is because I remember the big flume warn't finished when he first come [②] to the camp; but any way, he was the curiousest [③] man about always betting on anything that turned up you ever see, if he could get anybody to bet on the other side; and if he couldn't he'd change sides. Any way that suited the other man would suit him—any way just so's he got a bet, he was satisfied. But still he was lucky, uncommon lucky; he most always come out winner. He was always ready and laying for

① 惠勒在整个故事的讲述中使用的都是极不规范的语言。语言的不规范主要体现在发音、语法上。发音的不规范主要通过有意的单词误拼来体现，语法的不规范主要是体现在时态和词性变换上。

② come 应为 came。本段用法不规范之处还有：uncommon lucky(uncommonly lucky)，the boys here has seen (the boys here have seen)，the dangdest feller (the most damned fellow)，laid (lay)，come in (came in)，considerable better (considerably better)，before he thought says (before he thought said)，she don't anyway (she doesn't anyway)。

③ curious 的最高级应为 the most curious。

露笑脸，不皱眉头，从来就没改变过最初讲话时那种平和流畅的基调，也从未流露出一丝狂热的迹象，但整个冗长乏味的故事里始终流淌着一股感人至深的热诚和真挚。这明确地告诉我，他并不觉得这故事有什么荒谬可笑的地方，反而认为这是一件极为正经重要的事，并且很欣赏故事里的两位主角，视他们为运用计谋的超凡天才。我任由他径自说着，一次也没有打断。

“利奥尼达斯牧师。嗯，牧师利奥——喔，这儿曾经有个家伙的名字叫做吉姆·斯迈利，是四九年的冬天——或许是五〇年的春天——不知怎么的，我记不清啦，反正我认为不是这一年就是那一年，因为我记得他初到矿区时，大水渠还没完工。不管怎么说，他可是这附近最古怪的人，总喜欢拿你眼前的任何事打赌，只要他能找到人跟他赌对边。要是找不到，他换边赌也行。别人想怎么赌他就怎么赌——怎么赌都行，只要能让他赌，他就会很满意。可他倒也走运，出奇地走运，几乎场场都是赢家。他总是准备好等着赌上一把，甭管提到什么事儿，那家伙准会找人打赌，还让你随意选边，就像我刚才说的那样。

a chance; there couldn't be no solit'ry thing mentioned but that feller'd offer to bet on it[1], and take ary side you please, as I was just telling you. If there was a horse-race, you'd find him flush or you'd find him busted at the end of it; if there was a dog-fight, he'd bet on it; if there was a cat-fight, he'd bet on it; if there was a chicken-fight, he'd bet on it; why, if there was two birds setting on a fence, he would bet you which one would fly first; or if there was a camp-meeting, he would be there reg'lar to bet on Parson Walker, which he judged to be the best exhorter about here, and so he was too, and a good man. If he even see a straddle-bug start to go anywheres, he would bet you how long it would take him to get to—to wherever he was going to, and if you took him up, he would foller that straddle-bug to Mexico but what he would find out where he was bound for and how long he was on the road. Lots of the boys here has seen that Smiley; and can tell you about him. Why, it never made no difference to him—he'd bet on any thing—the dangdest feller. Parson Walker's wife laid very sick once, for a good while, and it seemed as if they warn't going to save her; but one morning he come in, and Smiley up and asked him how she was, and he said she was considerable better—thank the Lord for his inf'nit mercy—and coming on so smart that with the blessing of Prov'dence she'd get well yet; and Smiley, before he thought, says, 'Well, I'll resk two-and-a-half she don't anyway.'

① 这句话的规范说法是：there could be no solitary thing mentioned which that fellow would not offer to bet on. 这种用否定形式表示肯定意义的句子在口语中经常出现，起加强语气的作用。

要是有场赛马，赛后你就会发现他不是乐得脸红就是输得精光；要是狗儿打架，他会赌；要是猫儿打架，他会赌；要是鸡崽打架，他会赌；嘿，要是篱笆上站着两只鸟，他会跟你赌哪只会先飞；或者，要是有营地布道会，他通常准会在那儿拿沃克牧师来打赌，赌他是那一带最好的布道者，他也的确是这样，一个好人。甚至瞧见一只屎壳郎开始爬动，他也要跟你打赌它得花多久才能爬到——爬到它要去的地方，要是你同意跟他打赌，就算是跟着那只屎壳郎到墨西哥，他也要弄清它去什么地方，路上要走多久。这儿有许多小伙子都见过那个斯迈利，都能跟你说说关于他的事。咳，对他来说什么都一样——他什么都可以拿来赌——真是个大混球。有一次，沃克牧师的老婆病得很厉害，躺了好一阵子，好像是没得救了。可有天早晨，沃克牧师走了进来，斯迈利起来就问他老婆怎么样了，他说她好多了——感谢主的宽厚仁慈——而且恢复得还不错，上帝保佑，她肯定会康复的。可是，斯迈利想都没想，说：‘喂，我赌两块半，她肯定好不了。’

"Thish-yer Smiley [1] had a mare—the boys called her the fifteen-minute nag, but that was only in fun, you know, because of course she was faster than that—and he used to win money on that horse, for all she was so slow and always had the asthma, or the distemper, or the consumption, or something of that kind. They used to give her two or three hundred yards' start, and then pass her under way; but always at the fag end of the race she'd get excited and desperate like, and come cavorting and straddling up, and scattering her legs around limber, sometimes in the air, and sometimes out to one side among the fences, and kicking up m-o-r-e dust and raising m-o-r-e racket with her coughing and sneezing and blowing her nose—and always fetch up at the stand just about a neck ahead, as near as you could cipher it down.

"And he had a little small bull-pup, that to look at him you'd think he warn't worth a cent but to set around and look ornery and lay for a chance to steal something. But as soon as money was up on him he was a different dog; his under-jaw'd begin to stick out like the fo'castle of a steamboat, and his teeth would uncover and shine like the furnaces. And a dog might tackle him and bully-rag him, and bite him, and throw him over his shoulder two or three times, and Andrew Jackson—which was the name of the pup—Andrew Jackson would never let on but what he was satisfied, and hadn't expected nothing

① Thish-yer Smiley 应为 This here Smiley 或是 This Smiley。本段的类似不规范拼写还有：fo'castle (forecastle)，jest (just)，j'int (joint)，come out (came out)，pet holt (pet hold)，he see (he saw)，'peared (appeared)，sorter (sort of)，broke (broken)，laid down (lay down)，hisself (himself)，it don't (it doesn't)，under them circumstances (under these circumstances)，his'n (his)。

"这个斯迈利有匹母马——小伙子们都叫它'一刻钟老马',可你知道,那只是开开玩笑,因为它跑得当然要比这快——他过去常常靠那马赢钱,虽然那马跑得很慢,还老是发哮喘、马腺疫、肺病或是这样那样的病。他们通常让它先跑两三百码,然后中途超过它,可就在快到终点的时候,它总是会兴奋起来,死命地奔跑,它飞身腾跃,大步跨起,轻快自如地撒开四蹄,一会儿在空中飞腾,一会儿跑到围栏的另一侧,扬起越来越多的灰尘,发出越来越大的声响,又是咳嗽,又是打喷嚏,又是流鼻涕——还总是恰好超出一个头到达终点,刚好让你瞧个明白。

"他还有只丁点儿大的斗牛犬,看到它,你会觉得它一文不值,只会到处游荡,一脸卑劣样,好像随时都在伺机偷点什么。可只要赌注一押在它身上,它就变得不一样啦。它的下巴向前突出,像轮船的前甲板似的,它的牙露着,像火炉一般闪着光。别的狗可能就会扑向它,恐吓它,撕咬它,把它摔倒个两三次,而安德鲁·杰克逊[①]——这是那小狗的名字——安德鲁·杰克逊总是装作没什么不满意的样子,像是原本就没指望别的什么——

① 安德鲁·杰克逊(1767—1845),第七任美国总统。民主党创建者之一、新奥尔良之役战争英雄(1815)、首任佛罗里达州州长(1821),杰克逊式民主因他而得名。杰克逊又因作法强硬,被称为"老山胡桃"(Old Hickory)。其头像出现在二十美元的纸币上。

else[①]—and the bets being doubled and doubled on the other side all the time, till the money was all up; and then all of a sudden he would grab that other dog jest by the j'int of his hind leg and freeze to it—not chaw, you understand, but only just grip and hang on till they throwed up the sponge, if it was a year. Smiley always come out winner on that pup, till he harnessed a dog once that didn't have no hind legs, because they'd been sawed off in a circular saw, and when the thing had gone along far enough, and the money was all up, and he come to make a snatch for his pet holt, he see in a minute how he'd been imposed on, and how the other dog had him in the door, so to speak, and he 'peared surprised, and then he looked sorter discouraged-like, and didn't try no more to win the fight, and so he got shucked out bad. He give Smiley a look, as much as to say his heart was broke, and it was his fault, for putting up a dog that hadn't no hind legs for him to take holt of, which was his main dependence in a fight, and then he limped off a piece and laid down and died. It was a good pup, was that Andrew Jackson, and would have made a name for hisself if he'd lived, for the stuff was in him and he had genius—I know it, because he hadn't no opportunities to speak of, and it don't stand to reason that a dog could make such a fight as he could under them circumstances if he hadn't no talent. It always makes me feel sorry when I think of that last fight of his'n, and the way it turned out.

① hadn't expected nothing else 应为 had expected nothing else，本段的类似的不规范用法还有：hadn't no opportunities (had no opportunities)，if he hadn't no talent (if he had no talent)。

赌注一直成倍成倍地压在另一方，直到钱全都押上。然后，它会突然咬住那狗的后腿关节，紧紧咬着不放——不是啃，你知道，只是咬住不放，直到对方认输，哪怕是要咬上一年。斯迈利拿那小狗打赌总是赢，直到有一次斗上了一只没有后腿的狗，因为那狗的后腿让圆锯给锯掉了，打斗进行得差不多了，钱也全都押了上去，它张口正要咬它那爱咬的地方，可立马就意识到它上当了，也就是说，这狗把它给难住了，它显得很吃惊，然后就有了几分泄气的样子，不再尽力去打赢这架，结果它被咬得血肉模糊。它看了斯迈利一眼，似乎在说它很伤心，而这都是他的错，居然弄了一只没有后腿的狗来让它咬，而咬后腿可是它搏斗中的重要法宝。然后，它一瘸一拐地走到一边，倒下来，死了。它真是只好狗，那个安德鲁·杰克逊，它要是还活着，肯定早出名了，因为它有实力，有天赋——我知道的，说起来，它是没啥运气，可一条狗在那样的情况下还能那样搏斗，要是没些个才能，那可就真没法解释啦。一想起它最后的那场搏斗和那样的结局，我就总是觉得难过。

"Well, thish-yer Smiley had rat-tarriers[①], and chicken cocks, and tomcats and all them kind of things, till you couldn't rest, and you couldn't[②] fetch nothing for him to bet on but he'd match you. He ketched a frog one day, and took him home, and said he cal'lated to educate him; and so he never done nothing for three months but set in his back yard and learn that frog to jump. And you bet you he did learn him, too. He'd give him a little punch behind, and the next minute you'd see that frog whirling in the air like a doughnut—see him turn one summerset, or may be a couple, if he got a good start, and come down flat-footed and all right, like a cat. He got him up so in the matter of ketching flies, and kep' him in practice so constant, that he'd nail a fly every time as fur as he could see him. Smiley said all a frog wanted was education, and he could do 'most anything—and I believe him. Why, I've seen him set Dan'l Webster down here on this floor—Dan'l Webster was the name of the frog—and sing out, 'Flies, Dan'l, flies!' and quicker'n you could wink he'd spring straight up and snake a fly off'n the counter there, and flop down on the floor ag'in as solid as a gob of mud, and fall to scratching the side of his head with his hind foot as indifferent as if he hadn't no idea he'd been doin' any more'n any frog might do. You never see a frog so modest and straightfor'ard as he was, for all he was so gifted. And when it come to fair and square

① tarrier 应为 terrier。本段不规范的用法还有：ketched (caught)，cal'lated (calculated)，he never done nothing (he did nothing)，learn (taught)，you bet you (you bet)，kep' (kept)，as fur as (as far as)，'most (almost)，quicker'n (quicker than)，off'n (off on)，ag'in (again)，as indifferent (as indifferently)，doin' (doing)，more'n (more than)，straightfor' ard (straightforward)，when it come to (when it came to)。

② couldn't 此处应为 could。本段类似的错误还有：hadn't no idea (had no idea)。

“喔，这个斯迈利还养过会捉老鼠的小猎狗、小公鸡、小公猫和各种各样的动物，跟人赌个没完，不管你拿什么和他打赌，他总能赢你。有一天，他捉了只青蛙，把它带回家，还说打算要培养它。就这样，他三个月里啥也没干，就待在后院教那只青蛙跳。倒还真是把它给教会了。他只要在它后面轻轻一按，你立马就会看到那青蛙像个炸面包圈似的在空中旋转——看见它翻一个筋斗，要是起跳得好，还可能翻两个，落地干脆利落、稳稳当当，跟只猫似的。他教它那样跳起来抓苍蝇，还让它不停地练，练得每次它只要能看到苍蝇，就能一口捉住。斯迈利说只要训练，这青蛙几乎什么都能干——这话我信。嗨，我就曾看见过他把丹尼尔·韦伯斯特[①] 放在这儿的地板上——丹尼尔·韦伯斯特是那只青蛙的名字——大声喊，‘苍蝇，丹尼尔，苍蝇！’你眼还没来得及眨，它就径直跳起，把柜台上的一只苍蝇给卷到嘴里，又啪的一声落在地上，稳得跟团泥巴似的，还用它的后爪搔搔脑瓜边，满不在乎得好像它不知道自己比别的青蛙本领大。从没见过像它这么谦虚直率的青蛙，虽然它很有才。如果是在同一平面上正大光明地进行比赛，它只要一跳，就能比你见过的其他任何同种类的青蛙跳得更高。要知道，在同一平面上比跳是它的强项，如果是比这个，只要斯迈利还有一分钱，他也会把钱押在它身上。斯迈利为他的青蛙感到特别自豪，这也难怪，那些出过门、去过很多地方的家伙都说，他那青蛙比他们见过的任何一只都要强。

① 丹尼尔·韦伯斯特（1782—1852），美国政治家、演说家、法学家、辉格党（美国共和党前身）领袖。曾两次担任国务卿一职，在宪法学方面有许多经典论述。

jumping on a dead level, he could get over more ground at one straddle than any animal of his breed you ever see. Jumping on a dead level was his strong suit, you understand; and when it come to that, Smiley would ante up money on him as long as he had a red. Smiley was monstrous proud of his frog, and well he might be, for fellers that had traveled and been everywheres, all said he laid over any frog that ever they see.

"Well, Smiley kep' the beast in a little lattice box, and he used to fetch him down-town sometimes and lay for a bet. One day a feller—a stranger in the camp, he was—come acrost [1] him with his box, and says:

" 'What might it be that you've got in the box?'

"And Smiley says, sorter indifferent-like, 'It might be a parrot, or it might be a canary, maybe, but it ain't—it's only just a frog.'

"And the feller took it, and looked at it careful, and turned it round this way and that, and says, 'H'm—so 'tis. Well, what's he good for?'

" 'Well,' Smiley says, easy and careless, 'he's good enough for one thing, I should judge—he can outjump any frog in Calaveras County.'

"The feller took the box again, and took another long, particular look, and give it back to Smiley, and says, very

① come acrost 应为 came across 或 comes across，以下不规范的用法还有：I don't see no p'ints (I don't see any points)，better'n (better than)，'em (them)，ain't (are)，a amature (an amateur)，Anyways (anyway)，ain't (haven't)，set down (sat down)，git (get; go)，hysted up (hoisted up)，it warn't no use (it was no use)，he couldn't no more stir than (he coulnt't stir any more than)，he didn't have no idea (he had no idea)，throw'd off (threw off)，there ain't (there isn't)，'pears (appears)，nap (nape)，yaller (yellow)，bannanner (banana)。

“唔，斯迈利把那东西放在一个小笼子里，常常带着它到闹市区跟人打赌。一天，一个家伙——矿区里的一个陌生人——碰见斯迈利拿着笼子，就问：

“‘你那笼子里的会是个啥东西呢？’

“斯迈利有点漫不经心地说：‘这可能是只鹦鹉，也可能是只金丝雀，可都不是——这只是一只青蛙。’

“那家伙拿起笼子，仔细看着，把它转来转去，说：‘嗯——真是只青蛙。唔，它有什么用？’

“‘喔，’斯迈利满不在乎地随口说道，‘它有一件顶强的本领，我敢说——它比卡拉维拉斯县里的任何一只青蛙跳得都要好。’

“那家伙再次拿起笼子，仔仔细细地又看了很久，然后还给了斯迈利，不慌不忙地说：‘唔，我可看不出这青蛙有哪点比别的青蛙强。’

deliberate, 'Well,' he says, 'I don't see no p'ints about that frog that's any better'n any other frog.'

" 'Maybe you don't,' Smiley says. 'Maybe you understand frogs and maybe you don't understand 'em; maybe you've had experience, and maybe you ain't only a amature, as it were. Anyways, I've got my opinion, and I'll resk forty dollars that he can outjump any frog in Calaveras county.'

"And the feller studied a minute, and then says, kinder sad-like, 'Well, I'm only a stranger here, and I ain't got no frog; but if I had a frog, I'd bet you.'

"And then Smiley says, 'That's all right—that's all right—if you'll hold my box a minute, I'll go and get you a frog.' And so the feller took the box, and put up his forty dollars along with Smiley's, and set down to wait.

"So he set there a good while thinking and thinking to himself, and then he got the frog out and prized his mouth open and took a teaspoon and filled him full of quail-shot—filled him pretty near up to his chin—and set him on the floor. Smiley he went to the swamp and slopped around in the mud for a long time, and finally he ketched a frog, and fetched him in, and give him to this feller, and says:

" 'Now, if you're ready, set him alongside of Dan'l, with his fore paws just even with Dan'l's, and I'll give the word.' Then he says, 'One—two—three—git!' and him and the feller touched up the frogs from behind, and the new frog hopped off lively, but Dan'l give a heave, and hysted up his shoulders—so—like a Frenchman, but it warn't no use—he couldn't budge;

“‘也许你看不出来，’斯迈利说，‘也许你懂青蛙，也许你不懂。或者说，也许你经验丰富，也许你只是个外行。不管怎么说，这是我的看法，我赌四十美元，赌它比卡拉维拉斯县里的任何一只青蛙跳得都要好。’

“那家伙考虑了一会儿，然后开了口，显得有些苦恼：‘嗯，我在这儿人生地不熟，也没有青蛙，要是我有一只，肯定跟你赌。’

“接着斯迈利说：‘没关系——没关系——要是你帮我看会儿笼子，我就去给你抓只青蛙来。’于是，那个人拿过笼子，把他的四十美元和斯迈利的钱放在了一块儿，坐下来等着。

“他坐了好一阵子，心里不停地盘算着，后来，他把青蛙取了出来，掰开它的嘴，拿起茶匙，灌了它一肚子的打鸟铅弹——都快灌到嗓子眼了——然后把它放在地上。斯迈利去了沼泽地，在泥地里转悠了很久，终于抓到了一只青蛙，带回来交给了这家伙，说：

“‘现在，要是你准备好了，就把它放在丹尼尔的旁边，前爪要和丹尼尔的刚好一样齐，我来发口令，’接着，他说，‘一——二——三——开始！’他和那家伙就从后面按了下各自的青蛙，那只新抓的青蛙欢快地跳了起来，可丹尼尔使了使劲，耸起了肩——就这样——像个法国人似的，可是没用——它动不了，跟座教堂似的牢牢扎在那儿，它一动也不动，跟船抛了锚似的。斯迈利大吃一惊，还

he was planted as solid as a church, and he couldn't no more stir than if he was anchored out. Smiley was a good deal surprised, and he was disgusted too, but he didn't have no idea what the matter was, of course.

"The feller took the money and started away; and when he was going out at the door, he sorter jerked his thumb over his shoulder—so—at Dan'l, and says again, very deliberate, 'Well,' he says, 'I don't see no p'ints about that frog that's any better'n any other frog.'

"Smiley he stood scratching his head and looking down at Dan'l a long time, and at last he says, 'I do wonder what in the nation that frog throw'd off for—I wonder if there ain't something the matter with him—he 'pears to look mighty baggy, somehow.' And he ketched Dan'l by the nap of the neck, and hefted him, and says, 'Why blame my cats if he don't weigh five pound!' and turned him upside down and he belched out a double handful of shot. And then he see how it was, and he was the maddest man—he set the frog down and took out after that feller, but he never ketched him. And—"

[Here Simon Wheeler heard his name called from the front yard, and got up to see what was wanted.] And turning to me as he moved away, he said: "Just set where you are, stranger, and rest easy—I ain't going to be gone a second."

But, by your leave, I did not think that a continuation of the history of the enterprising vagabond Jim Smiley would be likely to afford me much information concerning the Rev. Leonidas W. Smiley, and so I started away.

很气愤，但是他当然不知道这是怎么回事。

“那家伙拿起钱就走了，快要走出门时，他从肩上竖起拇指——就这样——指着丹尼尔，又不慌不忙地说了一遍：‘唔，我可看不出这青蛙有哪点比别的青蛙强。’

“斯迈利站着，搔着脑袋，向下盯着丹尼尔看了好长一段时间，最后他说：‘真奇怪，这青蛙到底是为什么故意输掉——不知道是不是出了什么事——不知怎么的，它看起来鼓鼓的。’他拎起丹尼尔的后颈，掂了掂，说：‘它要是没有五磅重才怪呢！’他把青蛙头朝下倒过来，它一下子吐出两把子弹。他这才明白了是怎么回事，气得发疯——他放下青蛙，跑出去追那家伙，可怎么也没追上。于是——”

（这时，西蒙·惠勒听到前院有人在喊他，便起身去看看有什么事。）他离开时还转身对我说：“就待在这儿，外乡人，放心——我就去一会儿。”

不过，对不起，我认为再继续听那富有进取精神的流浪汉吉姆·斯迈利的那些过往，也不可能给我提供多少关于利奥尼达斯·W.斯迈利牧师的消息，所以我起身离开了。

At the door I met the sociable Wheeler returning, and he buttonholed me and recommenced:

"Well, thish-yer Smiley had a yaller one-eyed cow that didn't have no tail, only just a short stump like a bannanner, and— "

However, lacking both time and inclination, I did not wait to hear about the afflicted cow, but took my leave.

在门口我碰到好客的惠勒回来了，他硬是拉着我接着讲了起来：

“喔，这个斯迈利还养过一头黄色的独眼母牛，没有尾巴，只有一截尾巴根，像只香蕉，而且——”

可是，我既没时间，也无兴趣，没等听完那头苦难母牛的故事，我就离开了。

A Fable
寓言一则

《寓言一则》（A Fable，1909）讲述的是动物们想从镜中观看一幅绝妙画作，结果没看到画却只看到了自己的故事。寓言借用吉卜林（Joseph Rudyard Kipling，1865–1936）《丛林故事》（The Jungle Book，1894）中的动物形象轻松诙谐地讲述一个简单而又深刻的哲理故事，叫人开怀大笑之余又回味无穷。王国维曾提出“有我之境”和“无我之境”的古诗创作美学思想，推及至其他文学形式的创作，亦莫不如此。而文学艺术的创作实质上又是“有我之境”居多，“以我观物，故物皆着我之色彩”。感人肺腑的作品总是与作者的生活、情感经历以及所处的历史时代息息相关，正如《哈克贝里·费恩历险记》的出现和成功与马克·吐温早年在密西西比河上的生活有着密不可分的关系。另一方面，经典文学作品的长存也离不开读者的解读。作为审美主体的读者在阅读文学作品时往往也少不了着上一些“我之色彩”，在他人的故事、异国的经历中总是期盼着看到自我的过去和将来，或是“感时花溅泪”，或是“恨别鸟惊心”。如果把众多优秀文学作品比作这则寓言故事中那幅美丽精巧的画作，那读者就可以说是通过想象力之镜来观看画作的动物了。文学作品只有制造出一定的空间距离，才能让人有想象的余地，作品才会显得更加有趣。但距离和想象似乎又为作品真义的显现笼上了一层美丽的面纱，读者该如何从镜中的“有我”看到镜中的“无我”呢？也正是如此，一部优秀的文学作品总是不为世人所忘，年复一年地为众读者反复细读，只为最终能窥见其真正的美丽容颜。

Once upon a time an artist who had painted a small and very beautiful picture placed it so that he could see it in the mirror. He said, "This doubles the distance and softens it, and it is twice as lovely as it was before."

The animals out in the woods heard of this through the housecat, who was greatly admired by them because he was so learned, and so refined and civilized, and so polite and high-bred, and could tell them so much which they didn't know before, and were not certain about afterward. They were much excited about this new piece of gossip, and they asked questions, so as to get at a full understanding of it. They asked what a picture was, and the cat explained.

"It is a flat thing," he said; "wonderfully flat, marvelously flat, enchantingly flat and elegant. And, oh, so beautiful!"

That excited them almost to a frenzy, and they said they would give the world to see it. Then the bear asked:

"What is it that makes it so beautiful?"

"It is the looks of it," said the cat.

This filled them with admiration and uncertainty, and they were more excited than ever. Then the cow asked:

"What is a mirror?"

"It is a hole in the wall," said the cat. "You look in it, and there you see the picture, and it is so dainty and charming and ethereal and inspiring in its unimaginable beauty that your head turns round and round, and you almost swoon with ecstasy."

The ass had not said anything as yet; he now began to throw doubts. He said there had never been anything as

很久很久以前，一位艺术家画了一幅小巧且异常美丽的画，并把它摆在可以从镜子里看到的地方。他说："这样使距离增加了一倍，画也变得柔和，比以前漂亮了一倍。"

外面森林里的动物们从家猫那里听说了这件事。家猫极受动物尊崇，因为他知识渊博、温文尔雅、谦虚懂礼，而且出身高贵，能告诉他们许多以前不知道、听了以后肯定也不清楚的事。他们对这条小道消息感到异常兴奋，还提了些问题，好对此有个全面了解。他们问什么是画，猫解释道：

"是一个扁平的东西，"他说，"令人惊叹地扁平，不可思议地扁平，令人迷醉地扁平和雅致。而且，噢，太美了！"

那些话让动物们激动得近乎疯狂，都说要不惜一切代价去看看那幅画。接着熊问：

"是什么使它这么美呢？"

"是它的外观。"猫说。

这让动物们赞叹不已又满脸困惑，他们从未像现在这么激动过。接着母牛问：

"镜子是什么？"

"是墙上的一个洞，"猫说，"你朝里看，就可以从那里看到那幅画，那种不可想象的美丽是如此精致、迷人、飘逸和震撼心灵，让你头晕目眩，兴奋得几乎要晕倒。"

目前为止驴子什么也没说，现在他开始怀疑了。他说以前从来就没有过这般美丽的东西，恐怕现在也没有。他说要是得用满满

beautiful as this before, and probably wasn't now. He said that when it took a whole basketful of sesquipedalian adjectives to whoop up a thing of beauty, it was time for suspicion.

It was easy to see that these doubts were having an effect upon the animals, so the cat went off offended. The subject was dropped for a couple of days, but in the meantime curiosity was taking a fresh start, and there was a revival of interest perceptible. Then the animals assailed the ass for spoiling what could possibly have been a pleasure to them, on a mere suspicion that the picture was not beautiful, without any evidence that such was the case. The ass was not troubled; he was calm, and said there was one way to find out who was in the right, himself or the cat: he would go and look in that hole, and come back and tell what he found there. The animals felt relieved and grateful, and asked him to go at once—which he did.

But he did not know where he ought to stand; and so, through error, he stood between the picture and the mirror. The result was that the picture had no chance, and didn't show up. He returned home and said:

"The cat lied. There was nothing in that hole but an ass. There wasn't a sign of a flat thing visible. It was a handsome ass, and friendly, but just an ass, and nothing more."

The elephant asked:

"Did you see it good and clear? Were you close to it?"

"I saw it good and clear, O Hathi, King of Beasts. I was so close that I touched noses with it."

一篮子冗长的形容词来吹嘘一个东西很美的话，那就是时候该怀疑它了。

显而易见，这样的疑虑在动物们身上产生了影响，因此猫不悦地离开了。这个话题搁置了几日，同时动物们的好奇心也重新滋长起来，他们的兴趣明显再次复苏。于是动物们责骂起驴子破坏了他们本来应有的乐趣，仅仅是因为怀疑那幅画不美丽，却没有任何证据来证明情况属实。驴子并不苦恼，他很镇定，说有一个办法可以弄清楚谁是对的，是他自己还是猫——他将去看看那个洞，然后回来说说在那里发现了什么。动物们既欣慰又感激，叫他立刻就去——而他也这么做了。

可是他不知道该站在哪儿，所以他就错误地站在了画和镜子之间。结果画根本就不可能、也没有出现在镜子里。他回到家后说道：

“猫撒了谎。那个洞里面只有一头驴子。那里根本就没有什么可以看得见的扁平东西。那是一头英俊的驴子，很友好，但只是一头驴子，其他什么都没有。”

大象问：

“你看清楚了吗？离它近吗？”

“我看得清清楚楚，哦，哈蒂[1]，万兽之王。我近得鼻子都贴在上面了。”

① 北印度语和梵语中的“大象”，象征着记忆力、智慧和力量。

"This is very strange," said the elephant; "the cat was always truthful before—as far as we could make out. Let another witness try. Go, Baloo, look in the hole, and come and report."

So the bear went. When he came back, he said:

"Both the cat and the ass have lied; there was nothing in the hole but a bear."

Great was the surprise and puzzlement of the animals. Each was now anxious to make the test himself and get at the straight truth. The elephant sent them one at a time.

First, the cow. She found nothing in the hole but a cow.

The tiger found nothing in it but a tiger.

The lion found nothing in it but a lion.

The leopard found nothing in it but a leopard.

The camel found a camel, and nothing more.

Then Hathi was wroth, and said he would have the truth, if he had to go and fetch it himself. When he returned, he abused his whole subjectry for liars, and was in an unappeasable fury with the moral and mental blindness of the cat. He said that anybody but a near-sighted fool could see that there was nothing in the hole but an elephant.

MORAL, BY THE CAT

You can find in a text whatever you bring, if you will stand between it and the mirror of your imagination. You may not see your ears, but they will be there.

“这可太奇怪了，”大象说，“猫以前一直都是很可信的——就我们所了解的而言。再派一个证人去试试吧。去吧，巴卢[①]，去那个洞看看，回来汇报。”

于是熊去了。他一回来就说：

“猫和驴子都撒了谎，那个洞里面只有一头熊。”

动物们都极为惊奇和疑惑。现在他们个个都急切地想亲自去测试一番，以便弄清真相。大象每次只派出他们中的一个。

首先去的是母牛。她在洞里面只看到一头母牛。

老虎在那里只看到一只老虎。

狮子在那里只看到一只狮子。

豹子在那里只看到一只豹子。

骆驼在那里看到一只骆驼，别的什么都没有。

哈蒂勃然大怒，说如果非得他亲自去一趟的话，那么他会自己前往、弄清真相。他一回来就骂他所有的臣民都是骗子，还对猫在道德和认知上的盲目表现出了不可抑制的愤怒。他说除了近视的傻瓜，所有人都可以看到那个洞里面只有一头大象。

寓意，猫曰

站在文本和自我想象力的镜子中间，你会在文本中发现你所带来的任何东西。你也许看不到你的耳朵，但它们就在那里。

---

① 普什图语中的“熊”。Hathi 和 Baloo 皆为英国小说家、1907年诺贝尔文学奖获得者吉卜林《丛林故事》中的动物名。

The Californian's Tale
加利福尼亚人的故事

《加利福尼亚人的故事》（The Californian's Tale，1893）讲述的是"我"在美国西部矿区四处淘金时遇到的一件奇事。

19世纪50年代末正是美国加州淘金热潮消退之时，许多失落的人们相继离去，曾经兴旺的小镇也变得逐渐荒芜。"我"四处淘金，却一无所获，疲惫之时却忽遇一处鲜花环绕的旧日矿工村舍。主人好客地邀"我"进屋，"我"也欣然而入。故事的场景此时切换到一处处似幻亦真的温馨家庭画面，屋里摆设整洁舒适，丈夫在提到自己的妻子时也是爱意浓浓。为了一睹女主人的绰约风姿，"我"留了下来，时间在这艰难时世难得的幸福之中仿佛也停滞了下来。日子缓慢地流逝，就在最后"我"以为可以一睹女主人芳容的时候，却发现早在十九年前这位优雅可人的女士就已经失踪了，而这位看似幸福的丈夫实则已精神失常多年。结尾之处，时间的巨大落差和空间的内外对比共同呈现出了一个破碎虚空的如梦人生。

这是一篇有别于马克·吐温惯常嬉笑讥讽风格的另类小说，虽然在讲述故事的过程中仍然少不了其天性中固有的幽默因子，但结尾时一切真相大白，哀伤凄婉之情毕现，读完令人唏嘘不已。

正如武陵渔人之入桃花源，瑞普·凡·温克尔(Rip Van Winkle)之入山谷，人生就这样在时空的幻化之中演绎出了一场场叫人慨叹的黄粱美梦。

Thirty-five years ago I was out prospecting on the Stanislaus, tramping all day long with pick and pan and horn, and washing a hatful of dirt here and there, always expecting to make a rich strike, and never doing it. It was a lovely region, woodsy, balmy, delicious, and had once been populous, long years before, but now the people had vanished and the charming paradise was a solitude. They went away when the surface diggings gave out. In one place, where a busy little city with banks and newspapers and fire companies and a mayor and aldermen had been, was nothing but a wide expanse of emerald turf, with not even the faintest sign that human life had ever been present there. This was down toward Tuttletown. In the country neighborhood thereabouts, along the dusty roads, one found at intervals the prettiest little cottage homes, snug and cozy, and so cobwebbed with vines snowed thick with roses that the doors and windows were wholly hidden from sight—sign that these were deserted homes, forsaken years ago by defeated and disappointed families who could neither sell them nor give them away. Now and then, half an hour apart, one came across solitary log cabins of the earliest mining days, built by the first gold-miners, the predecessors of the cottage-builders. In some few cases these cabins were still occupied; and when this was so, you could depend upon it that the occupant was the very pioneer who had built the cabin; and you could depend on another thing, too—that he was there because he had once had his opportunity to go home to the States rich, and had not done it; had rather lost his wealth, and had then in his humiliation

三十五年前，我曾外出到斯坦尼斯洛斯县[①] 去寻矿，带着鹤嘴锄、淘金盘和号角整日漂泊，在各处淘洗了许多矿砂，总是期望能找到金矿，发笔横财，可从未如愿。那是个风景秀美的地区，树木繁茂、空气芬芳、气候宜人，许多年前，这里人口稠密，可现在，人烟渐渺，迷人的天堂成了荒僻之地。他们把表层矿石挖完之后，就离开了这里。这儿有个地方曾经是一个热闹的小城，有银行、报社、消防队、市长和市议员，可如今，除了一片辽阔的翠绿草皮，这里什么也没有，甚至看不出丝毫有人居住过的痕迹。这地方通向塔特尔镇[②] 。在这乡野四邻附近，沿着尘土飞扬的道路，你会不时地瞧见一些极其漂亮小巧的村舍居所，看起来既舒适又温馨，墙上藤蔓蜿蜒密布，玫瑰花开得层层叠叠，把门窗全都遮住了——这表明这是些废弃的房屋。多年前，一些家庭遭受挫折、深感失望，他们既卖不掉也送不掉这些房屋，便只有遗弃了。偶尔，间隔半小时，还会看到一些采矿初期留下的荒凉小木屋，都是由第一批淘金者所搭建的，也就是那些村舍建造者的前辈。在极少数的情况下，这些小木屋仍会有人居住。若是这样，那就可以肯定住这儿的人就是建造这间木屋的拓荒者。可以肯定的还有另一件事——他在这儿，是因为他曾有机会腰缠万贯地回到美国的家，可他没有回去，结果反倒失去了所有的财产，羞愧之际，便决心断掉与家乡亲戚朋友的一切往来。

① 斯坦尼斯洛斯县，位于加利福尼亚州的中央谷(Central Valley)。
② 塔特尔镇，位于加利福尼亚州的图奥勒米县(Tuolumne)，现已不存在。

resolved to sever all communication with his home relatives and friends, and be to them thenceforth as one dead. Round about California in that day were scattered a host of these living dead men—pride-smitten poor fellows, grizzled and old at forty, whose secret thoughts were made all of regrets and longings—regrets for their wasted lives, and longings to be out of the struggle and done with it all.

It was a lonesome land! Not a sound in all those peaceful expanses of grass and woods but the drowsy hum of insects; no glimpse of man or beast; nothing to keep up your spirits and make you glad to be alive. And so, at last, in the early part of the afternoon, when I caught sight of a human creature, I felt a most grateful uplift. This person was a man about forty-five years old, and he was standing at the gate of one of those cozy little rose-clad cottages of the sort already referred to. However, this one hadn't a deserted look; it had the look of being lived in and petted and cared for and looked after; and so had its front yard, which was a garden of flowers, abundant, gay, and flourishing. I was invited in, of course, and required to make myself at home—it was the custom of the country.

It was delightful to be in such a place, after long weeks of daily and nightly familiarity with miners' cabins—with all which this implies of dirt floor, never-made beds, tin plates and cups, bacon and beans and black coffee, and nothing of ornament but war pictures from the Eastern illustrated papers tacked to the log walls. That was all hard, cheerless, materialistic desolation, but here was a nest which had aspects to rest the

从那时起，对他们而言，他便成了个死人。那时候，加利福尼亚州到处都散居着大批这样的活死人——自尊心严重受创的可怜家伙，四十岁便已头发花白、未老先衰，隐秘的内心充满着悔恨和渴望——悔恨的是他们虚度的年华，渴望的是从这挣扎中逃脱，结束所有的一切。

这是一片荒凉的土地！在那大片大片静谧的草丛和树林中，除了令人昏昏欲睡的昆虫嗡嗡声，根本就听不到丝毫的声响，看不见丁点儿人影或兽迹，也没有什么能使你精神振奋，让你觉得活着有乐趣。所以，在这个下午的早些时候，当我终于瞥见一个人时，我顿时满心感激，精神振奋起来。这是个四十五岁左右的男人，他正站在一栋前面提到过的那样布满玫瑰的舒适小村舍的大门口。可是，这栋房子看上去并不荒芜。它看起来是有人居住的，得到了主人的喜爱、关怀和照料。前院也是如此，那是个花园，鲜花品种丰富、姹紫嫣红、花繁叶茂。他邀我进了屋，当然了，还叫我不要拘束——这是那地方的风俗。

走进这样一个地方可真叫人高兴，尤其是好几个星期日日夜夜混在矿工木屋，熟悉了那里的全部之后——肮脏的地板，从没整理过的床铺，锡制的盘子和杯子，熏肉、豆子和清咖啡，除了木头墙上钉着的从东部图片新闻报上剪下的战争图片外，就再也没有别的装饰品了。一切都显得艰苦、沉闷和穷困荒凉，可这儿却是个舒适的住所，有许多地方可以让疲倦的眼睛得到休息，使人性中的某种东西得到恢复，尤其是在长期挨饿之后，一旦遇到了艺术品，不论它们

tired eye and refresh that something in one's nature which, after long fasting, recognizes, when confronted by the belongings of art, howsoever cheap and modest they may be, that it has unconsciously been famishing and now has found nourishment. I could not have believed that a rag carpet could feast me so, and so content me; or that there could be such solace to the soul in wall-paper and framed lithographs, and bright-colored tidies and lamp-mats, and Windsor chairs, and varnished what-nots, with sea-shells and books and china vases on them, and the score of little unclassifiable tricks and touches that a woman's hand distributes about a home, which one sees without knowing he sees them, yet would miss in a moment if they were taken away. The delight that was in my heart showed in my face, and the man saw it and was pleased; saw it so plainly that he answered it as if it had been spoken.

"All her work," he said, caressingly; "she did it all herself—every bit," and he took the room in with a glance which was full of affectionate worship. One of those soft Japanese fabrics with which women drape with careful negligence the upper part of a picture-frame was out of adjustment. He noticed it, and rearranged it with cautious pains, stepping back several times to gauge the effect before he got it to suit him. Then he gave it a light finishing pat or two with his hand, and said: "She always does that. You can't tell just what it lacks, but it does lack something until you've done that—you can see it yourself after it's done, but that is all you know; you can't find out the law of it. It's like the finishing pats a mother gives the child's hair

是多么的廉价和朴素，这种人性中的东西就会意识到它已经不知不觉挨了好长时间的饿，而现在总算是找到营养了。真不敢相信一条破旧的地毯就能让我如此享受、如此心满意足；真不敢相信墙纸和镶框版画，亮色的罩布和灯垫，温莎椅[①]，摆放着海贝、书籍和瓷花瓶的涂漆古董架子，以及女人亲手在家四处随意摆放物品和点缀房间时所留下的痕迹，竟能如此慰藉我的灵魂。看见这些东西时，你不会留意它们的存在，可要是拿掉它们，又会马上怀念起来。我心中的喜悦流露在了脸上，那男人见了很是高兴，这喜悦之情看着肯定很明显，因为他回答得就好像我已经说出来了似的。

“全都是她的活儿，”他说着，一脸爱意，“全都是她自己做的——全部。”他一眼扫视了整个房间，眼里满是深情的敬意。在画框上端，盖着一件柔软的日本织物，那是女人们看似随意实则小心地用来做装饰的。他注意到了它有点歪了，便小心翼翼地调整起来，好几次都退后几步来估量摆放的效果，直到满意为止。最后他用手在那上面轻轻拍了一两下，说：“她总是那样做。你也说不清到底缺什么，可是你没那样做之前，又的确是缺些东西——做完后，你自己也能明白，可那也就是你所知道的全部了。你发现不了其中的规律。我估计，这就像是一个母亲给孩子梳理完头发之后最后再拍拍那样。我常常看她整理这些东西，都完全可以按照她的方式来弄了，尽管我对这其中的规律一无所知。但是她知道。她既知道为什

① 温莎椅，18世纪流行于英美的一种细骨靠椅。

after she's got it combed and brushed, I reckon. I've seen her fix all these things so much that I can do them all just her way, though I don't know the law of any of them. But she knows the law. She knows the why and the how both; but I don't know the why; I only know the how."

He took me into a bedroom so that I might wash my hands; such a bedroom as I had not seen for years: white counterpane, white pillows, carpeted floor, papered walls, pictures, dressing-table, with mirror and pin-cushion and dainty toilet things; and in the corner a wash-stand, with real china-ware bowl and pitcher, and with soap in a china dish, and on a rack more than a dozen towels—towels too clean and white for one out of practice to use without some vague sense of profanation. So my face spoke again, and he answered with gratified words:

"All her work; she did it all herself—every bit. Nothing here that hasn't felt the touch of her hand. Now you would think—But I mustn't talk so much."

By this time I was wiping my hands and glancing from detail to detail of the room's belongings, as one is apt to do when he is in a new place, where everything he sees is a comfort to his eye and his spirit; and I became conscious, in one of those unaccountable ways, you know, that there was something there somewhere that the man wanted me to discover for myself. I knew it perfectly, and I knew he was trying to help me by furtive indications with his eye, so I tried hard to get on the right track, being eager to gratify him. I failed several times, as I could see out of the corner of my eye without being told; but at

么，也知道该怎样做。可我不知道为什么，我只知道怎样做。”

他领我进了一间卧室让我洗手。我已经有许多年没见过这样的卧室了：白色的床单、白色的枕头，铺着地毯的地板，贴着墙纸的四壁，图画，带着镜子、针插和精致梳妆用品的梳妆台。角落里立着个脸盆架，上面放着正宗的陶瓷脸盆和水罐，瓷盘上放着肥皂，架子上挂着十来条毛巾——这些毛巾又白又干净，没用惯的人用起来，心里肯定会有一种说不清的亵渎感。于是我的表情再次泄露了心中的话语，他也心满意足地回答说：

“全都是她的活儿，全都是她自己做的——全部。这儿没有哪件东西是没被她的手碰过的。现在你会认为——可是，我不该说这么多。”

这时，我正在擦手，同时仔仔细细地打量房间里的每一个细节，就像一个人到了新地方，看到那里每件东西对他都是一种视觉和精神上的抚慰时，往往就会那样做。而且，我察觉到，你知道，有种说不清的感觉，觉得这儿某处有件东西是这个男人希望我能自己发现的。我完全清楚这点，还知道他正试着用眼神来暗示我，我也竭力地想走上正确的路线，迫切地想让他满意。我失败了好几次，不用他说，我从眼角也能瞥出来。终于，我知道应该是直视前方的那个东西——从他那无形之中流露出的喜悦我就知道是它了。他爆发出开心的笑声，搓着双手，大声叫道：

last I knew I must be looking straight at the thing—knew it from the pleasure issuing in invisible waves from him. He broke into a happy laugh, and rubbed his hands together, and cried out:

"That's it! You've found it. I knew you would. It's her picture."

I went to the little black-walnut bracket on the farther wall, and did find there what I had not yet noticed—a daguerreotype-case. It contained the sweetest girlish face, and the most beautiful, as it seemed to me, that I had ever seen. The man drank the admiration from my face, and was fully satisfied.

"Nineteen her last birthday," he said, as he put the picture back; "and that was the day we were married. When you see her—ah, just wait till you see her!"

"Where is she? When will she be in?"

"Oh, she's away now. She's gone to see her people. They live forty or fifty miles from here. She's been gone two weeks today."

"When do you expect her back?"

"This is Wednesday. She'll be back Saturday, in the evening—about nine o'clock, likely."

I felt a sharp sense of disappointment.

"I'm sorry, because I'll be gone then," I said, regretfully.

"Gone? No—why should you go? Don't go. She'll be so disappointed."

She would be disappointed—that beautiful creature! If she had said the words herself they could hardly have blessed me more. I was feeling a deep, strong longing to see her—a longing

"就是它！你找到啦。我就知道你会找到的。这是她的相片。"

我朝镶在远处墙上的那个黑色胡桃木小托架走去，的确在那儿找到了一个我未曾留意的东西——一个装着银版法[①]照片的相框。相框里镶着一张最可爱的少女的脸，似乎也是我曾经见过的最美丽的。这个男人尽情地享受着我脸上流露的羡慕之情，感到十分满足。

"上次她十九岁生日时拍的，"他一边说，一边把照片放了回去，"也是我俩结婚的日子。要是你见着她——哈，就等着见她吧！"

"她在哪儿？什么时候能回家？"

"噢，她现在出门了，去见她家里人了。他们住在离这儿四五十英里远的地方。到今天为止，她已经离开两周了。"

"那你预计她什么时候会回来？"

"今天是星期三。她星期六会回来，晚上——大约九点钟，可能吧。"

我深感失望。

"很遗憾，因为那时我就要走了。"我遗憾地说。

"走？不行——为什么要走？别走。她会很失望的。"

她会失望——那个美人儿！要是她亲口说出这些话，我可就再幸福不过了。我有一种深切强烈的渴望想见到她——这渴望是如

① 达盖尔银版法，一种早期的照相术，把像照在易感光的镀银金属版上。

so supplicating, so insistent, that it made me afraid. I said to myself: "I will go straight away from this place, for my peace of mind's sake."

"You see, she likes to have people come and stop with us—people who know things, and can talk—people like you. She delights in it; for she knows—oh, she knows nearly everything herself, and can talk, oh, like a bird—and the books she reads, why, you would be astonished. Don't go; it's only a little while, you know, and she'll be so disappointed."

I heard the words, but hardly noticed them, I was so deep in my thinkings and strugglings. He left me, but I didn't know. Presently he was back, with the picture case in his hand, and he held it open before me and said:

"There, now, tell her to her face you could have stayed to see her, and you wouldn't."

That second glimpse broke down my good resolution. I would stay and take the risk. That night we smoked the tranquil pipe, and talked till late about various things, but mainly about her; and certainly I had had no such pleasant and restful time for many a day. The Thursday followed and slipped comfortably away. Toward twilight a big miner from three miles away came—one of the grizzled, stranded pioneers—and gave us warm salutation, clothed in grave and sober speech. Then he said:

"I only just dropped over to ask about the little madam, and when is she coming home. Any news from her?"

"Oh, yes, a letter. Would you like to hear it, Tom?"

此恳切，如此急迫，连我自己都觉得害怕起来。我心想："为了心中的安宁，我得马上离开这里。"

"知道吗，她喜欢有人来和我们一起住——那些见识广又能说的人——像你这样的人。她以此为乐，因为她知道——哦，她几乎什么都知道，而且还很能说，哦，就像鸟儿一样——还有她读的那些书，哎呀，你会惊呆的。别走，你知道，不会等多久，不然，她会很失望的。"

我听着这些话，却没怎么在意，我已陷入了沉思，内心苦苦挣扎着。他离开我时我也不知道。不一会儿，他手里拿着相框回来了，在我面前敞着，说道：

"好，现在，请你当着她的面说，你本来是可以留下来见她的，可你不愿意。"

这第二眼便击溃了我本已下定的决心。我愿留下来冒这个险。那天晚上，我们安静地抽着烟斗，天南地北地聊到很晚，但主要聊的还是她。的确，我已经有许多天没有感到这般愉快闲适了。接着是星期四，也舒适地晃过去了。黄昏时分，一位住在三英里外的大个子矿工过来了——他是头发花白、无依无靠的拓荒者中的一位——以一种严肃、冷静的口吻跟我们热情地打了个招呼。接着，他说：

"我只是顺便过来问问年轻太太的情况，还有，她什么时候回来。有她的消息吗？"

"啊，有的，一封信。你想听吗，汤姆？"

"Well, I should think I would, if you don't mind, Henry!"

Henry got the letter out of his wallet, and said he would skip some of the private phrases, if we were willing; then he went on and read the bulk of it—a loving, sedate, and altogether charming and gracious piece of handiwork, with a postscript full of affectionate regards and messages to Tom, and Joe, and Charley, and other close friends and neighbors.

As the reader finished, he glanced at Tom, and cried out:

"Oho, you're at it again! Take your hands away, and let me see your eyes. You always do that when I read a letter from her. I will write and tell her."

"Oh no, you mustn't, Henry. I'm getting old, you know, and any little disappointment makes me want to cry. I thought she'd be here herself, and now you've got only a letter."

"Well, now, what put that in your head? I thought everybody knew she wasn't coming till Saturday."

"Saturday! Why, come to think, I did know it. I wonder what's the matter with me lately? Certainly I knew it. Ain't we all getting ready for her? Well, I must be going now. But I'll be on hand when she comes, old man!"

Late Friday afternoon another gray veteran tramped over from his cabin a mile or so away, and said the boys wanted to have a little gaiety and a good time Saturday night, if Henry thought she wouldn't be too tired after her journey to be kept up.

"Tired? She tired! Oh, hear the man! Joe, you know she'd sit up six weeks to please any one of you!"

When Joe heard that there was a letter, he asked to have it

"好吧，我想是的，要是你不介意的话，亨利！"

亨利从钱夹里拿出信，说要是我们不介意的话，他想跳过一些私密话。接着，他继续读起了信里的主要部分——深情、恬静，总而言之，那是一件迷人、高雅的手工艺品，后面还有附言，满是捎给汤姆、乔、查理及其他亲密友邻的深情问候和消息。

读完后，他瞥了一眼汤姆，叫了起来：

"啊哈，你又这样了！把手拿开，让我瞧瞧你的眼睛。每次读完一封她的来信，你就总是那样。我要写信告诉她。"

"唉，别，这可不行，亨利。你知道，我老了，任何小小的失望都会让我想哭。我本来以为她回来了，可现在你只有一封信。"

"啊，喂，你怎么会那么想？我以为大家都知道她星期六才回来。"

"星期六！哎呀，想起来了，我的确是知道的。真奇怪，最近我是怎么了？我当然是知道的。我们不是要准备迎接她吗？好吧，现在我得走了。不过，她回来时我会到的，老朋友！"

星期五下午晚些时候，另一位头发灰白的老矿工从他那离这儿一英里左右的木屋里走了过来，他说兄弟们想在星期六晚上乐上一小会儿，开心一番，要是亨利觉得她旅行回来再参加聚会不觉得累的话。

"累？她累！噢，瞧你说的！乔，你知道，为了让你们每个人都高兴，她可是宁愿六个星期都不睡觉！"

乔听说有一封信，便要求念来听听，信中捎给他的那些充满爱

read, and the loving messages in it for him broke the old fellow all up; but he said he was such an old wreck that that would happen to him if she only just mentioned his name. "Lord, we miss her so!" he said.

Saturday afternoon I found I was taking out my watch pretty often. Henry noticed it, and said, with a startled look:

"You don't think she ought to be here soon, do you?"

I felt caught, and a little embarrassed; but I laughed, and said it was a habit of mine when I was in a state of expectancy. But he didn't seem quite satisfied; and from that time on he began to show uneasiness. Four times he walked me up the road to a point whence we could see a long distance; and there he would stand, shading his eyes with his hand, and looking. Several times he said:

"I'm getting worried, I'm getting right down worried. I know she's not due till about nine o'clock, and yet something seems to be trying to warn me that something's happened. You don't think anything has happened, do you?"

I began to get pretty thoroughly ashamed of him for his childishness; and at last, when he repeated that imploring question still another time, I lost my patience for the moment, and spoke pretty brutally to him. It seemed to shrivel him up and cow him; and he looked so wounded and so humble after that, that I detested myself for having done the cruel and unnecessary thing. And so I was glad when Charley, another veteran, arrived toward the edge of the evening, and nestled up to Henry to hear the letter read, and talked over the preparations for the welcome.

意的话语让这位老兄完全崩溃了。可是，他说他就是这样一个老废物，只要她提一下他的名字，他就难免不会变成那样。“天啊，我们可真想她啊！”他说。

星期六下午，我发现自己老是频繁地掏出手表来看。亨利察觉到了，面带惊讶地说：

“你不会以为她这么快就会到的，是吧？”

我被说中了，觉得有点尴尬。但是我笑了起来，解释说这是我有所期待时的一种习惯。但他似乎并不是很相信。从那时起，他就开始露出不安的神情。他四次拉着我一起走上大道，走到一处可以看得很远的地方。然后，他就站着在那儿，手搭凉棚，望着什么。好几次他都说：

“我有些担心了，我真的有些担心了。我知道不到九点左右她是不会到的，可好像有什么总想警告我出事了。你觉得没出什么事，是吧？”

我开始为他的孩子气而感到万分羞愧。最后，当他再次重复那个犹如哀求一般的问题时，我一下子失去了耐心，非常粗鲁地冲他说了一些话。这似乎让他变得萎缩胆怯起来。并且，在那之后，他看起来很受伤，还显得很谦卑，让我憎恨起自己做了这么残酷而又多余的事。所以，临近傍晚，当另一个老矿工查理到来时，我感到非常高兴。他紧挨在亨利身边听他念信，还不停地说着欢迎会的准备事宜。查理一句接一句地说出些热情亲切的话语，竭尽全力地想驱散他朋友心中的不祥预感和忧虑。

Charley fetched out one hearty speech after another, and did his best to drive away his friend's bodings and apprehensions.

"Anything happened to her? Henry, that's pure nonsense. There isn't anything going to happen to her; just make your mind easy as to that. What did the letter say? Said she was well, didn't it? And said she'd be here by nine o'clock, didn't it? Did you ever know her to fail of her word? Why, you know you never did. Well, then, don't you fret; she'll be here, and that's absolutely certain, and as sure as you are born. Come, now, let's get to decorating—not much time left."

Pretty soon Tom and Joe arrived, and then all hands set about adorning the house with flowers. Toward nine the three miners said that as they had brought their instruments they might as well tune up, for the boys and girls would soon be arriving now, and hungry for a good, old-fashioned break-down. A fiddle, a banjo, and a clarinet—these were the instruments. The trio took their places side by side, and began to play some rattling dance-music, and beat time with their big boots.

It was getting very close to nine. Henry was standing in the door with his eyes directed up the road, his body swaying to the torture of his mental distress. He had been made to drink his wife's health and safety several times, and now Tom shouted:

"All hands stand by! One more drink, and she's here!"

Joe brought the glasses on a waiter, and served the party. I reached for one of the two remaining glasses, but Joe growled

"她出什么事了？亨利，这完全是瞎说。她不会出什么事的。你就只管放心吧。信上说了什么？说她很好，不是吗？还说九点钟她就会回来，不是吗？你什么时候见过她说话不算数？唉，你知道从来就没有过的。好啦，喏，别烦躁不安了。她会回来的，那是绝对肯定、毫无疑问的事儿。来，现在我们该开始布置了——没多少时间啦。"

很快，汤姆和乔也来了，然后所有人都开始用花装饰起了房子。快九点时，这三位矿工说，既然他们都把自己的乐器带来了，那最好还是演奏起来，因为小伙子和姑娘们马上就要到了，都渴望着好好地跳一场老式的跺脚曳步舞[①]呢。一把小提琴、一把班卓琴[②]和一支单簧管——这便是所有的乐器。三重奏的成员并排坐好，接着就开始演奏起了一些轻快活泼的舞曲，还踏着大靴子打起了拍子。

就快要到九点了。亨利站在门口，两眼直直地盯着前面的大路，他的身体因内心的煎熬而摇晃起来。大家让他为妻子的健康和安全干了好几次杯，现在，汤姆又叫了起来：

"大伙儿准备好了！再喝一杯，她就回来了！"

乔用托盘给大家端来酒水。我伸手去拿剩下两杯中的一杯，可

① 跺脚曳步舞，一种喧闹而轻快的美国乡村舞蹈。
② 班卓琴，上部形似吉他，下部形似铃鼓，有四弦或五弦，用手指或拨子弹奏。据传班卓琴是由非洲黑人的民族弹拨乐器发展而来，现已是美国移民音乐文化的代言。

under his breath:

"Drop that! Take the other."

Which I did. Henry was served last. He had hardly swallowed his drink when the clock began to strike. He listened till it finished, his face growing pale and paler; then he said:

"Boys, I'm sick with fear. Help me—I want to lie down!"

They helped him to the sofa. He began to nestle and drowse, but presently spoke like one talking in his sleep, and said: "Did I hear horses' feet? Have they come?"

One of the veterans answered, close to his ear: "It was Jimmy Parrish come to say the party got delayed, but they're right up the road a piece, and coming along. Her horse is lame, but she'll be here in half an hour."

"Oh, I'm so thankful nothing has happened!"

He was asleep almost before the words were out of his mouth. In a moment those handy men had his clothes off, and had tucked him into his bed in the chamber where I had washed my hands. They closed the door and came back. Then they seemed preparing to leave; but I said: "Please don't go, gentlemen. She won't know me; I am a stranger."

They glanced at each other. Then Joe said:

"She? Poor thing, she's been dead nineteen years!"

"Dead?"

"That or worse. She went to see her folks half a year after she was married, and on her way back, on a Saturday evening, the Indians captured her within five miles of this place, and she's never been heard of since."

是乔低声吼道：

“放下那杯！拿另一杯。”

我照做了。亨利是最后一个拿酒杯的。他刚饮完酒，钟就敲起来了。他一直听到钟声敲完，脸色也变得越来越苍白，然后他说：

“兄弟们，我害怕得要死。帮帮我——我想躺下！”

他们把他扶到沙发。他靠在上面打起了盹，可是，不一会儿做梦似的讲起话来：“我是不是听见马蹄声了？他们来了吗？”

其中一个老矿工贴着他的耳朵说：“是吉米·帕里什过来说聚会得推迟了，不过他们就在路上不远处，正朝这儿来。她的马瘸了，不过半个小时后她就会到。”

“噢，没出什么事可真是谢天谢地！”

话还没说完，他就几乎睡着了。不一会儿，这些身边的人帮他脱下衣服，把他抬上床，给他盖好被子，让他睡在我先前洗手的那个房间。他们关上门，走了出来。接着，他们似乎准备离开了。可是我说：“请别走，先生们。她不认识我，我是个生客。”

他们互相看了一眼。然后乔说：

“她？可怜的人儿，她都死了十九年了！”

“死了？”

“死了，或是更糟，婚后半年她去看望她的亲人，星期六晚上，在回来的途中，被印第安人在离这儿不到五英里的地方给捉走了，从此就再也没听到过她的消息了。”

"And he lost his mind in consequence?"

"Never has been sane an hour since. But he only gets bad when that time of year comes round. Then we begin to drop in here, three days before she's due, to encourage him up, and ask if he's heard from her, and Saturday we all come and fix up the house with flowers, and get everything ready for a dance. We've done it every year for nineteen years. The first Saturday there was twenty-seven of us, without counting the girls; there's only three of us now, and the girls are all gone. We drug him to sleep, or he would go wild; then he's all right for another year—thinks she's with him till the last three or four days come round; then he begins to look for her, and gets out his poor old letter, and we come and ask him to read it to us. Lord, she was a darling!"

“结果他就疯了吗？”

“从那以后，他一刻也没清醒过。不过，只是到了每年的这个时候他的情况才会变得那么糟。于是，我们会在她本来要回来的前三天过来看看，给他鼓劲，问他是不是有她的消息，而到了星期六，我们就会全都过来用花把这屋子装扮一番，备好舞会上用的一切东西。十九年来，我们每年都这样做。第一次星期六办的时候，不算上姑娘们，一共有二十七人。现在只剩下我们三个人了，姑娘们全都走了。我们给他吃药让他睡着，不然他会发狂的。这样，下一年他就会没问题——以为她跟他在一起，直到那一刻到来的最后三四天前。然后，他就会开始找她，拿出他那封可怜的旧信，我们也会过来叫他读给我们听。天哪，她真是一位可爱的人啊！”

Cannibalism in the Cars
火车上的食人族

《火车上的食人族》（Cannibalism in the Cars, 1868）讲述了一列火车中途突遇暴雪，车上的乘客被困在荒无人烟的大草原上，孤立无援，最后迫于饥饿做出了吃人的决定。

小说中被困的乘客，言行举止全然一副政客的模样。他们来自美国各地，享有平等的言论自由，构成了一个微型的美国社会。他们有强烈的民主意识，较高的政治素养，深谙当时国会的选举制度。即便是在极端恶劣的生存条件下，依然能够迅速达成一致，选出主席、委员会，并组成议会；制定并遵循一套完整的游戏规则，从提名候选人，提交修正案，到公开的唇枪舌剑，再到最后的投票选出结果，一切进行得井然有序，让人很容易联想到现实的政治生活。不同的是，小说中选举的目的却是为了“吃人”。

将“吃人”和政治联系在一起，本身具有很强烈的讽刺意味。小说以荒诞不经的情节、尖刻辛辣的语言，矛头直接指向当时的政治生活。以民主标榜的美国政治制度成了使“吃人”这一野蛮行径合法化的工具。道貌岸然的政客们充当了刽子手的角色，津津乐道地讨论着谁的肉质更为鲜美；而被选为佳肴美羹的人们只能任人宰割，无力维护自己的权益，这是对民主有力的讽刺。另外，小说结尾告诉读者，这场惨绝人寰的民主选举原来只不过是一位精神疯癫的政治家的臆想，让人不禁想到——难道政治家都疯了吗？还是只有疯了的政治家才会说实话？

I visited St. Louis lately, and on my way West, after changing cars at Terre Haute, Indiana, a mild, benevolent-looking gentleman of about forty-five, or maybe fifty, came in at one of the way-stations and sat down beside me. We talked together pleasantly on various subjects for an hour, perhaps, and I found him exceedingly intelligent and entertaining. When he learned that I was from Washington, he immediately began to ask questions about various public men, and about Congressional affairs; and I saw very shortly that I was conversing with a man who was perfectly familiar with the ins and outs of political life at the Capital, even to the ways and manners, and customs of procedure of Senators and Representatives in the Chambers of the national Legislature. Presently two men halted near us for a single moment, and one said to the other:

"Harris, if you'll do that for me, I'll never forget you, my boy."

My new comrade's eye lighted pleasantly. The words had touched upon a happy memory, I thought. Then his face settled into thoughtfulness—almost into gloom. He turned to me and said, "Let me tell you a story; let me give you a secret chapter of my life—a chapter that has never been referred to by me since its events transpired. Listen patiently, and promise that you will not interrupt me."

I said I would not, and he related the following strange adventure, speaking sometimes with animation, sometimes with melancholy, but always with feeling and earnestness.

不久前，我访问了圣路易斯。西行途中，我在印第安纳州的特雷霍特站转车。之后，从一个小站上来一位大约四十五岁，或者可能五十岁的先生，坐在我旁边。他性情温和、相貌和善。我们就各类话题一起愉快地聊了一个钟头左右，我发现他非常聪明风趣。当他得知我来自华盛顿[①]时，立即问起了诸位政界人物和国会事务。我很快明白，与我谈话的这个人深谙首都政治生活的方方面面，甚至深谙国家立法机关中参议员和众议员[②]办事的方法习惯及程序惯例。这时，有两个人在我们附近逗留了片刻，其中一人对另一个说：

“哈里斯，要是你帮我那个忙，我永远都不会忘了你，哥们儿。”

我的新同伴眼睛一亮，露出喜悦的神色。我料想，这句话让他回想起了一段快乐的往事。接着，他陷入了沉思——脸上的表情近乎忧郁。他转过头对我说道：“听我给你讲个故事吧，听我告诉你我这辈子最隐秘的一页——自从出了事，这一段生活我从未提起过。耐心听，而且你得保证不会打断我。”

我说我不会的，于是他讲述了下面那段离奇的经历，时而说得生动活泼，时而说得忧郁沮丧，但始终情绪饱满、郑重其事。

---

① 华盛顿，美国首都。文中陌生人得知“我”来自首都，故主动聊起了政治话题。
② Senators and Representatives 分别指参议员和众议员（或州议员）。美国国会由两院组成，即参议院和众议院，为国家最高的立法机关。两院中参议员任期为六年，众议员任期为两年。

On the 19th of December, 1853, I started from St. Louis on the evening train bound for Chicago. There were only twenty-four passengers, all told. There were no ladies and no children. We were in excellent spirits, and pleasant acquaintanceships were soon formed. The journey bade fair to be a happy one; and no individual in the party, I think, had even the vaguest presentiment of the horrors we were soon to undergo.

At 11 P.M. it began to snow hard. Shortly after leaving the small village of Welden, we entered upon that tremendous prairie solitude that stretches its leagues on leagues① of houseless dreariness far away toward the Jubilee Settlements. The winds, unobstructed by trees or hills, or even vagrant rocks, whistled fiercely, across the level desert, driving the falling snow before it like spray from the crested waves of a stormy sea. The snow was deepening fast; and we knew, by the diminished speed of the train, that the engine was plowing through it with steadily increasing difficulty. Indeed, it almost came to a dead halt sometimes, in the midst of great drifts that piled themselves like colossal graves across the track. Conversation began to flag. Cheerfulness gave place to grave concern. The possibility of being imprisoned in the snow, on the bleak prairie, fifty miles from any house, presented itself to every mind, and extended its depressing influence over every spirit.

At two o'clock in the morning I was aroused out of an uneasy slumber by the ceasing of all motion about me. The appalling truth flashed upon me instantly—we were captives

① league: 里格，旧时长度单位，约为3英里。文中形容地域的广袤。

1853年12月19日，我从圣路易斯出发，乘夜班火车前往芝加哥。车上一共才二十四名乘客，没有妇女和孩子。我们心情极佳，很快就认识了，打成一片。这有望成为一次愉快的旅行，我想，一群人中没有人对我们即将经受的噩梦有丝毫模糊的预感。

夜里十一点，下起了大雪。我们离开名为韦尔登的小村庄不久，就驶入了那茫茫沉寂的大草原。它渺无人烟，一片凄凉，一直延伸到远方的朱比利定居点。没有树，也没有山，甚至没有零落的石块的阻挡，风猛烈地呼啸着穿过平坦的荒原，驱赶着飘落的雪片，就像汹涌的大海里浪头上溅起的水花。雪很快越积越深，我们从火车减慢的速度知道，引擎正推动着火车在积雪中前行，越来越费力。实际上大雪堆积在铁轨上，犹如巨冢一般，列车从中间穿过，有时几乎完全停止。聊天开始变得枯燥无味。轻松愉快被忧心忡忡取代。方圆五十英里了无人烟，我们可能会被大雪困在荒凉的大草原上。这种想法浮现在每个人的心头，沮丧的心情蔓延开来，影响到每一个人。

凌晨两点，周围的一切活动沉寂下来，我被从不安的睡梦中惊醒，突然想到了一个可怕的事实——我们被大雪困住了！“所有人都去帮忙！”每个人都赶忙起身从命。大家出了车厢，进入暴风雪

in a snow-drift! "All hands to the rescue!" Every man sprang to obey. Out into the wild night, the pitchy darkness, the billowy snow, the driving storm, every soul leaped, with the consciousness that a moment lost now might bring destruction to us all. Shovels, hands, boards—anything, everything that could displace snow, was brought into instant requisition. It was a weird picture, that small company of frantic men fighting the banking snows, half in the blackest shadow and half in the angry light of the locomotive's reflector.

One short hour sufficed to prove the utter uselessness of our efforts. The storm barricaded the track with a dozen drifts while we dug one away. And worse than this, it was discovered that the last grand charge the engine had made upon the enemy had broken the fore-and-aft shaft of the driving-wheel! With a free track before us we should still have been helpless. We entered the car wearied with labor, and very sorrowful. We gathered about the stoves, and gravely canvassed our situation. We had no provisions whatever—in this lay our chief distress. We could not freeze, for there was a good supply of wood in the tender. This was our only comfort. The discussion ended at last in accepting the disheartening decision of the conductor, viz., that it would be death for any man to attempt to travel fifty miles on foot through snow like that. We could not send for help, and even if we could it would not come. We must submit, and await, as patiently as we might, succor or starvation! I think the stoutest heart there felt a momentary chill when those words were uttered.

之夜，外面漆黑一片，雪花漫天，狂风大作。我们明白，现在耽搁一分钟，可能就会给所有人带来灭顶之灾。铁锹、赤手、木板——任何东西，凡是可以铲雪的东西马上都被派上了用场。这是不可思议的一幕，一小群疯狂的人在与铺天盖地的大雪搏斗，一半在漆黑无比的暗影里，一半在火车头愤怒的灯光下。

短短一个钟头足以证明我们的努力完全是徒劳的。我们才铲去一堆雪，暴雪就又堆起了十来堆堵住铁轨。更糟糕的是，我们发现，火车头对敌人发起的最后一次主要进攻折断了连接驱动轮的纵轴。就算前面是条畅通无阻的车轨，我们也没辙。我们精疲力竭地走进车厢，忧心忡忡。大伙聚在火炉旁，心情沉重地谈论我们的处境。没有任何食物——这是最令我们头疼的一点。我们不会挨冻，因为在列车的煤水车厢备有足够的木柴。这算是我们唯一的宽慰。讨论结束了，最后大家接受了列车长令人沮丧的结论，即任何人试图在那么大的雪中徒步行走五十英里，都会是死路一条。我们无法派人求救，就算能，救援也到不了。我们只有听任摆布，尽量耐心地等待，等着获救或者等着被饿死！我想，听说那些话的时候，最坚强的心也会瞬间变凉。

Within the hour conversation subsided to a low murmur here and there about the car, caught fitfully between the rising and falling of the blast; the lamps grew dim; and the majority of the castaways settled themselves among the flickering shadows to think—to forget the present, if they could—to sleep, if they might.

The eternal night—it surely seemed eternal to us—wore its lagging hours away at last, and the cold gray dawn broke in the east. As the light grew stronger the passengers began to stir and give signs of life, one after another, and each in turn pushed his slouched hat up from his forehead, stretched his stiffened limbs, and glanced out of the windows upon the cheerless prospect. It was cheerless, indeed!—not a living thing visible anywhere, not a human habitation; nothing but a vast white desert; uplifted sheets of snow drifted hither and thither before the wind—a world of eddying flakes shutting out the firmament above.

All day we moped about the cars, saying little, thinking much. Another lingering dreary night—and hunger.

Another dawning—another day of silence, sadness, wasting hunger, hopeless watching for succor that could not come. A night of restless slumber, filled with dreams of feasting—wakings distressed with the gnawings of hunger.

The fourth day came and went—and the fifth! Five days of dreadful imprisonment! A savage hunger looked out at every eye. There was in it a sign of awful import—the foreshadowing of a something that was vaguely shaping itself in every heart—a something which no tongue dared yet to frame into words.

不到一个小时，谈话减弱为车内四处的窃窃私语，时不时湮没在强弱交织的狂风中。灯光变得昏暗，大多数受难者躺在忽明忽暗的灯影下思索——图的是忘记当下，如果他们能做到的话——图的是睡觉，如果他们可以的话。

漫漫长夜——在我们眼中，确实显得漫长——终于把拖拖拉拉的时间磨蹭过去了。天气寒冷，灰白的天空从东方亮起。随着光线逐渐增强，乘客们陆续醒来，显出生命的迹象。人们一个个向上推了推耷拉下来的帽子，伸了伸僵硬的四肢，然后望着窗外凄凉的景象。就是凄凉，千真万确！四周看不到一个生命，看不到一户人家，只有白茫茫的一片荒原。隆起的层层积雪被风刮得到处都是——一个大雪纷飞的世界，暴雪遮天蔽日。

一整天，我们没精打采地在车厢里闲荡，说话很少，想了很多。又一个漫长可怕的黑夜——还有饥饿。

又一个黎明——又一天的静寂、悲伤、蚀人的饥饿，绝望地期待着无法到达的救援。一个无眠的夜晚，人们纷纷做着盛宴的美梦——醒来却因饥饿的吞噬而沮丧不已。

第四天来了，走了——接着第五天！五天可怕的囚禁！每只眼睛都露出极度饥饿的凶光，隐含着一种可怕的意味——预示着在每个人心里一个想法正隐约形成——一个还没人敢说出来的想法。

The sixth day passed—the seventh dawned upon as gaunt and haggard and hopeless a company of men as ever stood in the shadow of death. It must out now! That thing which had been growing up in every heart was ready to leap from every lip at last! Nature had been taxed to the utmost—she must yield. RICHARD H. GASTON of Minnesota, tall, cadaverous, and pale, rose up. All knew what was coming. All prepared—every emotion, every semblance of excitement was smothered—only a calm, thoughtful seriousness appeared in the eyes that were lately so wild.

"Gentlemen: It cannot be delayed longer! The time is at hand! We must determine which of us shall die to furnish food for the rest!"

MR. JOHN J. WILLIAMS of Illinois rose and said: "Gentlemen—I nominate the Rev. James Sawyer of Tennessee."

MR. WM. R. ADAMS of Indiana said: "I nominate Mr. Daniel Slote of New York."

MR. CHARLES J. LANGDON: "I nominate Mr. Samuel A. Bowen of St. Louis."

MR. SLOTE: "Gentlemen—I desire to decline in favor of Mr. John A. Van Nostrand, Jun., of New Jersey."

MR. GASTON: "If there be no objection, the gentleman's desire will be acceded to."

MR. VAN NOSTRAND objecting, the resignation of Mr. Slote was rejected. The resignations of Messrs. ① Sawyer and Bowen were also offered, and refused upon the same grounds.

① Messrs.= Messieurs, 意思是"各位先生",置于一系列男子姓名前。

第六天过去了——第七天黎明降临时，一群瘦弱、憔悴、无望的人仍旧站在死亡的阴影之中。现在必须说出来！最后，那个在每个人心中不断膨胀的念头随时都会从嘴里蹦出来！本能已经忍到了极点——它必须屈服。明尼苏达州的理查德·H.加斯顿，一个高个、憔悴、面色苍白的人站了起来。大家都明白将会发生什么。大家都准备好了——每一种情感，每一种近似于兴奋的情感都被压制着——此前疯狂的眼睛中流露出的只有平静和若有所思的严肃。

"先生们，不能再拖了！时间紧迫！我们必须决定我们中间哪些人要死，做其他人的食物。"

伊利诺伊州的约翰·J.威廉斯先生站起来说："先生们——我提名田纳西州的詹姆士·索亚牧师。"

印第安纳州的威廉姆·R.亚当斯先生说："我提名纽约的丹尼尔·斯罗特先生。"

查尔斯·J.兰登先生："我提名圣路易斯的塞缪尔·A.鲍恩先生。"

斯罗特先生："先生们——我实不敢当。我支持新泽西的小约翰·A.范·诺斯特兰先生。"

加斯顿先生："如果没人反对，那么这位先生的请求将会被接受。"

范·诺斯特兰先生反对，斯罗特先生的放弃请求被拒绝。索亚和鲍文两位先生也提出了放弃请求，均以同样的理由遭到拒绝。

MR. A. L. BASCOM of Ohio: "I move that the nominations now close, and that the House proceed to an election by ballot."

MR. SAWYER: "Gentlemen—I protest earnestly against these proceedings. They are, in every way, irregular and unbecoming. I must beg to move that they be dropped at once, and that we elect a chairman of the meeting and proper officers to assist him, and then we can go on with the business before us understandingly."

MR. BELL of Iowa: "Gentlemen—I object. This is no time to stand upon forms and ceremonious observances. For more than seven days we have been without food. Every moment we lose in idle discussion increases our distress. I am satisfied with the nominations that have been made—every gentleman present is, I believe—and I, for one, do not see why we should not proceed at once to elect one or more of them. I wish to offer a resolution—"

MR. GASTON: "It would be objected to, and have to lie over one day under the rules, thus bringing about the very delay you wish to avoid. The gentleman from New Jersey—"

MR. VAN NOSTRAND: "Gentlemen—I am a stranger among you; I have not sought the distinction that has been conferred upon me, and I feel a delicacy—"

MR. MORGAN of Alabama (interrupting): "I move the previous question."

The motion was carried, and further debate shut off, of course. The motion to elect officers was passed, and under it Mr. Gaston was chosen chairman, Mr. Blake, secretary, Messrs.

俄亥俄州的 A.L. 巴斯科姆先生："我提议提名到此结束，下面由议会[1]进行投票选举。"

索亚先生："先生们——我坚决反对这些做法。这完全不正规、不合适。我提议立即取消这些做法，并且提议我们选举出一位会议主席和适合协助他工作的干事。然后，我们才能合理地处理眼前的事情。"

爱荷华州的贝尔先生："先生们——我反对。现在不是拘泥于形式和刻板规章的时候，因为我们已经七天多没有进食了。在无谓的讨论中浪费的每一分钟只会增加我们的痛苦。我赞成已经做出的提名——我相信，在座的每位先生都会赞成——但是有一点我不明白，为什么不立即从他们中选出一个或更多的人来呢？我想提出一种解决方案——"

加斯顿先生："这会遭到反对，并且按照规定，这得留着以后讨论，这样的话就会出现你不愿看到的那种延误。那位新泽西的先生——"

范·诺斯特兰先生："先生们——我们萍水相逢，我从未奢求过赋予我的这份殊荣，我担心的是——"

亚拉巴马州的摩根先生（插话道）："我提议回到前面的问题。"

该动议被采纳，更多的争论自然停了下来。选举干事的动议被通过了。根据动议，加斯顿先生被选为主席，布莱克先生为秘书，

① 为国家最高立法机关。作者在小说中多次使用"议会""选举""候选人""投票""提名""修正案"等政治生活方面的词汇，意在影射西方的民主政治。

Holcomb, Dyer, and Baldwin a committee on nominations, and Mr. R. M. Howland, purveyor, to assist the committee in making selections.

A recess of half an hour was then taken, and some little caucusing followed. At the sound of the gavel the meeting reassembled, and the committee reported in favor of Messrs. George Ferguson of Kentucky, Lucien Herrman of Louisiana, and W. Messick of Colorado as candidates. The report was accepted.

MR. ROGERS of Missouri: "Mr. President—The report being properly before the House now, I move to amend it by substituting for the name of Mr. Herrman that of Mr. Lucius Harris of St. Louis, who is well and honorably known to us all. I do not wish to be understood as casting the least reflection upon the high character and standing of the gentleman from Louisiana—far from it. I respect and esteem him as much as any gentleman here present possibly can; but none of us can be blind to the fact that he has lost more flesh during the week that we have lain here than any among us—none of us can be blind to the fact that the committee has been derelict in its duty, either through negligence or a graver fault, in thus offering for our suffrages a gentleman who, however pure his own motives may be, has really less nutriment in him—"

THE CHAIR: "The gentleman from Missouri will take his seat. The Chair cannot allow the integrity of the committee to be questioned save by the regular course, under the rules. What action will the House take upon the gentleman's motion?"

霍尔库姆先生、戴尔先生和鲍德温先生为提名委员会委员，还有R.M.豪兰先生承办伙食，协助委员会做决定。

休会半个小时后，接着召开了几场小规模的预备会议。随着木槌的声音，会议开始。委员会报告同意肯塔基州的乔治·弗格森先生、路易斯安那州的卢西恩·赫尔曼先生和科罗拉多州的W.梅西克先生为候选人。该报告被采纳。

密苏里州的罗杰斯先生："主席先生——趁现在议会正好在讨论该报告，我提议做些修改，把赫尔曼先生换成被我们大家熟知和尊敬的来自圣路易斯的卢修斯·哈里斯先生。我不希望此举被认为是在诋毁那位来自路易斯安那州的先生的崇高人格和名望——绝非如此。我和这里在场的诸位一样，尊重并敬佩他。但是我们谁也不能对事实熟视无睹，被困在这里的一周当中，他比我们任何人瘦得都要厉害——我们谁也不能对委员会的失职熟视无睹。它不是玩忽职守，就是犯下更严重的错误，才会不负责任地为我们的投票提供了这么一位先生，无论他本人的动机多么的单纯，他实在是没有什么营养——"

主席："密苏里州的这位先生请就座。除非按照规定通过正规的程序，否则本席不能允许委员会的公正遭到质疑。议会对这位先生的动议有什么要做的吗？"

MR. HALLIDAY of Virginia: "I move to further amend the report by substituting Mr. Harvey Davis of Oregon for Mr. Messick. It may be urged by gentlemen that the hardships and privations of a frontier life have rendered Mr. Davis tough; but, gentlemen, is this a time to cavil at toughness? Is this a time to be fastidious concerning trifles? Is this a time to dispute about matters of paltry significance? No, gentlemen, bulk is what we desire, substance, weight, bulk—these are the supreme requisites now—not talent, not genius, not education. I insist upon my motion."

MR. MORGAN (excitedly): "Mr. Chairman—I do most strenuously object to this amendment. The gentleman from Oregon is old, and furthermore is bulky only in bone—not in flesh. I ask the gentleman from Virginia if it is soup we want instead of solid sustenance? if he would delude us with shadows? if he would mock our suffering with an Oregonian specter? I ask him if he can look upon the anxious faces around him, if he can gaze into our sad eyes, if he can listen to the beating of our expectant hearts, and still thrust this famine-stricken fraud upon us? I ask him if he can think of our desolate state, of our past sorrows, of our dark future, and still unpityingly foist upon us this wreck, this ruin, this tottering swindle, this gnarled and blighted and sapless vagabond from Oregon's inhospitable shores? Never!" [Applause.]

The amendment was put to vote, after a fiery debate, and lost. Mr. Harris was substituted on the first amendment. The balloting then began. Five ballots were held without a choice.

弗吉尼亚州的韩礼德先生：“我提议进一步修改报告，把梅西克先生换成俄勒冈州[1]的哈维·戴维斯先生。先生们可能会坚持认为，艰苦贫乏的边疆生活已经使戴维斯先生变得难嚼；但是先生们，这是指摘难嚼的时候吗？这是对小事挑三拣四的时候吗？这是在微不足道的事情上争来争去的时候吗？不，先生们，块头才是我们想要的，食物、体重、块头——这些是现在最必要的条件——不是才干，不是智慧，不是技能。我坚持我的提议。”

摩根先生（激动地）：“主席先生——我极力反对这项修正。来自俄勒冈州的那位先生老了，而且只是骨头块儿大——并不是肉多。我问问这位来自弗吉尼亚州的先生，是否我们需要的是清汤，而不是实实在在的食物？是否他想用假象蒙骗我们？是否他想用个俄勒冈州的瘦鬼嘲弄我们的痛苦？我问问他，是否能看看周围一张张焦虑的面孔，是否能直视我们忧伤的眼睛，是否能听到我们期盼的心在跳动，却还硬塞给我们这个饥饿不堪的骗子？我问问他能否想想我们悲惨的状况，想想我们过去的悲痛，想想我们黯淡的未来，却还无情地塞给我们这具枯骸，这个废物，这个踉踉跄跄的骗子，这个皱巴巴、干瘪瘪、病蔫蔫，来自俄勒冈州荒凉海岸的盲流？绝对不行！”（掌声）

一番激烈的争论之后，该修正案被交付表决，但未被通过。根据第一项修正案，哈里斯先生成了替补。随后投票开始。投了五次都没有结果。第六次哈里斯先生当选，除了他自己之外，其他人全

① 俄勒冈州，位于美国西北海岸，西临太平洋。在作者生活的时代，该州为偏远的西部边疆地区。

On the sixth, Mr. Harris was elected, all voting for him but himself. It was then moved that his election should be ratified by acclamation, which was lost, in consequence of his again voting against himself.

MR. RADWAY moved that the House now take up the remaining candidates, and go into an election for breakfast. This was carried.

On the first ballot there was a tie, half the members favoring one candidate on account of his youth, and half favoring the other on account of his superior size. The President gave the casting vote for the latter, Mr. Messick. This decision created considerable dissatisfaction among the friends of Mr. Ferguson, the defeated candidate, and there was some talk of demanding a new ballot; but in the midst of it a motion to adjourn was carried, and the meeting broke up at once.

The preparations for supper diverted the attention of the Ferguson faction from the discussion of their grievance for a long time, and then, when they would have taken it up again, the happy announcement that Mr. Harris was ready drove all thought of it to the winds.

We improvised tables by propping up the backs of car-seats, and sat down with hearts full of gratitude to the finest supper that had blessed our vision for seven torturing days. How changed we were from what we had been a few short hours before! Hopeless, sad-eyed misery, hunger, feverish anxiety, desperation, then; thankfulness, serenity, joy too deep for utterance now. That I know was the cheeriest hour of my

都投了赞成票。然后，有人提议以口头表决的方式批准他的当选，这一提议因他再次投了自己的反对票而未被通过。

瑞德威先生提议，现在议会继续加上其余候选人，选出早餐的人选。该提议被通过。

首轮投票出现平局，一半成员支持某位候选人，因为其风华正茂；一半支持另一位候选人，因为其个头较大。主席把决定性的一票[1]投给了后者梅西克先生。这一决定在败方弗格森先生的朋友当中引起了相当大的不满，还有人要求再投一轮。但是在这期间，通过了休会的动议，随即散会。

晚餐的准备工作转移了弗格森派的注意力，很长一段时间内，他们停止了忿恨不平的议论。后来，在他们又要重新开始时，得知了哈里斯先生已经做好这个开心的消息，并将对落选的所有关注全都抛到了九霄云外。

我们支起车座后背，临时拼凑成桌子坐下来，心里充满了感激之情。历经七天的折磨，我们做梦都在期盼着这顿最美味的晚餐。跟短短几个小时之前相比，我们的变化可真大啊！那时的我们失望、愁容满面、饥饿难耐、焦躁不安、绝望透顶；现在的我们满怀感激、内心平静、开心得无以言表。我知道那是我坎坷的一生中最快乐的时刻。我们牢狱般的车厢周围，风在怒号，疯狂地刮起雪花，

① 决定票，指赞成或反对票数相等时会议主席所投的起决定作用的票。

eventful life. The winds howled, and blew the snow wildly about our prison-house, but they were powerless to distress us any more. I liked Harris. He might have been better done, perhaps, but I am free to say that no man ever agreed with me better than Harris, or afforded me so large a degree of satisfaction. Messick was very well, though rather high-flavored, but for genuine nutritiousness and delicacy of fiber, give me Harris. Messick had his good points—I will not attempt to deny it, nor do I wish to do it—but he was no more fitted for breakfast than a mummy would be, sir—not a bit. Lean?—why, bless me!—and tough? Ah, he was very tough! You could not imagine it—you could never imagine anything like it.

"Do you mean to tell me that—"

"Do not interrupt me, please. After breakfast we elected a man by the name of Walker, from Detroit, for supper. He was very good. I wrote his wife so afterward. He was worthy of all praise. I shall always remember Walker. He was a little rare, but very good. And then the next morning we had Morgan of Alabama for breakfast. He was one of the finest men I ever sat down to—handsome, educated, refined, spoke several languages fluently—a perfect gentleman—he was a perfect gentleman, and singularly juicy. For supper we had that Oregon patriarch, and he was a fraud, there is no question about it—old, scraggy, tough, nobody can picture the reality. I finally said, gentlemen, you can do as you like, but I will wait for another election. And Grimes of Illinois said, 'Gentlemen, I will wait also. When you elect a man that has something to recommend him, I shall be

但它再也无法使我们焦虑。我喜欢哈里斯。或许，他本来可以被做得更好吃些。但是坦率地说，没有谁比哈里斯更适合我的口味，或给了我更大的满足。梅西克非常可口，虽然相当受青睐，但是要论起实际的营养价值和肉质的美味，还得说哈里斯。梅西克有他的优点——我并不否认这一点，我也不想这样做——但是，做早餐的话，他并不比木乃伊好到哪儿去，老兄——一点儿也不。瘦吗？——啊，我的天哪！难嚼吗？——哎，他真难嚼啊！你无法想象——你永远无法想象那样的东西。

“难道你要告诉我——”

“请别打断我。早饭之后，我们选了个名叫沃克、来自底特律的人作为晚餐。他很不错。事后我写信给他妻子这么说的。任何夸奖他都当之无愧。我会永远记住沃克的。他稍嫩了点儿，但是还不错。接着，第二天早晨，我们早餐吃了亚拉巴马州的摩根。他是我吃过的最优秀的人之一——英俊、有文化、文雅、能流利地说几种语言——一位出色的绅士——他是一位出色的绅士，而且很有油水。晚饭我们吃了俄勒冈州的那个老家伙，他是个骗子，这点毋庸置疑——年迈、皮包骨头、难嚼，没人说得清楚。最后我说，先生们，你们爱怎么办就怎么办吧，而我要等下一次选举。伊利诺伊州的格兰姆斯也说：‘先生们，我也要等。等你们选个物有所值的人，我再和你们一起享用。’显然，人们很快对俄勒冈州的戴维斯普遍感到不满意。于是，为了保持住我们吃哈里斯以来一直有的好盼头，我们又召集了一场选举，结果佐治亚州的贝克当选。他相当棒！得啦，得啦——之后，我们吃了杜利特尔，还有霍金斯，还有麦克尔罗伊

glad to join you again.' It soon became evident that there was general dissatisfaction with Davis of Oregon, and so, to preserve the good will that had prevailed so pleasantly since we had had Harris, an election was called, and the result of it was that Baker of Georgia was chosen. He was splendid! Well, well—after that we had Doolittle, and Hawkins, and McElroy (there was some complaint about McElroy, because he was uncommonly short and thin), and Penrod, and two Smiths, and Bailey (Bailey had a wooden leg, which was clear loss, but he was otherwise good), and an Indian boy, and an organ-grinder, and a gentleman by the name of Buckminster—a poor stick of a vagabond that wasn't any good for company and no account for breakfast. We were glad we got him elected before relief came."

"And so the blessed relief did come at last?"

"Yes, it came one bright, sunny morning, just after election. John Murphy was the choice, and there never was a better, I am willing to testify; but John Murphy came home with us, in the train that came to succor us, and lived to marry the widow Harris—"

"Relict of—"

"Relict of our first choice. He married her, and is happy and respected and prosperous yet. Ah, it was like a novel, sir—it was like a romance. This is my stopping-place, sir; I must bid you good-by. Any time that you can make it convenient to tarry a day or two with me, I shall be glad to have you. I like you, sir; I have conceived an affection for you. I could like you as well as I liked Harris himself, sir. Good day, sir, and a pleasant

（大家对麦克尔罗伊有些抱怨，因为他太矮太瘦），还有彭罗德，还有两位史密斯，还有贝利（贝利有一条木头腿，这无疑是个损失，但是除此之外他还可以），还有个印第安小伙儿，还有个手摇风琴师，还有个叫勃克明斯特的先生——是个穷鬼流浪汉，根本没法交往，也没法做早餐。我们很高兴在他被选中之前救援来了。"

"那么该死的救援最终真的来了？"

"是的，在一个天气晴朗、阳光明媚的早晨来的，那时我们刚选举完。约翰·墨菲当选，再也没有比他更强的了，我愿意作证。约翰·墨菲同我们一起，乘坐前来营救我们的火车回家了，还活着娶了哈里斯的遗孀——"

"谁的遗孀——"

"第一个被我们选中的那人。他娶了她，现在依旧幸福快乐、受人尊敬、生活富裕。啊，这像部小说，伙计——这像部浪漫小说。我到站了，伙计。我必须跟你说再见了，随便你什么时候有空，就来我这儿住上一两天，我会很高兴见到你的。我喜欢你，伙计，我已经深深地喜欢上了你。我会像喜欢哈里斯那样喜欢你的，伙计。祝你愉快，伙计，祝你旅途愉快。"

journey."

He was gone. I never felt so stunned, so distressed, so bewildered in my life. But in my soul I was glad he was gone. With all his gentleness of manner and his soft voice, I shuddered whenever he turned his hungry eye upon me; and when I heard that I had achieved his perilous affection, and that I stood almost with the late Harris in his esteem, my heart fairly stood still!

I was bewildered beyond description. I did not doubt his word; I could not question a single item in a statement so stamped with the earnestness of truth as his; but its dreadful details overpowered me, and threw my thoughts into hopeless confusion. I saw the conductor looking at me. I said, "Who is that man?"

"He was a member of Congress once, and a good one. But he got caught in a snow-drift in the cars, and like to have been starved to death. He got so frost-bitten and frozen up generally, and used up for want of something to eat, that he was sick and out of his head two or three months afterward. He is all right now, only he is a monomaniac[①], and when he gets on that old subject he never stops till he has eat up[②] that whole car-load of people he talks about. He would have finished the crowd by this time, only he had to get out here. He has got their names as pat as A B C[③]. When he gets them all eat up but himself, he always says: 'Then the hour for the usual election for breakfast having

① monomaniac: 偏执狂，一种精神疾病，临床特征主要表现为妄想。
② 这是不规范的用法，准确地说应该是"...has eaten up..."。
③ ABC 意为"最简单的知识，基础知识"，如短语 as easy as ABC 形容极简单。与之类似，此处 as pat as ABC 形容脱口而出，毫不犹豫。

他走了。这辈子我从未感到过如此惊愕、焦虑和困惑。但是我打心眼儿里高兴他走了。虽然他态度和蔼、声音轻柔，但是每当他那饥饿的眼睛看着我时，就会令我发抖；而且当听说我获得了他危险的倾爱，并被他与死去的哈里斯相提并论时，我的心脏几乎停止了跳动。

我的困惑难以形容。我不怀疑他的话，他讲得那么真切，我无法质疑其中任何一点。可是那骇人的细节使我无法忍受，这将我的思维抛入绝望的混乱之中。我看见列车长在盯着我。我说："那人是谁？"

"他以前是个国会议员，还是个不错的议员。但他曾被大雪困在火车上，差点儿饿死。他被冻伤，几乎僵硬，精疲力竭，亟须食物，为此害了一场病，两三个月里神志不清。他现在痊愈了，只是患上了偏执狂，一提到那个老话题，不把谈到的一车人都吃光就不会罢休。这一次，若不是得在这儿下车，他会吃光那帮人。他们的名字他背得滚瓜烂熟。当吃光所有人、只剩下他自己时，他总是说：'后来又到了平常选举早餐的时候，没人反对，我顺利当选，之后，没人反对，我退出。因此我在这里。'"

arrived; and there being no opposition, I was duly elected, after which, there being no objections offered, I resigned. Thus I am here.' "

I felt inexpressibly relieved to know that I had only been listening to the harmless vagaries of a madman instead of the genuine experiences of a bloodthirsty cannibal.

得知我听到的不过是个疯子无伤大雅的臆想，而并非嗜血的食人者的真实经历，我感到无以言表的轻松。

The Stolen White Elephant

被偷的白象①

① Left out of A Tramp Abroad, because it was feared that some of the particulars had been exaggerated, and that others were not true. Before these suspicious had been proven groundless, the book had gone to press. M. T.
该故事被从《海外旅者》中删掉，因为有人担心有些情节被夸大，而另外有些情节不实。等到这些怀疑被证实并无根据时，该书业已付梓。——马克·吐温原注

《被偷的白象》(The Stolen White Elephant，1882)讲述了“我”聘请著名的布伦特探长查找失窃白象的下落的故事。在他的指挥下，众多侦探奔走各地，通过各种途径总算找回失物，而此时它早已死去多日；“我”也为支付侦查的巨额费用倾家荡产。

故事的情节主要通过“我”和布伦特两人在办公室的对话展开。其中“我”是马克·吐温笔下典型的叙述者，表情严肃，一本正经，似乎根本不知道案情的玄机所在，只是听从所谓专业人士的讲解，对案情并无明确的判断。但故事的主角布伦特平静的外表下隐藏的不是冷峻的智慧，而是无可救药的自负和愚蠢。由他做出的一系列判断，事后都被证明是荒谬的。小说用一个无知的普通人衬托了一个更为无知和蠢笨的侦探，达到对后者的讽刺效果。

小说通过对比，突出故事前后内容之间的不协调，从而达到讽刺的效果。起初侦探布伦特一再强调行动务必高度保密，但次日清早行动计划就全部见诸报端，并带有详细的说明，甚至有他本人的评论。布伦特肯定无疑的嫌犯，实际上早已不在人世。原本信誓旦旦要抓到凶手、找回大象的“名侦探”，到头来却不得不花大价钱与罪犯妥协。侦探们不远千里、不辞辛苦四处追踪调查，孰不知大象的尸体就躺在自家的地下室里。这个结局也将先前所有的调查结论都统统推翻。侦探们所谓的智慧在对比中被瓦解得支离破碎，更显出他们的愚蠢。

在《被偷的白象》中，马克·吐温不动声色地对这帮侦探，尤其是对布伦特探长的自负和愚蠢进行了辛辣的讽刺。侦探们寻找白象忙得越是不可开交，读者就越会觉得他们荒谬可笑。

1

The following curious history was related to me by a chance railway acquaintance. He was a gentleman more than seventy years of age, and his thoroughly good and gentle face and earnest and sincere manner imprinted the unmistakable stamp of truth upon every statement which fell from his lips. He said:

You know in what reverence the royal white elephant of Siam is held by the people of that country. You know it is sacred to kings, only kings may possess it, and that it is, indeed, in a measure even superior to kings, since it receives not merely honor but worship. Very well; five years ago, when the troubles concerning the frontier line arose between Great Britain and Siam, it was presently manifest that Siam had been in the wrong. Therefore every reparation was quickly made, and the British representative stated that he was satisfied and the past should be forgotten. This greatly relieved the King of Siam, and partly as a token of gratitude, but partly also, perhaps, to wipe out any little remaining vestige of unpleasantness which England might feel toward him, he wished to send the Queen a present—the sole sure way of propitiating an enemy, according to Oriental ideas. This present ought not only to be a royal one, but transcendently royal. Wherefore, what offering could be so meet as that of a white elephant? My position in the Indian civil service was such that I was deemed peculiarly worthy of the honor of conveying the present to her Majesty. A ship was fitted

一

下面这段离奇的故事是一位在火车上邂逅的人告诉我的。他是位七十多岁的先生，面容尤其慈祥和蔼，态度尤其认真诚恳，这就使他嘴里的每一句话都带着毋庸置疑的真实感。他说：

要知道，暹罗[1]的皇家白象是多么地受那个国家的人崇敬。要知道它对于国王来说是神圣的，只有国王才配拥有。在某种程度上，它的地位甚至高于国王，因为它受到的不仅仅是尊敬，还有崇拜。好啦，五年前，大不列颠和暹罗在边界线问题上发生了摩擦，很快证明是暹罗错了，因而它迅速做出各项赔偿。英国代表说他很满意，还说过去的事情应该被忘掉。这让暹罗国王大大松了一口气。于是部分出于表达感激，部分可能也是为了消除英国对他残存的任何细小的不满，他想要送给英国女王一份礼物——根据东方的观点，这是获得对方原谅唯一稳妥的做法。这份礼物不仅应该高贵，而且应该异乎寻常的高贵。因此，有什么礼物能比白象更合适呢？我在印度政府的相关部门供职，所以被认为特别适合担当起这份殊荣，把这份礼物运送给女王陛下。我、我的随从、官员和照料大象的侍者乘坐的船整装出发，并如期到达纽约港。然后我将负责的皇家白象安置在泽西城内一所体面的住处。为了让白象的体力得到恢复，我们有必要逗留一段时间，然后再继续航行。

① 暹罗，泰国的旧称。

out for me and my servants and the officers and attendants of the elephant, and in due time I arrived in New York harbor and placed my royal charge in admirable quarters in Jersey City. It was necessary to remain awhile in order to recruit the animal's health before resuming the voyage.

All went well during a fortnight—then my calamities began. The white elephant was stolen! I was called up at dead of night and informed of this fearful misfortune. For some moments I was beside myself with terror and anxiety; I was helpless. Then I grew calmer and collected my faculties. I soon saw my course—for, indeed, there was but the one course for an intelligent man to pursue. Late as it was, I flew to New York and got a policeman to conduct me to the headquarters of the detective force. Fortunately I arrived in time, though the chief of the force, the celebrated Inspector Blunt, was just on the point of leaving for his home. He was a man of middle size and compact frame, and when he was thinking deeply he had a way of knitting his brows and tapping his forehead reflectively with his finger, which impressed you at once with the conviction that you stood in the presence of a person of no common order. The very sight of him gave me confidence and made me hopeful. I stated my errand. It did not flurry him in the least; it had no more visible effect upon his iron self-possession than if I had told him somebody had stolen my dog. He motioned me to a seat, and said, calmly:

"Allow me to think a moment, please."

So saying, he sat down at his office table and leaned his

两周当中一切顺利——接着我的灾难开始了。白象被偷了！深更半夜我被叫醒，得知了这一可怕的厄运。一时间，我惊骇万分，焦灼不已，不知道怎么办好。后来我冷静了一些，定了定神，很快想到了一条出路——因为聪明人其实只有一条路可走。尽管很晚了，我还是飞到纽约，由一位警察领着到了侦缉总部。幸好我来得及时，侦缉队队长、赫赫有名的布伦特督察正要起身回家。他中等身材，身体结实，沉思的时候眉毛拧在一起，并不停地用手指敲着额头，立刻就给人留下了深刻的印象，让你相信站在你面前的人不一般。看他一眼，我就有了信心，充满了希望。我说明了来意。那丝毫没有令他慌乱，看不出对他有什么影响，他镇定自若，就好像我只不过告诉他有人偷了我的狗而已。他示意我坐下，冷静地说：

“请允许我想一下。”

说着，他在办公桌旁坐下来，一只手支着头。几个办事员正在

head upon his hand. Several clerks were at work at the other end of the room; the scratching of their pens was all the sound I heard during the next six or seven minutes. Meantime the inspector sat there, buried in thought. Finally he raised his head, and there was that in the firm lines of his face which showed me that his brain had done its work and his plan was made. Said he—and his voice was low and impressive:

"This is no ordinary case. Every step must be warily taken; each step must be made sure before the next is ventured. And secrecy must be observed—secrecy profound and absolute. Speak to no one about the matter, not even the reporters. I will take care of them; I will see that they get only what it may suit my ends to let them know." He touched a bell; a youth appeared. "Alaric, tell the reporters to remain for the present." The boy retired. "Now let us proceed to business—and systematically. Nothing can be accomplished in this trade of mine without strict and minute method."

He took a pen and some paper. "Now—name[①] of the elephant?"

"Hassan Ben Ali Ben Selim Abdallah Mohammed Moisé Alhammal Jamsetjejeebhoy Dhuleep Sultan Ebu Bhudpoor."

"Very well. Given name?"

"Jumbo."

"Very well. Place of birth?"

① name 包括了我们所说的姓和名，而下文的 given name 仅指名的部分。

房间的另一头忙碌。在接下来的六七分钟里，我只听到钢笔沙沙的声音。此时，督察坐在那儿，陷入了沉思。最后，他抬起头，面容坚定，向我表明他已经思考完毕，拟定好了计划。他说——声音低沉，令人印象深刻：

"这不是个普通的案子。每一步都必须谨慎行事，每一步都必须确保无误，然后才能进行下一步。而且务必要保密——高度保密、绝对保密。不要告诉任何人，甚至是记者。我来对付他们，我保证，他们得到的消息只是为了达到我的目的才透露给他们的。"他按了下铃，进来一个年轻人。"阿拉里克，告诉记者们先等会儿。"小伙子出去了。"现在让我们继续谈正事——系统地谈谈。干我这一行，没有严谨缜密的方法，什么事也做不成。"

他拿了一杆笔和一些纸。"好吧——大象的全名？"

"哈森·本·阿里·本·赛利姆·阿布达拉·穆罕默德·莫伊兹·阿尔哈梅尔·詹姆塞特杰吉布霍伊·杜利浦·苏丹·埃布·布德普尔。"

"好的。叫什么？"

"蓝宝[①]。"

"好的。出生地？"

① Jumbo 原本是美国巴纳姆马戏团里一头著名大象的名字。它是一只大型非洲象，于1861年在法属苏丹（French Sudan）诞生，曾先后被引进至巴黎动物园和伦敦动物园，1882年由美国巴纳姆马戏团收购，1885年为救一头小象而被火车撞死。现在 Jumbo 则用来指体大而笨拙的人、动物或物件，有"庞然大物"之意。

"The capital city of Siam."

"Parents living?"

"No—dead."

"Had they any other issue[①] besides this one?"

"None. He was an only child."

"Very well. These matters are sufficient under that head. Now please describe the elephant, and leave out no particular, however insignificant—that is, insignificant from your point of view. To men in my profession there are no insignificant particulars; they do not exist."

I described—he wrote. When I was done, he said:

"Now listen. If I have made any mistakes, correct me."

He read as follows:

"Height, 19 feet; length from apex of forehead insertion of tail, 26 feet; length of trunk, 16 feet; length of tail, 6 feet; total length, including trunk and tail, 48 feet; length of tusks, 91/2 feet; ears in keeping with these dimensions; footprint resembles the mark left when one upends a barrel in the snow; color of the elephant, a dull white; has a hole the size of a plate in each ear for the insertion of jewelry, and possesses the habit in a remarkable degree of squirting water upon spectators and of maltreating with his trunk not only such persons as he is acquainted with, but even entire strangers; limps slightly with his right hind leg, and has a small scar in his left armpit caused by a former boil; had on, when stolen, a castle containing seats for fifteen persons, and a gold-cloth saddle-blanket the size of

① issue 在法律用语里有"子女，后代，后嗣"的意思。

“暹罗首都。”

“父母还在吗？”

“不在——死了。”

“它们除了这个还有别的孩子吗？”

“没有。它是独生子。”

“好的。这个方面这些情况就够了。现在请描述一下那头象，别漏了细节，无论它们多么微不足道——就是说，在你眼中微不足道。对于我这一行的人来说，没有微不足道的细节；那不存在。”

我描述着——他写着。当我讲完了，他说道：

“现在听好。要是我哪点弄错了，就纠正我。”

他所读如下：

“身高，19英尺；额顶到尾稍的长度，26英尺；鼻长，16英尺；尾长，6英尺；包括鼻子和尾巴在内的总长度，48英尺；象牙长度，9.5英尺；耳朵与这些尺寸保持一致；脚印像竖放在雪地上的桶留下的印迹；象的颜色，灰白色；每只耳朵上有个盘子大小的洞，备穿珠宝之用，而且特别喜欢向观众喷水，特别喜欢拿鼻子捉弄人，不只是捉弄它认识的人，甚至还捉弄完全陌生的人；右边的后腿略跛，左腋窝处有一小块以前生疖子留下的疤；被偷的时候，象背上有一个带十五人座位的塔楼和一张普通地毯大小的金丝鞍垫。”

an ordinary carpet."

There were no mistakes. The inspector touched the bell, handed the description to Alaric, and said:

"Have fifty thousand copies of this printed at once and mailed to every detective office and pawnbroker's shop on the continent." Alaric retired. "There—so far, so good. Next, I must have a photograph of the property."

I gave him one. He examined it critically, and said:

"It must do, since we can do no better; but he has his trunk curled up and tucked into his mouth. That is unfortunate, and is calculated to mislead, for of course he does not usually have it in that position." He touched his bell.

"Alaric, have fifty thousand copies of this photograph made the first thing in the morning, and mail them with the descriptive circulars."

Alaric retired to execute his orders. The inspector said:

"It will be necessary to offer a reward, of course. Now as to the amount?"

"What sum would you suggest?"

"To begin with, I should say—well, twenty-five thousand dollars. It is an intricate and difficult business; there are a thousand avenues of escape and opportunities of concealment. These thieves have friends and pals everywhere—"

"Bless me, do you know who they are?"

The wary face, practised in concealing the thoughts and feelings within, gave me no token, nor yet the replying words, so quietly uttered:

准确无误。督察按了下铃，把那张写着白象特征的纸递给阿拉里克，说：

“马上去把这个印五万份，然后寄给北美洲大陆上各个侦缉办公室和当铺。”阿拉克里出去了。“瞧——目前还不错[1]。接下来，我要有一张失物的照片。”

我给了他一张。他一丝不苟地端详了一番，然后说：

“就它得了，既然我们没有更好的，只是它的鼻子卷着，塞在嘴里。真不走运，这很可能会误导我们，因为它的鼻子平时肯定不在那个位置。”他按了下铃。

“阿拉里克，明天一早先把这张照片印五万份，然后同那张大象特征的传单一起寄出去。”

阿拉里克执行他的命令去了。督察说：

“当然悬赏将是少不了的。那么金额有多少呢？”

“您认为多少合适？”

“开始的话，我估计——好吧，两万五千美金。这是件复杂棘手的事，有上千种逃跑的路线和藏匿的机会。这些贼到处都有朋友和同伙——”

“天啊，您知道他们是谁吗？”

督察那副谨慎的面孔习惯将思想和感情隐藏起来，并没有给我提示，也没有回答我，而是非常平静地说：

① 这是布伦特探长询问记录时的一句口头禅。

"Never mind about that. I may, and I may not. We generally gather a pretty shrewd inkling of who our man is by the manner of his work and the size of the game he goes after. We are not dealing with a pickpocket or a hall thief now, make up your mind to that. This property was not 'lifted' by a novice. But, as I was saying, considering the amount of travel which will have to be done, and the diligence with which the thieves will cover up their traces as they move along, twenty-five thousand may be too small a sum to offer, yet I think it worth while to start with that."

So we determined upon that figure as a beginning. Then this man, whom nothing escaped which could by any possibility be made to serve as a clue, said:

"There are cases in detective history to show that criminals have been detected through peculiarities, in their appetites. Now, what does this elephant eat, and how much?"

"Well, as to what he eats—he will eat anything. He will eat a man, he will eat a Bible—he will eat anything between a man and a Bible."

"Good—very good, indeed, but too general. Details are necessary—details are the only valuable things in our trade. Very well—as to men. At one meal—or, if you prefer, during one day—how many men will he eat, if fresh?"

"He would not care whether they were fresh or not; at a single meal he would eat five ordinary men.

"Very good; five men; we will put that down. What nationalities would he prefer?"

"He is indifferent about nationalities. He prefers

“别管那个。我可能知道，也可能不知道。我们通常根据罪犯的作案手法和他要偷的赃物大小，搜集一些蛛丝马迹，判断出谁是我们要找的人。我们要对付的不是个扒手，也不是个入室盗窃的贼，你要清楚这一点。这个东西不是被新手‘顺手牵走’的。但正如我所说，考虑到将要跑很远的路，窃贼逃跑途中会精心掩盖他们的踪迹，两万五可能给得太少了，但我觉得开始的时候是够用了。”

于是，我们决定开始的时候就给那笔数目。任何可能成为线索的事都逃不过此人的眼睛，接着他说：

“侦缉史上有案例显示，通过罪犯的饮食癖好曾找到过他们。好吧，这头象吃什么，吃多少？”

“噢，关于它吃什么——它什么都吃。它吃人，它吃《圣经》——它吃介于人和《圣经》之间的任何东西。”

“不错——确实很不错，但是太笼统了。必要的是细节——细节才是我们这行唯一有价值的东西。好吧——说说人吧，一顿——或者随你的便，一天——若是新鲜的，它要吃多少人？”

“它不会在乎他们是不是新鲜。单就一顿，它要吃五个普通人。”

“很不错，五个人，我们要记下来。它喜欢吃哪些国籍的？”

“它对国籍不感兴趣。它喜欢吃认识的人，但也不歧视陌生

acquaintances, but is not prejudiced against strangers."

"Very good. Now, as to Bibles. How many Bibles would he eat at a meal?"

"He would eat an entire edition."

"It is hardly succinct enough. Do you mean the ordinary octavo, or the family illustrated?"

"I think he would be indifferent to illustrations; that is, I think he would not value illustrations above simple letterpress."

"No, you do not get my idea. I refer to bulk. The ordinary octavo Bible weighs about two pound and a half, while the great quarto with the illustrations weighs ten or twelve. How many Doré Bibles would he eat at a meal?"

"If you knew this elephant, you could not ask. He would take what they had."

"Well, put it in dollars and cents, then. We must get at it somehow. The Doré costs a hundred dollars a copy, Russia leather, beveled."

"He would require about fifty thousand dollars' worth—say an edition of five hundred copies."

"Now that is more exact. I will put that down. Very well; he likes men and Bibles; so far, so good. What else will he eat? I want particulars."

"He will leave Bibles to eat bricks, he will leave bricks to eat bottles, he will leave bottles to eat clothing, he will leave clothing to eat cats, he will leave cats to eat oysters, he will leave oysters to eat ham, he will leave ham to eat sugar, he will leave sugar to eat pie, he will leave pie to eat potatoes, he will leave potatoes to eat

人。”

“很不错。那么说说《圣经》吧，它一顿要吃多少本《圣经》？”

“他要吃掉整整一个版次。”

“这不够准确。你指的是普通的八开本，还是家庭用的插图本呢？”

“我觉得它对插图不感兴趣，也就是说，我觉得它不会把插图看得比简单的文字部分更重要。”

“不是，你没听懂我的意思。我说的是重量。普通的八开本《圣经》大约重两磅半，而带插图的大本四开本重10磅或者12磅。多雷[①]插图本《圣经》它一顿要吃多少本呢？”

“您要是了解这头大象，就不会问了。有什么它就吃什么。”

“好吧，那么就用钱来表示。无论如何我们得把这弄清楚。多雷插图本《圣经》100美元一本，俄国皮子包的，斜面剪裁。”

“它大约需要价值五万美元的《圣经》——也就是五百本的一个版次。”

“这就确切多了。我要记下来。好的，它喜欢吃人和《圣经》，目前还不错。别的它还吃什么吗？我要具体的情况。”

“有砖头它就不吃《圣经》，有瓶子它就不吃砖头，有衣服它就不吃瓶子，有猫它就不吃衣服，有牡蛎它就不吃猫，有火腿它就不吃牡蛎，有糖它就不吃火腿，有馅饼它就不吃糖，有土豆它就不吃馅饼，

① 多雷（Gustave Doré，1833–1883），法国插图画家，擅长木版画，曾经为《圣经》作过插图。

bran; he will leave bran to eat hay, he will leave hay to eat oats, he will leave oats to eat rice, for he was mainly raised on it. There is nothing whatever that he will not eat but European butter, and he would eat that if he could taste it."

"Very good. General quantity at a meal—say about—"

"Well, anywhere from a quarter to half a ton."

"And he drinks—"

"Everything that is fluid. Milk, water, whisky, molasses, castor oil, camphene, carbolic acid—it is no use to go into particulars; whatever fluid occurs to you set it down. He will drink anything that is fluid, except European coffee."

"Very good. As to quantity?"

"Put it down five to fifteen barrels—his thirst varies; his other appetites do not."

"These things are unusual. They ought to furnish quite good clues toward tracing him."

He touched the bell.

"Alaric, summon Captain Burns."

Burns appeared. Inspector Blunt unfolded the whole matter to him, detail by detail. Then he said in the clear, decisive tones of a man whose plans are clearly defined in his head and who is accustomed to command:

"Captain Burns, detail Detective Jones, Davis, Halsey, Bates, and Hackett to shadow the elephant."

"Yes, sir."

"Detail Detectives Moses, Dakin, Murphy, Rogers, Tupper, Higgins, and Bartholomew to shadow the thieves."

有麦麸它就不吃土豆，有干草它就不吃麦麸，有燕麦它就不吃干草，有大米它就不吃燕麦，因为它主要是吃大米长大的。除了欧洲的黄油，没有它不吃的，但它要是能尝尝黄油的话，也会吃的。”

“很不错。通常一顿的饭量——大致地说——”

“嗯，1/4吨到1/2吨之间，都有可能。”

“另外它喝——”

“所有液体的东西。牛奶、水、威士忌、糖蜜、蓖麻油、松脂、石碳酸——不用再细说了，不管什么液体，你想到了都记下来。除了欧洲的咖啡，任何液体的东西它都喝。”

“很不错。关于数量呢？”

“就写五到十五桶吧——它渴的程度会不一样。它别的胃口没什么变化。”

“这些情况不一般，应该会为追踪它提供非常好的线索。”

他按了下铃。

“阿拉里克，叫彭斯队长过来。”

彭斯来了，布伦特督察向他详细介绍了整个事件。然后，他俨然一副计划了然于胸的样子，像个惯于发号施令的人，用清楚坚定的声调说：

“彭斯队长，派探员琼斯、戴维斯、哈尔西、贝茨和哈克特追踪白象。”

“是，长官。”

“派探员摩西、达金、墨菲、罗杰斯、塔珀、希金斯和巴塞洛缪追踪盗贼。”

"Yes, sir."

"Place a strong guard—A guard of thirty picked men, with a relief of thirty—over the place from whence the elephant was stolen, to keep strict watch there night and day, and allow none to approach—except reporters—without written authority from me."

"Yes, sir."

"Place detectives in plain clothes in the railway, steamship, and ferry depots, and upon all roadways leading out of Jersey City, with orders to search all suspicious persons."

"Yes, sir."

"Furnish all these men with photograph and accompanying description of the elephant, and instruct them to search all trains and outgoing ferryboats and other vessels."

"Yes, sir."

"If the elephant should be found, let him be seized, and the information forwarded to me by telegraph."

"Yes, sir."

"Let me be informed at once if any clues should be found—footprints of the animal, or anything of that kind."

"Yes, sir."

"Get an order commanding the harbor police to patrol the frontages vigilantly."

"Yes, sir."

"Despatch detectives in plain clothes over all the railways, north as far as Canada, west as far as Ohio, south as far as Washington."

"Yes, sir."

“是，长官。”

“安排一支强有力的警卫队——由精选的三十人组成的警卫队，另备三十人轮班——在大象被盗的地方，昼夜严密监守，没有我的书面批准，不允许任何人靠近——记者除外。”

“是，长官。”

“在火车站、轮船和渡船口岸，以及通向泽西城[①]外的所有道路上安排便衣侦探，命令他们搜查所有的可疑人员。”

“是，长官。”

“把大象的照片和相应的描述配发给所有这些人，命令他们搜查所有火车及外出的渡船和其他船只。”

“是，长官。”

“倘若发现大象就捉住它，并发电报向我汇报。”

“是，长官。”

“发现任何线索立即通知我——该动物的脚印，或诸如此类的任何东西。”

“是，长官。”

“传令要求口岸警察仔细巡查沿河地带。”

“是，长官。”

“向所有铁路沿线派遣便衣侦探，北至加拿大，西至俄亥俄，南至华盛顿。”

“是，长官。”

① 泽西城，美国新泽西州东北部的一个城市。

"Place experts in all the telegraph offices to listen to all messages; and let them require that all cipher despatches be interpreted to them."

"Yes, sir."

"Let all these things be done with the utmost secrecy—mind, the most impenetrable secrecy."

"Yes, sir."

"Report to me promptly at the usual hour."

"Yes, sir."

"Go!"

"Yes, sir."

He was gone.

Inspector Blunt was silent and thoughtful a moment, while the fire in his eye cooled down and faded out. Then he turned to me and said in a placid voice:

"I am not given to boasting, it is not my habit; but—we shall find the elephant."

I shook him warmly by the hand and thanked him; and I felt my thanks, too. The more I had seen of the man the more I liked him and the more I admired him and marveled over the mysterious wonders of his profession. Then we parted for the night, and I went home with a far happier heart than I had carried with me to his office.

2

Next morning it was all in the newspapers, in the minutest

“在所有的电报局里安排专家，接听所有电文，并让他们提出申请，要求把所有的密码电文译给他们。”

“是，长官。”

“所有这些事都要绝对保密——注意，绝对不能走漏半点风声。”

“是，长官。”

“平时及时向我汇报。”

“是，长官。”

“行动！”

“是，长官。”

他离开了。

布伦特督察一言不发，沉思了片刻。他眼中的激情冷却，随后消失了。然后他转向我，平静地说：

“不是吹牛，我没那习惯。但是——我们一定会找到大象。”

我热情地握着他的手，打心底感谢他。这个人我越看就越喜欢，就越钦佩，就越惊叹他的职业的神秘与奇妙。当夜我们告了别。我回家时的心情远比进入他办公室时快乐。

二

次日清早，一切都见诸报端，包括最最微小的细节。报纸上甚

detail. It even had additions—consisting of Detective This, Detective That, and Detective The Other's "Theory" as to how the robbery was done, who the robbers were, and whither they had flown with their booty. There were eleven of these theories, and they covered all the possibilities; and this single fact shows what independent thinkers detectives are. No two theories were alike, or even much resembled each other, save in one striking particular, and in that one all the other eleven theories were absolutely agreed. That was, that although the rear of my building was torn out and the only door remained locked, the elephant had not been removed through the rent, but by some other (undiscovered) outlet. All agreed that the robbers had made that rent only to mislead the detectives. That never would have occurred to me or to any other layman, perhaps, but it had not deceived the detectives for a moment. Thus, what I had supposed was the only thing that had no mystery about it was in fact the very thing I had gone furthest astray in. The eleven theories all named the supposed robbers, but no two named the same robbers; the total number of suspected persons was thirty-seven. The various newspaper accounts all closed with the most important opinion of all—that of Chief Inspector Blunt. A portion of this statement read as follows:

The chief knows who the two principals are, namely, "Brick" Duffy and "Red" McFadden. Ten days before the robbery was achieved he was already aware that it was to be attempted, and had quietly proceeded to shadow these two noted villains; but unfortunately on the night in question their

至还有增加的内容——包括这侦探、那侦探和某某侦探的"推测"，其中谈到了盗窃是怎么发生的、谁是窃贼以及他们带着赃物逃往了何方。有十一种这样的推测，囊括了所有可能性。这一事实表明，侦探是多么有独立见解的思想家啊。没有哪两种推测是一样的，甚至没有两种推测彼此相似，除了一点惹人注意的细节之外。在这点上，所有十一种推测完全一致。也就是说，虽然我的房子后墙有豁口，并且唯一的门仍然紧锁着，但是大象并非从豁口处被偷走，而是另有其他的出口（未被发现）。这些推测一致认为，窃贼制造那个豁口只是为了误导侦探。我或是其他任何外行可能怎么也想不到这一点，但这压根也骗不了侦探。这样一来，我原以为唯一一件毋庸置疑的事，事实上正是我被迷惑最深的事。虽然十一种推测都指出了有嫌疑的窃贼，但是没有哪两种说的一样，被怀疑的共有三十七人。报纸上的各种报道都以所有观点中最重要的一个——布伦特探长的观点结尾。这一说法部分如下：

探长知道两名主犯是谁，就是"砖头"杜飞和"红"麦克法登。该盗窃案发生的10天前，他已经得知了他们的企图，并开始暗中跟踪这两个出了名的恶棍；不过可惜的是，案发当晚他们的踪迹消失了，还没来得及找到，东西——也就是大象就不见了。

track was lost, and before it could be found again the bird was flown—that is, the elephant.

Duffy and McFadden are the boldest scoundrels in the profession[①]; the chief has reasons for believing that they are the men who stole the stove out of the detective headquarters on a bitter night last winter—in consequence of which the chief and every detective present were in the hands of the physicians before morning, some with frozen feet, others with frozen fingers, ears, and other members.

When I read the first half of that I was more astonished than ever at the wonderful sagacity of this strange man. He not only saw everything in the present with a clear eye, but even the future could not be hidden from him. I was soon at his office, and said I could not help wishing he had had those men arrested, and so prevented the trouble and loss; but his reply was simple and unanswerable:

"It is not our province to prevent crime, but to punish it. We cannot punish it until it is committed."

I remarked that the secrecy with which he had begun had been marred by the newspapers; not only all our facts but all our plans and purposes had been revealed; even all the suspected persons had been named; these would doubtless disguise themselves now, or go into hiding.

"Let them. They will find that when I am ready for them my hand will descend upon them, in their secret places, as unerringly as the hand of fate. As to the newspapers, we must

① profession 本意是"职业",这里指专门从事盗窃的勾当。

杜飞和麦克法登是道上最胆大妄为的恶棍。探长有理由相信，去年冬天的一个严寒之夜，就是他们从侦缉总部偷走了火炉——结果还没到早上，探长和里面的所有探员就都到医生那儿报到去了。有的冻伤了脚，还有的冻伤了手指、耳朵等其他部位。

当读完前半部分，我比以前更加惊叹于这个陌生人的绝顶聪明。他不但目光锐利，一眼就看透了当前的每一件事，而且将来的事也瞒不住他。我立即到了他的办公室，说我简直希望他已经抓到了那些人，这样就会免去麻烦和损失。但他的回答很简单，而且无可争辩：

“我们的职责不是避免犯罪，而是惩治犯罪。我们只有在其作案的时候才能惩治它。”

我说，他初步行动的秘密已经被报纸破坏了。不光是我们掌握的所有情况，还有我们所有的计划和目标都被泄露了，甚至所有的怀疑对象也被指了出来。现在，这些人无疑会改头换面，或是躲藏起来。

“随他们的便。他们会发现，如果我准备抓他们，我的手会在他们的藏身之处落在他们身上，像命运之手一样准确无误。至于报纸，我们必须跟他们搞好关系。名气、声誉、经常被公众提到——

keep in with them. Fame, reputation, constant public mention—these are the detective's bread and butter. He must publish his facts, else he will be supposed to have none; he must publish his theory, for nothing is so strange or striking as a detective's theory, or brings him so much wonderful respect; we must publish our plans, for these the journals insist upon having, and we could not deny them without offending. We must constantly show the public what we are doing, or they will believe we are doing nothing. It is much pleasanter to have a newspaper say, 'Inspector Blunt's ingenious and extraordinary theory is as follows,' than to have it say some harsh thing, or, worse still, some sarcastic one."

"I see the force of what you say. But I noticed that in one part of your remarks in the papers this morning you refused to reveal your opinion upon a certain minor point."

"Yes, we always do that; it has a good effect. Besides, I had not formed any opinion on that point, anyway."

I deposited a considerable sum of money with the inspector, to meet current expenses, and sat down to wait for news. We were expecting the telegrams to begin to arrive at any moment now. Meantime I reread the newspapers and also our descriptive circular, and observed that our twenty-five thousand dollars reward seemed to be offered only to detectives. I said I thought it ought to be offered to anybody who would catch the elephant. The inspector said:

"It is the detectives who will find the elephant, hence the reward will go to the right place. If other people found the

这些是侦探的谋生之道。他必须公开他掌握的情况，不然会被认为什么也没掌握。他必须公开他的推测，因为没有什么会像侦探的推测那么离奇，那么吸引人，或给他带来那么多非同寻常的重视。我们必须公开我们的计划，因为这些东西是报纸坚持要得到的。我们要是拒绝的话，准会得罪他们。我们必须经常告诉公众我们在做什么，否则他们会认为我们什么也没做。听报纸说‘布伦特督察巧妙而非凡的推测如下’，总比听它说些难听话，或者更糟糕的是，说些刻薄话要好得多。”

“我知道您说的意思。但是我注意到今天早上的报纸，您在上面的一段评论中拒绝对某个小问题发表您的想法。”

“是的，我们一直这么做，那样效果很好。再说，我对那个问题也还没什么想法。”

我向督察支付了一笔数目不小的钱，用来偿付当前的开支，然后坐下来等待消息。现在我们就等着电报随时发过来。同时我重新把报纸和登载我们描述的传单又读了一遍，发现我们那两万五千美元的奖金好像只是给侦探的。我说，我认为应该把它奖给任何抓到大象的人。督察说：

“将来找到大象的人就是侦探，因此奖金会被用到合适的地方。倘若其他人找到了它，那只可能是因为监视侦探，并且利用了从他

animal, it would only be by watching the detectives and taking advantage of clues and indications stolen from them, and that would entitle the detectives to the reward, after all. The proper office of a reward is to stimulate the men who deliver up their time and their trained sagacities to this sort of work, and not to confer benefits upon chance citizens who stumble upon a capture without having earned the benefits by their own merits and labors."

This was reasonable enough, certainly. Now the telegraphic machine in the corner began to click, and the following despatch was the result:

FLOWER STATION, N. Y.[①], 7.30 A.M.

HAVE GOT A CLUE. FOUND A SUCCESSION OF DEEP TRACKS ACROSS A FARM NEAR HERE. FOLLOWED THEM TWO MILES EAST WITHOUT RESULT; THINK ELEPHANT WENT WEST. SHALL NOW SHADOW HIM IN THAT DIRECTION.

DARLEY, DETECTIVE

"Darley's one of the best men on the force," said the inspector. "We shall hear from him again before long."

Telegram No. 2 came:

BARKER'S, N. J., 7.40 A.M.

JUST ARRIVED. GLASS FACTORY BROKEN OPEN HERE DURING NIGHT, AND EIGHT HUNDRED BOTTLES TAKEN. ONLY WATER IN LARGE QUANTITY NEAR HERE IS FIVE MILES

① N. Y. 是 New York 的缩写，即纽约州；后文中出现的 N. J. 是 New Jersey 的缩写，即新泽西州；L. I. 是 Illinois 的缩写，即伊利诺伊州；PA. 是 Pennsylvania 的缩写，即宾夕法尼亚州；CT. 是 Connecticut 的缩写，即康涅狄格州；MICH. 是 Michigan 的缩写，即密歇根州。

们那儿偷来的线索和提示。而那样的话，奖金终究还得归侦探所有。悬赏本来的作用就在于激励人们为这种工作花费时间，发挥他们训练有素的机警，而不是向幸运的市民发放好处。他们只是碰巧撞上了猎物，而不是靠自己的能力和劳动得来的。”

当然，这话很有道理。这时，角落里的电报机响了起来，收到的是下面这封急件：

鲜花车站，纽约，上午7：30

获得线索。发现一串深深的足迹穿过附近的农庄。循之向东两英里，无果；认为象已向西。现在该方向追踪。

探员 达利

“达利是警队里最出色的，”督察说，“不久我们将会再次收到他的消息。”

第二封电报到了：

贝克家，新泽西州，上午7：40

刚到。本地玻璃厂夜间被撬，八百只瓶子被盗。附近唯一水源较多的地方距此五英里。将前往。象必口渴。皆系空瓶。

探员 贝克

DISTANT. SHALL STRIKE FOR THERE. ELEPHANT WILL BE THIRSTY. BOTTLES WERE EMPTY.

BAKER, DETECTIVE

"That promises well, too," said the inspector. "I told you the creature's appetites would not be bad clues."

Telegram No. 3:

TAYLORVILLE, I. L., 8.15 A.M.

A HAYSTACK NEAR HERE DISAPPEARED DURING NIGHT. PROBABLY EATEN. HAVE GOT A CLUE, AND AM OFF.

HUBBARD, DETECTIVE

"How he does move around!" said the inspector "I knew we had a difficult job on hand, but we shall catch him yet."

FLOWER STATION, N. Y., 9 A.M.

SHADOWED THE TRACKS THREE MILES WESTWARD. LARGE, DEEP AND RAGGED. HAVE JUST MET A FARMER WHO SAYS THEY ARE NOT ELEPHANT TRACKS. SAYS THEY ARE HOLES WHERE HE DUG UP SAPLINGS FOR SHADETREES WHEN GROUND WAS FROZEN LAST WINTER. GIVE ME ORDERS HOW TO PROCEED.

DARLEY, DETECTIVE

"Aha! A confederate of the thieves! The thing grows warm," said the inspector.

He dictated the following telegram to Darley:

ARREST THE MAN AND FORCE HIM TO NAME HIS PALS. CONTINUE TO FOLLOW THE TRACKS—TO THE PACIFIC IF NECESSARY.

CHIEF BLUNT

“那也很有希望，”督察说，“我告诉过你，那家伙的胃口不失为好线索。”

第三封电报：

泰勒维尔，伊利诺伊州，上午8：15

附近一堆干草夜间失踪。或被食。获得线索，吾去。

探员 哈伯德

“它怎么到处跑啊！”督察说。“我就知道手里这活儿很棘手，但我们一定会捉住它。”

鲜花车站，纽约，上午9：00

向西追踪3英里。足迹大而深，凸凹不平。刚遇一农夫，说那并非大象足迹，乃去年冬天大地上冻时，他为了栽林荫树挖树苗留下的坑。指示下一步怎么办。

探员 达利

“啊哈！窃贼的同党！案情明朗了。”督察说道。

他口述以下电报发给达利：

逮捕此人，逼其供出同伙。继续追踪——不惜追到太平洋[1]。

探长 布伦特

① 纽约位于美国东部，太平洋在北美大陆西边，两者相距甚远；这里所说的追到太平洋表示要坚决追踪到底。

Next telegram:

CONEY POINT, PA., 8.45 A.M.

GAS OFFICE BROKEN OPEN HERE DURING NIGHT AND THREE MONTHS' UNPAID GAS BILLS TAKEN. HAVE GOT A CLUE AND AM AWAY.

MURPHY, DETECTIVE

"Heavens!" said the inspector; "would he eat gas bills?"

"Through ignorance—yes; but they cannot support life. At least, unassisted."

Now came this exciting telegram:

IRONVILLE, N. Y., 9.30 A.M.

JUST ARRIVED. THIS VILLAGE IN CONSTERNATION. ELEPHANT PASSED THROUGH HERE AT FIVE THIS MORNING. SOME SAY HE WENT EAST, SOME SAY WEST, SOME NORTH, SOME SOUTH—BUT ALL SAY THEY DID NOT WAIT TO NOTICE PARTICULARLY. HE KILLED A HORSE; HAVE SECURED A PIECE OF IT FOR A CLUE. KILLED IT WITH HIS TRUNK; FROM STYLE OF BLOW, THINK HE STRUCK IT LEFT-HANDED. FROM POSITION IN WHICH HORSE LIES, THINK ELEPHANT TRAVELED NORTHWARD ALONG LINE OF BERKLEY RAILWAY. HAS FOUR AND A HALF HOURS' START, BUT I MOVE ON HIS TRACK AT ONCE.

HAWES, DETECTIVE

I uttered exclamations of joy. The inspector was as self-contained as a graven image. He calmly touched his bell.

"Alaric, send Captain Burns here."

Burns appeared.

"How many men are ready for instant orders?"

下一封电报：

科尼角，宾夕法尼亚州，上午8：45

此处油气办公室夜间被撬，3个月的未付油气账单被盗。获得线索，吾去。

探员 墨菲

“天啊！”督察说，“他吃油气账单吗？”

“因为无知吧——是啊，可那不可能维持生命。至少不能独立维持生命。”

这时，来了这条令人兴奋的电报：

艾恩维尔，纽约，上午9：30

刚到。该村人心惶惶。今晨五时象经由此地。有人说他向东，有人说向西，有人说向北，有人说向南——但是他们都说没来得及看清楚。它杀死一匹马，已取其残片作为线索。它用象鼻将其杀死，从攻击的方式来看，料它从左翼袭击。从马躺的位置来看，料象已沿伯克利铁路北去。象出发四个半小时，我即刻沿其足迹追赶。

探员 霍斯

我高兴地欢呼起来。督察像尊雕像一样不动声色。他镇定地按了下铃。

“阿拉里克，叫彭斯队长过来。”

彭斯来了。

“有多少人准备随时待命。”

"Ninety-six, sir."

"Send them north at once. Let them concentrate along the line of the Berkley road north of Ironville."

"Yes, sir."

"Let them conduct their movements with the utmost secrecy. As fast as others are at liberty, hold them for orders."

"Yes, sir."

"Go!"

"Yes, sir."

Presently came another telegram:

SAGE CORNERS, N. Y., 10.30.

JUST ARRIVED, ELEPHANT PASSED THROUGH HERE AT 8.15. ALL ESCAPED FROM THE TOWN BUT A POLICEMAN. APPARENTLY ELEPHANT DID NOT STRIKE AT POLICEMAN, BUT AT THE LAMP-POST. GOT BOTH. I HAVE SECURED A PORTION OF THE POLICEMAN AS CLUE.

STUMM, DETECTIVE

"So the elephant has turned westward," said the inspector. "However, he will not escape, for my men are scattered all over that region."

The next telegram said:

GLOVER'S, 11.15.

JUST ARRIVED. VILLAGE DESERTED, EXCEPT SICK AND AGED. ELEPHANT PASSED THROUGH THREE-QUARTERS OF AN HOUR AGO. THE ANTITEMPERANCE MASS-MEETING WAS IN SESSION; HE PUT HIS TRUNK IN AT A WINDOW AND WASHED IT OUT WITH WATER FROM CISTERN. SOME SWALLOWED

"九十六人，长官。"

"立即派他们向北。让他们集中在艾恩维尔北部的伯克利铁路沿线。"

"是，长官。"

"告诉他们行动高度保密。其他的人一没事，便令他们原地待命。"

"是，长官。"

"行动！"

"是，长官。"

一会儿，传来另一封电报：

塞奇科纳斯，纽约，10：30

刚到。8点15分象经过此地。除一名警察外，所有人均已逃离此镇。显然象并非攻击警察，而是灯柱。两者均被击中。我已取警察残肢作为线索。

探员 斯顿姆

"那么大象已经调头向西了，"督察说，"无论如何它跑不掉了，因为我的人遍布在整个区域。"

下一条电报说：

格拉弗，11：15

刚到。村庄被弃，只剩病人和老人。三刻钟前象经由此地。反禁酒群众大会正在召开；它将鼻子伸进一扇窗户，用从蓄水池里吸的水把屋子冲了个遍。有些人呛了水——一命呜呼，数人被淹死。探员克罗斯和奥肖内斯恰经过该镇，但向南去了——故未遇象。整个方圆数英里的区域惶恐不安——人们从家里逃出来，往哪跑都会

IT—SINCE DEAD; SEVERAL DROWNED. DETECTIVES CROSS AND O'SHAUGHNESSY WERE PASSING THROUGH TOWN, BUT GOING SOUTH—SO MISSED ELEPHANT. WHOLE REGION FOR MANY MILES AROUND IN TERROR—PEOPLE FLYING FROM THEIR HOMES. WHEREVER THEY TURN MEET ELEPHANT, AND MANY ARE KILLED.

BRANT, DETECTIVE

I could have shed tears, this havoc so distressed me. But the inspector only said:

"You see—we are closing in on him. He feels our presence; he has turned eastward again."

Yet further troublous news was in store for us. The telegraph brought this:

HOGANSPORT, 12.19.

JUST ARRIVED. ELEPHANT PASSED THROUGH HALF AN HOUR AGO, CREATING WILDEST FRIGHT AND EXCITEMENT. ELEPHANT RAGED AROUND STREETS: TWO PLUMBERS GOING BY, KILLED ONE.—OTHER ESCAPED. REGRET GENERAL.

O'FLAHERY, DETECTIVE

"Now he is right in the midst of my men," said the inspector. "Nothing can save him."

A succession of telegrams came from detectives who were scattered through New Jersey and Pennsylvania, and who were following clues consisting of ravaged barns, factories, and Sunday-school libraries, with high hopes—hopes amounting to certainties, indeed. The inspector said:

遇上象，多人遇害。

探员 布兰特

我的眼泪都要掉下来了，这场灾难让我非常难过。而督察只是说：

“你看——我们正在包围它。它觉察到了我们的存在，又调头向东了。”

但是更多不幸的消息还在等着我们。电报捎来了这条消息：

霍根斯波特，12：19

刚到。半小时前象经由此地，引起了极度的恐慌和骚乱。大象在街上肆虐：两名管工路过，一人遇害——另一人逃脱。普感痛惜。

探员 奥弗莱厄蒂

“现在，它周围都是我们的人了，”督察说，“它插翅难飞。”

分散在新泽西和宾夕法尼亚的侦探们发来了一连串的电报，他们正在追踪的线索包括被毁的谷仓、工厂和主日学校的图书馆，大家满怀希望——实际上几近于肯定。督察说：

"I wish I could communicate with them and order them north, but that is impossible. A detective only visits a telegraph office to send his report; then he is off again, and you don't know where to put your hand on him."

Now came this despatch:

BRIDGEPORT, CT., 12.15.

BARNUM OFFERS RATE OF $4,000 A YEAR FOR EXCLUSIVE PRIVILEGE OF USING ELEPHANT AS TRAVELING ADVERTISING MEDIUM FROM NOW TILL DETECTIVES FIND HIM. WANTS TO PASTE CIRCUS-POSTERS ON HIM. DESIRES IMMEDIATE ANSWER.

BOGGS, DETECTIVE

"That is perfectly absurd!" I exclaimed.

"Of course it is," said the inspector. "Evidently Mr. Barnum, who thinks he is so sharp, does not know me—but I know him."

Then he dictated this answer to the despatch:

MR. BARNUM'S OFFER DECLINED. MAKE IT $7,000 OR NOTHING.

CHIEF BLUNT

"There. We shall not have to wait long for an answer. Mr. Barnum is not at home; he is in the telegraph office—it is his way when he has business on hand. Inside of three—"

DONE.—P. T. BARNUM.

So interrupted the clicking telegraphic instrument. Before I could make a comment upon this extraordinary episode, the

“我真希望能联系上他们，命令他们向北，但那是不可能的。探员只有发情报的时候才在电报局，离开，你不知道去哪儿找他。”

这时，来了这封急件：

布里奇波特，康涅狄格州，12：15

巴纳姆[①]每年出4,000美元，购买用象做的流动广告传媒的独家使用权，期限从现在开始直到侦探找到它为止。拟在象身上粘贴传单海报。盼速回。

探员 博格斯

“那太荒唐了！”我大声叫道。

“可不是，”督察说，“显然巴纳姆先生以为自己很聪明，他不了解我——但我了解他。”

接着，他口述回复了那封急件：

拒绝巴纳姆的要求。要么出7,000美元，要么拉倒。

探长 布伦特

“得啦。等不了多久我们就会得到答复。巴纳姆先生没在家，他在电报局——他手头有事要办时，这是他的一贯做法——用不了三——”

成交。——P.T. 巴纳姆

咔咔响的电报机打断了他的话。我还没有来得及对这个特别

① 巴纳姆（Phineas Taylor Barnum，1810—1891），美国游艺节目演出经理人，以主办耸人听闻的游艺节目演出和奇人怪物展览而闻名。

following despatch carried my thoughts into another and very distressing channel:

BOLIVIA, N. Y., 12.50.

ELEPHANT ARRIVED HERE FROM THE SOUTH AND PASSED THROUGH TOWARD THE FOREST AT 11.50, DISPERSING A FUNERAL ON THE WAY, AND DIMINISHING THE MOURNERS BY TWO. CITIZENS FIRED SOME SMALL CANNON-BALLS INTO HIM, AND THEN FLED. DETECTIVE BURKE AND I ARRIVED TEN MINUTES LATER, FROM THE NORTH, BUT MISTOOK SOME EXCAVATIONS FOR FOOTPRINTS, AND SO LOST A GOOD DEAL OF TIME; BUT AT LAST WE STRUCK THE RIGHT TRAIL AND FOLLOWED IT TO THE WOODS. WE THEN GOT DOWN ON OUR HANDS AND KNEES AND CONTINUED TO KEEP A SHARP EYE ON THE TRACK, AND SO SHADOWED IT INTO THE BRUSH. BURKE WAS IN ADVANCE. UNFORTUNATELY THE ANIMAL HAD STOPPED TO REST; THEREFORE, BURKE HAVING HIS HEAD DOWN, INTENT UPON THE TRACK, BUTTED UP AGAINST THE ELEPHANT'S HIND LEGS BEFORE HE WAS AWARE OF HIS VICINITY. BURKE INSTANTLY AROSE TO HIS FEET, SEIZED THE TAIL, AND EXCLAIMED JOYFULLY, "I CLAIM THE RE—" BUT GOT NO FURTHER, FOR A SINGLE BLOW OF THE HUGE TRUNK LAID THE BRAVE FELLOW'S FRAGMENTS LOW IN DEATH. I FLED REARWARD, AND THE ELEPHANT TURNED AND SHADOWED ME TO THE EDGE OF THE WOOD, MAKING TREMENDOUS SPEED, AND I SHOULD INEVITABLY HAVE BEEN LOST, BUT THAT THE REMAINS OF THE FUNERAL PROVIDENTIALLY INTERVENED AGAIN AND DIVERTED HIS

的小插曲评论什么，下面这封急件就将我的注意带到了另一个令人非常担忧的地方。

玻利维亚镇，纽约，12：50

11点50分，象由南至，穿过此地朝森林走去，途中驱散了一支送葬队伍，两名送葬者丧生。市民向它发射数枚小炮弹，随后逃跑。十分钟后，我和伯克侦探从北边赶到，但误把一些坑穴当做脚印，因此浪费了很长时间。但最后我们发现了真正的踪迹，并循之进了树林。我们当时爬着走，一直死盯着足迹，这样追踪到灌木丛。伯克在前。不幸那畜生停下休息，伯克头低着，一心铺在足迹上，所以直到一头撞到象的后腿才知道周围的情况。伯克立刻站起来，抓住大象的尾巴，高兴地大叫："我得了赏——"话没说完，巨大的象鼻只一下，就将此勇士击倒在地，使其身裂而亡。我往后跑，大象调头追我，直追到树林边上，速度极快。若不是送葬队伍中幸存的人再次及时介入，转移了它的注意力，我一定劫数难逃。我刚获悉，那支送葬队伍现无一人生还，但这也没什么损失，因为死者众多又办了场葬礼。同时象再次失踪。

探员 穆罗尼

ATTENTION. I HAVE JUST LEARNED THAT NOTHING OF THAT FUNERAL IS NOW LEFT; BUT THIS IS NO LOSS, FOR THERE IS ABUNDANCE OF MATERIAL FOR ANOTHER. MEANTIME, THE ELEPHANT HAS DISAPPEARED AGAIN.

MULROONEY, DETECTIVE

we heard no news except from the diligent and confident detectives scattered about New Jersey, Pennsylvania, Delaware, and Virginia—who were all following fresh and encouraging clues—until shortly after 2 P.M., when this telegram came:

BAXTER CENTER, 2.15.

ELEPHANT BEEN HERE, PLASTERED OVER WITH CIRCUS-BILLS, ANY BROKE UP A REVIVAL, STRIKING DOWN AND DAMAGING MANY WHO WERE ON THE POINT OF ENTERING UPON A BETTER LIFE. CITIZENS PENNED UP AND ESTABLISHED A GUARD. WHEN DETECTIVE BROWN AND I ARRIVED, SOME TIME AFTER, WE ENTERED INCLOSURE AND PROCEEDED TO IDENTIFY ELEPHANT BY PHOTOGRAPH AND DESCRIPTION. ALL MASKS TALLIED EXACTLY EXCEPT ONE, WHICH WE COULD NOT SEE—THE BOIL-SCAR UNDER ARMPIT. TO MAKE SURE, BROWN CREPT UNDER TO LOOK, AND WAS IMMEDIATELY BRAINED—THAT IS, HEAD CRUSHED AND DESTROYED, THOUGH NOTHING ISSUED FROM DEBRIS. ALL FLED; SO DID ELEPHANT, STRIKING RIGHT AND LEFT WITH MUCH EFFECT. HE ESCAPED, BUT LEFT BOLD BLOOD-TRACK FROM CANNON-WOUNDS. REDISCOVERY CERTAIN. HE BROKE SOUTHWARD, THROUGH A DENSE FOREST.

BRENT, DETECTIVE

我们除了收到分散在新泽西、宾夕法尼亚、特拉华和弗吉尼亚那些努力而又自信的侦探发来的消息之外，再没别的收获——他们都在追踪新的、令人振奋的线索——直到下午两点多才来了这封电报：

巴克斯特中心，2：15

象来过此地，浑身贴满马戏团海报，驱散了一场奋兴会[①]，撞倒并伤及多人性命，而这些人原本即将开始更好的生活。市民们围成一圈，组成一道防线。稍后，我和布朗侦探赶到，我们进入圈内，根据照片和描述进一步确认大象的身份。除一点外，所有特征均吻合，而那一点我们看不到——即腋下生疖子留下的疤。为了弄清楚，布朗爬到下面去看，随即脑袋开花——即头碎而亡，不过没什么从尸体上流出。众人皆逃，大象亦左冲右撞，顿时大乱。虽已逃走，但因炮伤留下了显眼的血迹，定会被重新发现。它向南逃遁，进入浓密的森林。

探员 布郎特

① 奋兴会。一种由教会举办的宗教集会，通过祈祷、唱诗、讲道等方式使信徒得到奋兴，灵魂得到升华。

That was the last telegram. At nightfall a fog shut down which was so dense that objects but three feet away could not be discerned. This lasted all night. The ferryboats and even the omnibuses had to stop running.

3

Next morning the papers were as full of detective theories as before; they had all our tragic facts in detail also, and a great many more which they had received from their telegraphic correspondents. Column after column was occupied, a third of its way down, with glaring head-lines, which it made my heart sick to read. Their general tone was like this:

THE WHITE ELEPHANT AT LARGE! HE MOVES UPON HIS FATAL MARCH! WHOLE VILLAGES DESERTED BY THEIR FRIGHT-STRICKEN OCCUPANTS! PALE TERROR GOES BEFORE HIM, DEATH AND DEVASTATION FOLLOW AFTER! AFTER THESE, THE DETECTIVES! BARNS DESTROYED, FACTORIES GUTTED, HARVESTS DEVOURED, PUBLIC ASSEMBLAGES DISPERSED, ACCOMPANIED BY SCENES OF CARNAGE IMPOSSIBLE TO DESCRIBE! THEORIES OF THIRTY-FOUR OF THE MOST DISTINGUISHED DETECTIVES ON THE FORCES! THEORY OF CHIEF BLUNT!

"There!" said Inspector Blunt, almost betrayed into excitement, "this is magnificent! This is the greatest windfall that any detective organization ever had. The fame of it will travel to the ends of the earth, and endure to the end of time, and

那是最后一封电报。傍晚时分起了雾，雾浓得看不清三英尺之外的东西。浓雾持续了一夜。渡船，甚至公共汽车都被迫停运。

三

第二天早上，报纸像往常一样，上面净是些侦探的推测。他们还详细刊登了我们所有的悲剧事件，还有从电报通讯员那儿得来的大量细节。这些内容占了一个又一个专栏，达到三分之一的版面，带着醒目的标题，读起来让我心烦意乱。他们总体的腔调是这样的：

白象依旧在逃！继续它的毁灭之行！整个村庄被恐惧万分的居民废弃！在它之前是令人谈虎色变的恐怖，在它之后是死亡和毁灭！继之就是侦探！谷仓被毁，工厂被劫，庄稼收成被席卷一空，公众聚会被驱散，伴随着难以形容的屠杀场面！警队里三十四位最杰出探员的推测啊！布伦特探长的推测啊！

"瞧！"布伦特督察说，显得近乎激动，"太棒了！这是所有侦缉机构有过的最大的意外收获。它的名气将会传到天涯海角，并与日月同辉，还有我的名字在上面呐。"

my name with it."

But there was no joy for me. I felt as if I had committed all those red crimes, and that the elephant was only my irresponsible agent. And how the list had grown! In one place he had "interfered with an election and killed five repeaters." He had followed this act with the destruction of two pool fellows, named O'Donohue and McFlannigan, who had "found a refuge in the home of the oppressed of all lands only the day before, and were in the act of exercising for the first time the noble right of American citizens at the polls, when stricken down by the relentless hand of the Scourge of Siam." In another, he had "found a crazy sensation-preacher preparing his next season's heroic attacks on the dance, the theater, and other things which can't strike back, and had stepped on him." And in still another place he had "killed a lightning-rod agent." And so the list went on, growing redder and redder, and more and more heartbreaking. Sixty persons had been killed, and two hundred and forty wounded. All the accounts bore just testimony to the activity and devotion of the detectives, and all closed with the remark that "three hundred thousand citizen and four detectives saw the dread creature, and two of the latter he destroyed."

I dreaded to hear the telegraphic instrument begin to click again. By and by the messages began to pour in, but I was happily disappointed in they nature. It was soon apparent that all trace of the elephant was lost. The fog had enabled him to search out a good hiding-place unobserved. Telegrams from the most absurdly distant points reported that a dim vast mass had

但是我却高兴不起来。我觉得自己好像犯了所有那些血腥的罪行，而大象只不过是我不负责任的代理而已。名单增加得真快啊！在某个地方，它“搅乱了一场选举，杀死了五名重复投票者”。此举之后，它接着毁掉了两个可怜的家伙，即奥多诺休和麦克弗兰尼根，他们“前一天刚在世界受压迫者之家找到庇护，正在大选中首次行使美国公民神圣的权利，就被暹罗瘟神的无情之手击倒”。在另一个地方，它“发现一位疯狂的牧师正在针对舞会、剧院和其他无法反抗的东西做下一阶段的攻击准备，就从他身上踩了过去”。还有在另一个地方，它“杀死了一个避雷针推销员”。就这样名单继续增加，变得越来越血腥，越来越令人痛心。六十人遇害，二百四十人受伤。所有的报道都充分证明了侦探们的行动和献身精神，而且都在结尾处写道：“三十万市民和四位侦探目睹了这可怕的畜生，两名侦探被杀。”

电报机又咔咔地响了起来，我听到就害怕。不久，电文开始大量涌来，但我对它们的内容既开心又失望。很快我们就明白了，大象的所有踪迹都消失了。大雾使它能够找到一个好的藏身之处，不被发现。从最偏僻的远方传来的电报说，在某某时候，有人透过大雾瞥见一个模糊的庞然大物，并且“肯定是那头大象”。这个模糊的庞然大物在纽黑文、新泽西、宾夕法尼亚、纽约州腹地、布鲁克林

been glimpsed there through the fog at such and such an hour, and was "undoubtedly the elephant." This dim vast mass had been glimpsed in New Haven, in New Jersey, in Pennsylvania, in interior New York, in Brooklyn, and even in the city of New York itself! But in all cases the dim vast mass had vanished quickly and left no trace. Every detective of the large force scattered over this huge extent of country sent his hourly report, and each and every one of them had a clue, and was shadowing something, and was hot upon the heels of it.

But the day passed without other result.

The next day the same.

The next just the same.

The newspaper reports began to grow monotonous with facts that amounted to nothing, clues which led to nothing, and theories which had nearly exhausted the elements which surprise and delight and dazzle.

By advice of the inspector I doubled the reward.

Four more dull days followed. Then came a bitter blow to the poor, hard-working detectives—the journalists declined to print their theories, and coldly said, "Give us a rest."

Two weeks after the elephant's disappearance I raised the reward to seventy-five thousand dollars by the inspector's advice. It was a great sum, but I felt that I would rather sacrifice my whole private fortune than lose my credit with my government. Now that the detectives were in adversity, the newspapers turned upon them, and began to fling the most stinging sarcasms at them. This gave the minstrels an idea, and

区[1]，甚至在纽约市都曾被瞥见过！但是在所有事件中，这个模糊的庞然大物都迅速消失，不知去向。庞大侦缉队的全体侦探散布在这个幅员辽阔的国家，每小时发一份报告，并且他们每个人都有一条线索，都正在追踪着什么，都正在紧紧地尾随其后。

但是一天过去了，没有什么结果。

接下来的一天也一样。

再接下来还是一样。

报纸的报道开始变得千篇一律，写的尽是没用的事情、毫无价值的线索以及几乎将惊奇、快乐和赞叹消耗殆尽的推测。

在探长的建议下，我把赏金增加了一倍。

接下来的四天更加无聊。随后，那些可怜巴巴、卖力工作的侦探受到了一次沉重的打击——记者谢绝刊登他们的推测，还冷冰冰地说："让我们歇歇吧。"

白象失踪的两周后，在督察的建议下，我把赏金提高到了七万五千美元。虽然这是一笔巨大的数目，但是我觉得就算赔上全部家私，也不能辜负政府的信任。现在侦探们身陷逆境，报纸开始攻击他们，并对他们进行最尖刻的挖苦。这给了滑稽说唱演员[2]灵感，他们把自己打扮成侦探，在舞台上追寻大象，表现得极为荒诞。

① 布鲁克林，纽约市西南部的一个区。

② 滑稽说唱演员。这类剧团尤其活跃在美国内战以后，剧中主要由白人歌舞演员化装成黑人，表演滑稽的大众节目。

they dressed themselves as detectives and hunted the elephant on the stage in the most extravagant way. The caricaturists made pictures of detectives scanning the country with spyglasses, while the elephant, at their backs, stole apples out of their pockets. And they made all sorts of ridiculous pictures of the detective badge—you have seen that badge printed in gold on the back of detective novels, no doubt—it is a wide-staring eye, with the legend, "WE NEVER SLEEP." When detectives called for a drink, the would-be facetious barkeeper resurrected an obsolete form of expression and said, "Will you have an eye-opener?" All the air was thick with sarcasms.

But there was one man who moved calm, untouched, unaffected, through it all. It was that heart of oak, the chief inspector. His brave eye never drooped, his serene confidence never wavered. He always said:

"Let them rail on; he laughs best who laughs last."

My admiration for the man grew into a species of worship. I was at his side always. His office had become an unpleasant place to me, and now became daily more and more so. Yet if he could endure it I meant to do so also—at least, as long as I could. So I came regularly, and stayed—the only outsider who seemed to be capable of it. Everybody wondered how I could; and often it seemed to me that I must desert, but at such times I looked into that calm and apparently unconscious face, and held my ground.

About three weeks after the elephant's disappearance I was about to say, one morning, that I should have to strike my colors

在漫画家的画中，侦探们正拿着望远镜瞭望乡村，而大象就在他们身后，从他们的口袋中偷苹果。他们还画了很多种侦探徽章的搞笑图案——你肯定见过那种印在侦探小说背面的镏金徽章——是一只瞪大的眼睛，附有一句话："我们从来不睡。"当侦探叫了一杯饮料，有意要诙谐一把的酒吧老板会重新起用一种过时的说法："你想要一杯空肚酒[①]吗？"那整个神态满是挖苦。

但是有一个人始终显得冷静，不为所动，不受影响，那就是坚强的探长。他勇敢的眼睛从不下垂，他平静的信心从不动摇。他总是说：

"让他们抱怨去吧，笑到最后的人才笑得最好。"

我对此人的尊敬发展成了一种崇拜。我总是在他左右。他的办公室本来就是个令我讨厌的地方，现在这种感觉一天天变得更加强烈。但是如果他能忍受，那么我也打算忍下去——只要我还能受得了。所以我经常去，并待在那儿——或许我是唯一能做到这点的外人。大家都想知道我是怎么做到的，我常常觉得我必须放弃，但每到这种时候，我一看到那张平静、不动声色的脸，就坚持了下去。

白象失踪后的三周左右，一天早上，我正打算说我早该放弃、

① （早上醒来时喝的）空肚酒。该词与上文的"从不睡觉"形成反讽，被用来挖苦侦探。

and retire, when the great detective arrested the thought by proposing one more superb and masterly move.

This was to compromise with the robbers. The fertility of this man's invention exceeded anything I have ever seen, and I have had a wide intercourse with the world's finest minds. He said he was confident he could compromise for one hundred thousand dollars and recover the elephant. I said I believed I could scrape the amount together, but what would become of the poor detectives who had worked so faithfully? He said:

"In compromises they always get half."

This removed my only objection. So the inspector wrote two notes, in this form:

DEAR MADAME—YOUR HUSBAND CAN MAKE A LARGE SUM OF MONEY (AND BE ENTIRELY PROTECTED FROM THE LAW) BY MAKING AN IMMEDIATE, APPOINTMENT WITH ME.

CHIEF BLUNT

He sent one of these by his confidential messenger to the "reputed wife" of Brick Duffy, and the other to the reputed wife of Red McFadden.

Within the hour these offensive answers came:

YE OWLD FOOL: BRICK DUFFYS BIN DED 2 YERE.

BRIDGET MAHONEY

CHIEF BAT—RED MCFADDEN IS HUNG AND IN HEVING 18 MONTH. ANY ASS BUT A DETECTIVE KNOSE THAT.

MARY O'HOOLIGAN

"I had long suspected these facts," said the inspector; "this testimony proves the unerring accuracy of my instinct."

退出，这时那个伟大的侦探提出了一个更绝更妙的行动，打消了我的念头。

这个行动就是与盗贼妥协。我曾与世界上最聪明的人有过广泛的交流，但此人非凡的创造力是我从未见过的。他说他有信心以十万美元达成妥协，找回大象。我说我想能够凑齐这笔数目，但是工作那么兢兢业业、可怜的探员该怎么办呀？他说：

"妥协的话他们通常拿一半。"

这消除了我唯一的顾虑。然后督察写了两封信，形式如下：

亲爱的夫人——您的丈夫立即和我见上一面就可以赚一大笔钱（而且完全受法律保护）。

探长 布伦特

由他的心腹担当信使，一封寄给了砖头杜飞"传闻中的妻子"，另一封寄给了红麦克法登传闻中的妻子。

不到一个小时，来了这些火药味十足的回信：

你个老笨蛋：砖头杜飞都死两年了。

布里奇特·马奥尼

瞎子探长——红麦克法登被绞死了，在天堂十八个月了。除了侦探，是个傻子都知道。

玛丽·奥胡利根

"我早就怀疑这些事儿了，"督察说，"这份证词证明我的直觉准确无误。"

The moment one resource failed him he was ready with another. He immediately wrote an advertisement for the morning papers, and I kept a copy of it:

A.—xwblv. 242 N. Tjnd—fz328wmlg. Ozpo,—;2 m! ogw. Mum.

He said that if the thief was alive this would bring him to the usual rendezvous. He further explained that the usual rendezvous was a glare where all business affairs between detectives and criminals were conducted. This meeting would take place at twelve the next night.

We could do nothing till then, and I lost no time in getting out of the office, and was grateful indeed for the privilege.

At eleven the next night I brought one hundred thousand dollars in bank-notes and put them into the chief's hands, and shortly afterward he took his leave, with the brave old undimmed confidence in his eye. An almost intolerable hour dragged to a close; then I heard his welcome tread, and rose gasping and tottered to meet him. How his fine eyes flamed with triumph! He said:

"We've compromised! The jokers will sing a different tune to-morrow! Follow me!"

He took a lighted candle and strode down into the vast vaulted basement where sixty detectives always slept, and where a score were now playing cards to while the time. I followed close after him. He walked swiftly down to the dim and remote end of the place, and just as I succumbed to the pangs of suffocation and was swooning away he stumbled and

他一计不成，随即又生一计。他很快写了一条广告，刊登在早报上，我抄了一份：

A.—xwblv. 242 N. Tjnd—fz328wmlg. Ozpo,—;2 m! ogw. Mum.[1]

他说，如果那贼还活着，这会带他去碰头的地方。他进一步解释说，碰头的地方是侦探和罪犯之间从事一切交易的场所。这次见面将会定在次日午夜12点。

在那之前我们没事做，我迫不及待地走出办公室，并对这种特殊的待遇感到非常感激。

次日夜里11点，我带了十万美元的现金，交到探长手里。不久他便离开了，眼神勇敢而坚定。令人难以忍受的一个小时慢慢过去；此时我听到他款款的脚步，急忙站起来跑去迎接他。他漂亮的眼睛里闪耀着胜利的光芒！他说道：

"我们已经妥协了！开玩笑的家伙们明天得换换调子[2]了！跟我来！"

他拿了一支点着的蜡烛，大踏步走进宽敞的拱顶地下室，通常六十名探员在这里睡觉，这会儿二十几个人正在这儿打牌，消磨时间。我紧紧地跟在他后面，他飞步走到屋子阴暗、遥远的尽头。就在我受窒息的折磨、快要晕过去的时候，他绊了一跤，倒在了一个展

① 此句是接头的暗语。
② 改变调子，变卦。这里指那些人不能再说侦探们的坏话了，得变个态度。

fell over the outlying members of a mighty object, and I heard him exclaim as he went down:

"Our noble profession is vindicated. Here is your elephant!"

I was carried to the office above and restored with carbolic acid. The whole detective force swarmed in, and such another season of triumphant rejoicing ensued as I had never witnessed before. The reporters were called, baskets of champagne were opened, toasts were drunk, the handshakings and congratulations were continuous and enthusiastic. Naturally the chief was the hero of the hour, and his happiness was so complete and had been so patiently and worthily and bravely won that it made me happy to see it, though I stood there a homeless beggar, my priceless charge dead, and my position in my country's service lost to me through what would always seem my fatally careless execution of a great trust. Many an eloquent eye testified its deep admiration for the chief, and many a detective's voice murmured, "Look at him—just the king of the profession; only give him a clue, it's all he wants, and there ain't anything hid that he can't find." The dividing of the fifty thousand dollars made great pleasure; when it was finished the chief made a little speech while he put his share in his pocket, in which he said, "Enjoy it, boys, for you've earned it; and, more than that, you've earned for the detective profession undying fame."

A telegram arrived, which read:

MONROE, MICH., 10 P.M.

FIRST TIME I'VE STRUCK A TELEGRAPH OFFICE IN OVER THREE WEEKS. HAVE FOLLOWED THOSE FOOTPRINTS,

开的庞然大物上。我还听他倒下时大喊：

“我们崇高的职业得到了维护，你的白象在这儿！”

我被抬到上面的办公室里，恢复了神志。整个侦缉队涌了进来。接下来的那么一段洋洋得意的快乐时光，我以前从未见过。他们请来了记者，打开了成箱的香槟，举杯共庆，持续而热情地握手和祝贺。探长此刻自然成了英雄，他高兴得溢于言表。这是用耐心、努力和勇气换来的，连我看了都很高兴。尽管我站在那儿，像个无家可归的乞丐，我负责的无价之宝死了，还因为严重疏忽，我未能完成一项重托，丢了国家机关的差事。许多双饱含情绪的眼睛写满了对探长的钦佩，许多侦探低声咕哝着：“瞧瞧他——就像行业之王。只要给他一条线索，他只要这个，藏起来的东西没有他找不到的。”分享五万美元令人极为高兴。结束时，探长一面把他的那份塞到兜里，一面发表了一小段讲话。他说：“好好享受吧，伙计们，这是你们赢得的。不仅如此，你们还为侦缉行业赢得了不朽的声誉。”

一封电报传来，说道：

门罗，密歇根州，晚上 10：00

三周来我首次找到电报局。追踪到那些脚印，骑马穿过树林，千里迢迢来到这里。脚印每天都变得更深，更大，也更新。不必担

HORSEBACK, THROUGH THE WOODS, A THOUSAND MILES TO HERE, AND THEY GET STRONGER AND BIGGER AND FRESHER EVERY DAY. DON'T WORRY—INSIDE OF ANOTHER WEEK I'LL HAVE THE ELEPHANT. THIS IS DEAD SURE.

DARLEY, DETECTIVE.

The chief ordered three cheers for "Darley, one of the finest minds on the force," and then commanded that he be telegraphed to come home and receive his share of the reward.

So ended that marvelous episode of the stolen elephant. The newspapers were pleasant with praises once more, the next day, with one contemptible exception. This sheet said, "Great is the detective! He may be a little slow in finding a little thing like a mislaid elephant—he may hunt him all day and sleep with his rotting carcass all night for three weeks, but he will find him at last—if he can get the man who mislaid him to show him the place!"

Poor Hassan was lost to me forever. The cannon-shots had wounded him fatally, he had crept to that unfriendly place in the fog, and there, surrounded by his enemies and in constant danger of detection, he had wasted away with hunger and suffering till death gave him peace.

The compromise cost me one hundred thousand dollars; my detective expenses were forty-two thousand dollars more; I never applied for a place again under my government; I am a ruined man and a wanderer on the earth—but my admiration for that man, whom I believe to be the greatest detective the world has ever produced, remains undimmed to this day, and will so remain unto the end.

心——不出一周我就会抓到它。这点肯定无疑。

探员 达利

探长要求为“达利，队里最优秀的探员之一”干三杯，然后命令发电报叫他回来领他那份奖金。

关于被偷的白象那段非同寻常的故事就这样结束了。第二天，报纸上又一次出现赞誉之声，只有一家不值一提的小报例外。这份报纸说：“侦探真了不起啊！他找到被弃的大象这样的小东西可能稍慢了点儿——三周来，他整个白天在找，整个晚上却与大象腐烂的尸体睡在一起，不过总算是找到了——只要他能让抛弃大象的人指给他地方。”

我永远失去了可怜的哈森。炮弹对它造成了致命的创伤，雾中它爬到了那个不祥的地方，在那里，它被敌人包围，并时刻有被发现的危险，由于饥饿和疼痛，它渐渐衰弱，直到死亡给了它宁静。

妥协花了我十万美元，侦缉费用又花了四万二千多美元。在政府部门，我再无容身之处。我破产了，成了世间的一名流浪汉——但是我认为，那人是世上最伟大的侦探，我对他的崇敬之情至今未减一分，并将一直如此，直到我死。

A Dog's Tale
狗的自述

小说《狗的自述》（A Dog's Tale, 1903）从狗的视角，讲述了一条狗的悲惨故事。“我”是一条忠心耿耿的狗，曾经从大火中救出了主人家孩子的性命，但是自己却屡屡遭到不幸：先是被主人打折一条腿，后来又眼睁睁地看着自己的爱子命丧黄泉，最后在悲痛欲绝中奄奄一息。作品详细描写了“我”的所见所闻所感，将一条活生生的狗展现在了读者的面前。这是马克·吐温晚年创作的一篇带有悲剧色彩的小说，通过狗的遭遇反映出传统道德在当时社会中受到的冲击。

小说中的“我”是一条道德高尚的狗，至少具有三点人的美德。一是忠诚。“我”安分于自己眼下的生活，终日陪伴女主人，看护婴儿，或跟孩子们玩耍，为了家人甚至不惜献出自己的生命。二是勇敢。“我”面对熊熊烈火，所做的不是独自逃命，而是冒着危险救出了家中的婴儿。三是宽容。在厄运面前，“我”并无半句怨言及愤恨之情，只是默默地忍受。不论是遭到了主人的无理毒打而致残，还是目睹自己的爱子在实验室惨遭不幸，“我”都是独自在痛苦中煎熬。与狗相比，有些人却逊色了许多。小说中有一位冷酷的科学家，他不分青红皂白使一条无辜的狗终身残疾，却从未想过弥补这一过失。狗救了他的孩子，而他却将狗的孩子送上了实验台，其冷酷残忍令人痛心。道德在人身上泯灭了，反而在狗的身上体现了出来，这怎能不引起人的思索？

1

My father was a St. Bernard, my mother was a collie, but I am a Presbyterian. This is what my mother told me; I do not know these nice distinctions myself. To me they are only fine large words meaning nothing. My mother had a fondness for such; she liked to say them, and see other dogs look surprised and envious, as wondering how she got so much education. But, indeed, it was not real education; it was only show: she got the words by listening in the dining-room and drawing-room when there was company, and by going with the children to Sunday-school and listening there; and whenever she heard a large word she said it over to herself many times, and so was able to keep it until there was a dogmatic gathering in the neighborhood, then she would get it off, and surprise and distress them all, from pocket-pup to mastiff, which rewarded her for all her trouble. If there was a stranger he was nearly sure to be suspicious, and when he got his breath again he would ask her what it meant. And she always told him. He was never expecting this, but thought he would catch her; so when she told him, he was the one that looked ashamed, whereas he had thought it was going to be she. The others were always waiting for this, and glad of it and proud of her, for they knew what was going to happen, because they had had experience. When she told the meaning of a big word they were all so taken up with admiration that it never occurred to any dog to doubt if it was the right one; and that was natural, because, for one thing, she answered up

一

我父亲是圣伯纳犬[①]，母亲是柯利牧羊犬[②]，而我是长老会教友[③]。这是母亲告诉我的，我自己并不明白这些微妙的差别。在我看来，它们只不过是漂亮时髦的字眼，没有多大意义。我母亲热衷于这个，喜欢把它们挂在嘴边，喜欢看到别的狗露出吃惊和羡慕的表情，好像它们在纳闷，她怎么受过这么多教育。可是，这真的算不上什么实实在在的教育，只是显摆罢了。那些词有的是她在聚会时，从餐厅和客厅里听来的；有的是她跟孩子们去主日学校时，在那儿听来的；一听到时髦的字眼，她就在心里背很多遍，所以能把它记住。一直记到附近开宣讲会的时候，到那时她会说出来。从小型犬到大驯犬，所有的狗听了无不吃惊，心里不是个滋味儿，这也算是对她的一番苦功的回报。要是有条陌生的狗在，差不多肯定要起疑心。等他回过神儿，就会问她那个词什么意思。而她总会告诉人家。对此他万万想不到，只是以为会难住她；所以当她告诉他时，他倒成了面露愧色的一位，尽管他原以为羞愧的会是她。其他的狗总是等着这个时候，以此为乐，以她为荣。他们知道会发生什么，因为他们曾经有过教训。当她说了个大字眼的意思时，他们全都钦佩不已，甚至于从来就没有哪条狗会怀疑意思是不是对；那也难怪，一则她回答得非常快，像是一本字典在说话；再说，他们上哪儿弄明白意思对不对呢？因为她是那里唯一一条受过教育的狗。后来我逐渐长大，有一次，她背熟了"缺乏智力"这个词，而且整整一个星期她在不同的集会上表演得都相当卖力，制造了许多不快和沮丧；就是在这一次

① 圣伯纳犬，原产于丹麦的一种大型犬，历史上曾被用于恶劣气候条件下的搜索和救援工作。

② 柯利牧羊犬，原产于英国苏格兰地区，在牧羊和驱赶牲畜方面极具实用价值。

③ 这里母亲并不是为了说明"我"的教派，只是为了卖弄。从下文我们得知，母亲喜欢用一些听起来气派的词，并不管它们的意思。她给"我"的这个称呼也暗示了"我"善良的性格。

so promptly that it seemed like a dictionary speaking, and for another thing, where could they find out whether it was right or not? for she was the only cultivated dog there was. By and by, when I was older, she brought home the word Unintellectual, one time, and worked it pretty hard all the week at different gatherings, making much unhappiness and despondency; and it was at this time that I noticed that during that week she was asked for the meaning at eight different assemblages, and flashed out a fresh definition every time, which showed me that she had more presence of mind than culture, though I said nothing, of course. She had one word which she always kept on hand, and ready, like a life-preserver, a kind of emergency word to strap on when she was likely to get washed overboard in a sudden way—that was the word Synonymous. When she happened to fetch out a long word which had had its day weeks before and its prepared meanings gone to her dump-pile, if there was a stranger there of course it knocked him groggy for a couple of minutes, then he would come to, and by that time she would be away down the wind on another tack, and not expecting anything; so when he'd hail and ask her to cash in, I (the only dog on the inside of her game) could see her canvas flicker a moment—but only just a moment—then it would belly out taut and full, and she would say, as calm as a summer's day, "It's synonymous with supererogation," or some godless long reptile of a word like that, and go placidly about and skim away on the next tack, perfectly comfortable, you know, and leave that stranger looking profane and embarrassed, and the initiated

我注意到，在那周八场不同的集会上她都被问到该词的意思，但她每次脱口就给了一种新的解释。这让我明白了，她有的更多是遇事不慌的能力，而不是文化。不过我自然什么也没说。有个词她总是攥在手里准备救急，像件救生衣，一有被突然冲下水的危险，她就把它紧紧地绑在身上——那个词就是“同义”。有时，她偶然提到了几个星期前用过的一个长长的词，而为它准备好的意思已经进了她的废物堆。要是有条陌生的狗在那儿，一时半会儿自然会被蒙得晕头转向，然后他会反应过来。而那时，她就顺着风偏向另一个航向，料想出不了什么事情；所以当他叫着让她解释时，我（唯一了解她游戏内幕的狗）能看到她的帆抖动了片刻——仅仅就是片刻——然后完全拉紧扬起[①]。她会像夏日一样[②]平静地说：“该词与多此一举同义。”或是说一些诸如此类像爬虫一般邪恶冗长的词，然后平静地走来走去，飞快地掠过偏向下一个航向。你要知道，这尤为惬意。而那条狗则被丢在一边，显得粗俗难堪。知情的狗会一起用尾巴扑打着地面，脸上焕发出极度的喜悦。

① 本句使用暗喻的修辞，将母亲比作在风中航行的船，利用风灵活改变航向，出奇制胜。句中用了很多航海方面的术语，如 down the wind 顺风；tack 强风航行；canvas 帆布，这里指风帆；belly out 鼓胀，扬帆。

② 莎士比亚十四行诗中曾提到过 summer's day 这一短语，原句为“Shall I compare thee to a summer's day? Thou art more lovely and more temperate”。由此可见，summer's day 含有“秀丽、温和”之意。

slatting the floor with their tails in unison and their faces transfigured with a holy joy.

And it was the same with phrases. She would drag home a whole phrase, if it had a grand sound, and play it six nights and two matinées, and explain it a new way every time—which she had to, for all she cared for was the phrase; she wasn't interested in what it meant, and knew those dogs hadn't wit enough to catch her, anyway. Yes, she was a daisy! She got so she wasn't afraid of anything, she had such confidence in the ignorance of those creatures. She even brought anecdotes that she had heard the family and the dinner-guests laugh and shout over; and as a rule she got the nub of one chestnut hitched onto another chestnut, where, of course, it didn't fit and hadn't any point; and when she delivered the nub she fell over and rolled on the floor and laughed and barked in the most insane way, while I could see that she was wondering to herself why it didn't seem as funny as it did when she first heard it. But no harm was done; the others rolled and barked too, privately ashamed of themselves for not seeing the point, and never suspecting that the fault was not with them and there wasn't any to see.

You can see by these things that she was of a rather vain and frivolous character; still, she had virtues, and enough to make up, I think. She had a kind heart and gentle ways, and never harbored resentments for injuries done her, but put them easily out of her mind and forgot them; and she taught her children her kindly way, and from her we learned also to be brave and prompt in time of danger, and not to run away, but

短语也是一样的。若是它听着气派，她会把整条短语记熟，表演上六个晚场和两个下午场，而且每次都给出新的解释——她保准会这样做，因为她在乎的完全就是短语，对意思是什么不感兴趣。她知道那些狗根本没那么聪明能难得住她。是啊，她是最棒的！有了这个本事她什么都不怕。她对那帮家伙的无知非常有信心，甚至把听过的令家人和晚餐上的客人大呼大笑的趣事都记了下来；她还经常把精彩之处从一个老掉牙的笑话安到另一个老掉牙的笑话上，在那儿当然不合适，也不切题；并且她一说完精彩之处，就倒在地上来回打滚，发疯似的大笑大叫。可我看得出来，她在暗自奇怪，为什么故事不像她第一次听到时那么好笑。但是这并不碍事，别的狗也在打滚，也在汪汪大叫，私下里还为自己没有明白故事的意思而感到羞愧。它们万万不会想到错并不在他们身上，也就没什么要明白的。

从这些事你能看出来，她相当自负和轻浮；可是她也有优点，而且我认为她的优点足以弥补她的不足。她心地善良，举止文雅，绝不会因为自己受了伤害而记仇，只是轻轻地把它们从记忆中抹去，忘掉它们；她把自己的那份善良传承给了她的子女。而且从她身上我们还学到，在危险的时候要勇敢，要迅速，不要逃跑；当朋友或陌生人面临危险时，要尽全力提供帮助，不要因为计较可能会付出多大的代价而犹豫。她不是光嘴上说说，还用行动教育我们，那

face the peril that threatened friend or stranger, and help him the best we could without stopping to think what the cost might be to us. And she taught us not by words only, but by example, and that is the best way and the surest and the most lasting. Why, the brave thing she did, the splendid things! she was just a soldier; and so modest about it—well, you couldn't help admiring her, and you couldn't help imitating her; not even a King Charles spaniel could remain entirely despicable in her society. So, as you see, there was more to her than her education.

2

When I was well grown, at last, I was sold and taken away, and I never saw her again. She was broken-hearted, and so was I, and we cried; but she comforted me as well as she could, and said we were sent into this world for a wise and good purpose, and must do our duties without repining, take our life as we might find it, live it for the best good of others, and never mind about the results; they were not our affair. She said men who did like this would have a noble and beautiful reward by and by in another world, and although we animals would not go there, to do well and right without reward would give to our brief lives a worthiness and dignity which in itself would be a reward. She had gathered these things from time to time when she had gone to the Sunday-school with the children, and had laid them up in her memory more carefully than she had done with those other words and phrases; and she had studied them deeply, for her good

是最好、最可靠、也是最持久的方法。啊，她做的事情多么勇敢，多么了不起啊！她简直就是一个战士，并且对此非常谦虚——哎，你会禁不住佩服她，你会禁不住模仿她；就算是查尔斯王犬[①]和她在一起，也不能把她给看扁了。所以你知道，除了受良好的教育之外，她还有很多其他的优点。

二

后来，我长大了，被人买走，就再也没见过她。她的心都碎了，我也是，我们哭了。可是她极力安慰我，还说我们被派到这个世界上来，为的是一个明智善良的目的，必须无怨无悔地履行我们的职责，随遇而安。我们活着是为了他人最大的利益，千万不要计较得失，那不是我们操心的事。她说，像这样做的人迟早会在另一个世界里得到丰厚、美好的回报。虽然我们动物去不了那里，但是做好事、做善事而不求回报会使我们短暂的一生有价值、有尊严，这本身就是回报。她跟孩子们去主日学校时，经常听到这些东西，并且把它们记在脑子里，比记其他那些词和短语更认真。她已经把它们研究得很透彻，为她好，也为我们好。从这点可以看出来，她的脑子聪明，而且有思想，虽然里面有许多轻浮和虚荣的成分。

① 查尔斯王犬，原产于英国的一种小型犬，17世纪时深受英王查尔斯二世的宠爱，在宫里大受欢迎。

and ours. One may see by this that she had a wise and thoughtful head, for all there was so much lightness and vanity in it.

So we said our farewells, and looked our last upon each other through our tears; and the last thing she said—keeping it for the last to make me remember it the better, I think—was, "In memory of me, when there is a time of danger to another do not think of yourself, think of your mother, and do as she would do."

Do you think I could forget that? No.

3

It was such a charming home!—my new one; a fine great house, with pictures, and delicate decorations, and rich furniture, and no gloom anywhere, but all the wilderness of dainty colors lit up with flooding sunshine; and the spacious grounds around it, and the great garden—oh, greensward, and noble trees, and flowers, no end! And I was the same as a member of the family; and they loved me, and petted me, and did not give me a new name, but called me by my old one that was dear to me because my mother had given it me— Aileen Mavourneen. She got it out of a song; and the Grays knew that song, and said it was a beautiful name.

Mrs. Gray was thirty, and so sweet and so lovely, you cannot imagine it; and Sadie was ten, and just like her mother, just a darling slender little copy of her, with auburn tails down her back, and short frocks; and the baby was a year old, and plump and dimpled, and fond of me, and never could get enough

于是我们告别了，透过泪水看了彼此最后一眼。她说的最后一句话是——我想，她把它留到最后是要让我记得更牢——“为了纪念我，当他人遇到危险时，别想你自己，想想妈妈，想想她会怎么做。”

你说我能忘了那些话吗？不能。

三

多么迷人的家啊！——我的新家，是一幢漂亮的大房子，有画，有精美的装饰，还有富丽堂皇的家具，没有任何阴暗的角落。在充足的阳光下，到处闪耀着鲜艳的色彩；周围是片广阔的空地，还有一个大花园——啊，草地，高大的树木和鲜花，说也说不完！我跟家里的成员没什么两样，他们爱我，抚摸我，并没有给我起新名字，而是叫我原来的名字。我喜欢它，因为那是妈妈给我起的——艾琳·马弗尔宁。她从一首歌里听来的，格雷家的人也知道那首歌，说这是个好听的名字。

格雷夫人有30岁，非常迷人，非常漂亮，你简直无法想象；赛迪10岁，就像她妈妈一样，就是她妈妈可爱苗条的缩小版，红褐色的辫子垂在背上，穿了一件短短的连衣裙；宝宝有一岁，胖嘟嘟的，带着酒窝。他很喜欢我，总是不厌烦地拽我的尾巴，搂着我，笑起来天真无邪，非常开心；格雷先生38岁，瘦高个儿，英俊潇洒，脑门稍秃，

of hauling on my tail, and hugging me, and laughing out its innocent happiness; and Mr. Gray was thirty-eight, and tall and slender and handsome, a little bald in front, alert, quick in his movements, business-like, prompt, decided, unsentimental, and with that kind of trim-chiseled face that just seems to glint and sparkle with frosty intellectuality! He was a renowned scientist. I do not know what the word means, but my mother would know how to use it and get effects. She would know how to depress a rat-terrier with it and make a lap-dog look sorry he came. But that is not the best one; the best one was Laboratory. My mother could organize a Trust on that one that would skin the tax-collars off the whole herd. The laboratory was not a book, or a picture, or a place to wash your hands in, as the college president's dog said—no, that is the lavatory; the laboratory is quite different, and is filled with jars, and bottles, and electrics, and wires, and strange machines; and every week other scientists came there and sat in the place, and used the machines, and discussed, and made what they called experiments and discoveries; and often I came, too, and stood around and listened, and tried to learn, for the sake of my mother, and in loving memory of her, although it was a pain to me, as realizing what she was losing out of her life and I gaining nothing at all; for try as I might, I was never able to make anything out of it at all.

Other times I lay on the floor in the mistress's work-room and slept, she gently using me for a foot-stool, knowing it pleased me, for it was a caress; other times I spent an hour in the nursery, and got well tousled and made happy; other

反应敏捷，做事利索，有条不紊，麻利，有主见，不感情用事，脸上干干净净，看起来总是闪现着冰冷的智慧！他是位著名的科学家。虽然我不知道“科学家”这个词是什么意思，但是妈妈一定知道怎么用，还会收到效果。她一定知道怎么用它让捕鼠小猎犬[①]沮丧，让哈叭儿狗看上去后悔来这儿。但那还不是最棒的词，最棒的词是“实验室”。我的母亲能用那个词成立个托拉斯[②]，把一群狗的脖项圈都给扯下来。实验室不是一本书，不是一幅画，也不是像大学校长家的狗说的那样，是个洗手的地方——不是，洗手的地方叫盥洗室，实验室完全不一样，里面全是瓶瓶罐罐、电子器件、电线和奇怪的机器；每一周其他的科学家都会去那儿，坐在里面，用机器，讨论，进行他们所谓的实验和发现。我也经常去，站在一旁听，试图学点什么，为了我的母亲，为了深深地纪念她，虽然那对我是件痛苦的事，因为我认识到她一辈子费了那么多心血，而我却一无所获。尽管我费尽力气，却一点儿也听不懂。

有时候，我趴在女主人工作间的地板上睡觉。她温柔地把我当脚凳，知道我喜欢这样，因为这是爱抚；有时候，我在婴儿屋里待一个小时，浑身被弄得乱糟糟的，我却很开心；有时候，宝宝睡着了，保姆为宝宝的事出去几分钟，我就守在婴儿床旁边；有时候，我和

① 捕鼠小猎犬，一种小型犬，性格温顺，有较强的狩猎能力。
② 托拉斯，一种垄断组织的形式，由若干相关企业合并而成。这里比喻母亲和其他狗组成的联盟。

times I watched by the crib there, when the baby was asleep and the nurse out for a few minutes on the baby's affairs; other times I romped and raced through the grounds and the garden with Sadie till we were tired out, then slumbered on the grass in the shade of a tree while she read her book; other times I went visiting among the neighbor dogs—for there were some most pleasant ones not far away, and one very handsome and courteous and graceful one, a curly-haired Irish setter by the name of Robin Adair, who was a Presbyterian like me, and belonged to the Scotch minister.

The servants in our house were all kind to me and were fond of me, and so, as you see, mine was a pleasant life. There could not be a happier dog than I was, nor a gratefuler one. I will say this for myself, for it is only the truth: I tried in all ways to do well and right, and honor my mother's memory and her teachings, and earn the happiness that had come to me, as best I could.

By and by came my little puppy, and then my cup was full, my happiness was perfect. It was the dearest little waddling thing, and so smooth and soft and velvety, and had such cunning little awkward paws, and such affectionate eyes, and such a sweet and innocent face; and it made me so proud to see how the children and their mother adored it, and fondled it, and exclaimed over every little wonderful thing it did. It did seem to me that life was just too lovely to—

Then came the winter. One day I was standing a watch in the nursery. That is to say, I was asleep on the bed. The baby

赛迪在空地和花园追逐嬉戏，直到我们都精疲力竭，然后我就在树荫下的草地上睡觉，而她读她的书；有时候，我去找邻居家的狗串门——附近有些狗很讨人喜欢，有一条非常漂亮、非常谦和、非常优雅的卷毛爱尔兰赛特犬[①]，名叫罗宾·阿代尔，和我一样也是长老会教友，它是苏格兰牧师家的狗。

家里的用人对我很好，都很喜欢我。所以你看，我过得很开心。哪条狗也没有我快乐，哪条狗也没有我知足。我会对自己这么说，因为这不过就是事实："我竭尽全力地做好事、做善事，纪念我的母亲，铭记她的教诲，尽我最大的努力赢得了属于我的幸福。"

不久，我的小狗儿出生了，当时我乐坏了，非常幸福。它是一个非常可爱的小家伙，走起路来晃晃悠悠，身上那么光滑柔软，天鹅绒一般，小爪子那么讨人喜欢，眼睛那么脉脉含情，小脸那么天真可爱；看到孩子和他们的母亲那么喜欢它，爱抚它，为它做出的每一件奇妙的小事惊呼，我感到非常骄傲。我觉得生活真是太美好了，简直无法——

后来，冬天来了。有一天，我守候在婴儿屋里，也就是说我在床上睡觉。宝宝睡在靠着床边的婴儿床里，旁边是火炉。这种小床

① 爱尔兰赛特犬，毛多呈深红色，多用于狩猎。

was asleep in the crib, which was alongside the bed, on the side next the fireplace. It was the kind of crib that has a lofty tent over it made of gauzy stuff that you can see through. The nurse was out, and we two sleepers were alone. A spark from the wood-fire was shot out, and it lit on the slope of the tent. I supposed a quiet interval followed, then a scream from the baby woke me, and there was that tent flaming up toward the ceiling! Before I could think, I sprang to the floor in my fright, and in a second was half-way to the door; but in the next half-second my mother's farewell was sounding in my ears, and I was back on the bed again. I reached my head through the flames and dragged the baby out by the waist-band, and tugged it along, and we fell to the floor together in a cloud of smoke; I snatched a new hold, and dragged the screaming little creature along and out at the door and around the bend of the hall, and was still tugging away, all excited and happy and proud, when the master's voice shouted:

"Begone, you cursed beast!" and I jumped to save myself; but he was wonderfully quick, and chased me up, striking furiously at me with his cane, I dodging this way and that, in terror, and at last a strong blow fell upon my left foreleg, which made me shriek and fall, for the moment, helpless; the cane went up for another blow, but never descended, for the nurse's voice rang wildly out, "The nursery's on fire!" and the master rushed away in that direction, and my other bones were saved.

The pain was cruel, but, no matter, I must not lose any time; he might come back at any moment; so I limped on

上面支了一顶高高拱起的细纱帐子，一眼就能看到里面。保姆出去了，只留我们两个在睡觉。火堆里迸出一个火星，落在帐子的侧面，将帐子点着了。我觉得接下来的一会儿没什么动静，随后宝宝哇的一声把我吵醒。帐子烧得正旺，火苗直窜屋顶！我想都没想，惊慌之中跳到地上，随即朝门口冲去，但是猛然间，妈妈临别时的话在我耳边响起。于是我重新跳上床，头探进火中，叼住孩子的腰带，把他拖了出来，一个劲儿地拽，在滚滚浓烟中我们一同摔到地上。我重新衔起他，将这个哭喊的小家伙一路拖到门外，拖到过道的拐角处，还不停地往外拽。我满是兴奋、欢喜和骄傲，这时男主人的声音喊道：

“滚开，你这该死的畜生！”我跳起来就逃，可他快得惊人，追上我，用手杖狠狠地朝我打来。我左躲右闪，吓得要命。终于，一记重击落到了我左侧的前腿上。我惨叫一声，扑倒在地，此时已无力抵抗，手杖举了起来，眼看又是一击，但是没有落下来，因为保姆的声音急切地传来：“婴儿屋里着火了！”男主人朝那个方向跑了过去，我的皮肉才幸免于难。

虽然疼痛难忍，但我顾不上了，片刻也不容耽搁，他随时都会回来，于是，我三条腿一瘸一拐地朝过道的另一头走去，那儿有一条

three legs to the other end of the hall, where there was a dark little stairway leading up into a garret where old boxes and such things were kept, as I had heard say, and where people seldom went. I managed to climb up there, then I searched my way through the dark among the piles of things, and hid in the secretest place I could find. It was foolish to be afraid there, yet still I was; so afraid that I held in and hardly even whimpered, though it would have been such a comfort to whimper, because that eases the pain, you know. But I could lick my leg, and that did me some good.

For half an hour there was a commotion downstairs, and shoutings, and rushing footsteps, and then there was quiet again. Quiet for some minutes, and that was grateful to my spirit, for then my fears began to go down; and fears are worse than pains—oh, much worse. Then came a sound that froze me. They were calling me—calling me by names—hunting for me!

It was muffled by distance, but that could not take the terror out of it, and it was the most dreadful sound to me that I had ever heard. It went all about, everywhere, down there: along the halls, through all the rooms, in both stories, and in the basement and the cellar; then outside, and farther and farther away—then back, and all about the house again, and I thought it would never, never stop. But at last it did, hours and hours after the vague twilight of the garret had long ago been blotted out by black darkness.

Then in that blessed stillness my terrors fell little by little away, and I was at peace and slept. It was a good rest I had, but

昏暗的小楼梯，直通上面的阁楼。我听说阁楼上放着废旧箱子之类的东西，很少有人上去。我吃力地爬上去，然后在黑暗中摸索着穿过一堆堆的杂物，在我能找到的最隐秘的地方藏了起来。要是在那儿害怕就太傻了，可我还是害怕，非常害怕，我强忍着，甚至不敢低声哭泣，不过要是哭出来就舒服多了，因为你知道，哭会缓解疼痛。但是我还能舔舔自己的腿，这让我好受了点。

楼下一片混乱。喊叫声、跑动的脚步声持续了半个小时，后来又安静下来。安静了几分钟，这让我心里很感激，因为当时我的恐惧开始减弱，恐惧比疼痛更糟糕——哎，要糟糕得多。接着传来的一个声音让我一动也不敢动。他们在喊我——在喊我的名字——在找我！

喊声因为在远处听得不大清楚，可是那消除不了其中的恐怖，这是我听过的最可怕的声音。它到处都有，在每一个角落，在下面那儿：沿着过道，穿过所有的房间，回响在楼上楼下，回响在地下室和地窖里；然后到外面，到很远很远的地方——然后回来；又在房子里各处响起。我想它永远永远也不会停止，但是终于停下来了。这时已经过了很长时间，阁楼昏暗的光线早已被黑暗湮没。

后来在那片祥和的宁静中，我的恐惧一点一点地消失，我平静地睡着了。我休息得很好，可是天没亮就醒了。我觉得好多了，并

I woke before the twilight had come again. I was feeling fairly comfortable, and I could think out a plan now. I made a very good one; which was, to creep down, all the way down the back stairs, and hide behind the cellar door, and slip out and escape when the iceman came at dawn, while he was inside filling the refrigerator; then I would hide all day, and start on my journey when night came; my journey to—well, anywhere where they would not know me and betray me to the master. I was feeling almost cheerful now; then suddenly I thought: Why, what would life be without my puppy!

That was despair. There was no plan for me; I saw that; I must stay where I was; stay, and wait, and take what might come—it was not my affair; that was what life is—my mother had said it. Then—well, then the calling began again! All my sorrows came back. I said to myself, the master will never forgive. I did not know what I had done to make him so bitter and so unforgiving, yet I judged it was something a dog could not understand, but which was clear to a man and dreadful.

They called and called—days and nights, it seemed to me. So long that the hunger and thirst near drove me mad, and I recognized that I was getting very weak. When you are this way you sleep a great deal, and I did. Once I woke in an awful fright—it seemed to me that the calling was right there in the garret! And so it was: it was Sadie's voice, and she was crying; my name was falling from her lips all broken, poor thing, and I could not believe my ears for the joy of it when I heard her say:

"Come back to us—oh, come back to us, and forgive—it is

且现在能够想出个办法。我有了个很好的办法，就是悄悄地沿着后面的楼梯下去，躲在地窖门后，趁清晨送冰人进来装冰库的时候溜出去逃跑，然后藏一整天，等到夜里就动身，动身去——哎，随便去哪个没人认识我，不会把我出卖给主人的地方。现在，我甚至有点兴奋了，这时突然想到：啊，要是没了小狗，我可怎么活啊！

这真让人绝望。我没有办法，我知道，我必须留在这儿，留下来等着，忍受会发生的事情——这不是我操心的事，生活就是这样——我妈妈曾经说过。此时——哎，此时喊声又响了起来！我所有的痛苦重新涌上来。我自言自语道，主人永远也不会原谅我了。我不知道自己做了什么让他这般痛恨，这般绝情。不过我判断，这件事狗是理解不了的，而在人看来则一目了然，糟糕透顶。

他们喊啊喊啊——我觉得好像昼夜都在喊。这么长时间，饥渴快把我逼疯了，我知道我现在非常虚弱。你要是遇到这种情况，你会睡很长时间，于是我倒头就睡。有一次，我从极度的恐惧中醒来——我觉得喊声好像正从阁楼那儿传来！是这样的：是赛迪的声音，她正在哭，她嘴里正断断续续地叫着我的名字。可怜的人啊，听了她的话，我高兴得不敢相信自己的耳朵：

“回到我们身边吧——啊，回到我们身边吧，对不起——没有了

all so sad without our—"

I broke in with such a grateful little yelp, and the next moment Sadie was plunging and stumbling through the darkness and the lumber and shouting for the family to hear, "She's found, she's found!"

The days that followed—well, they were wonderful. The mother and Sadie and the servants—why, they just seemed to worship me. They couldn't seem to make me a bed that was fine enough; and as for food, they couldn't be satisfied with anything but game and delicacies that were out of season; and every day the friends and neighbors flocked in to hear about my heroism—that was the name they called it by, and it means agriculture. I remember my mother pulling it on a kennel once, and explaining it in that way, but didn't say what agriculture was, except that it was synonymous with intramural incandescence; and a dozen times a day Mrs. Gray and Sadie would tell the tale to newcomers, and say I risked my life to save the baby's, and both of us had burns to prove it, and then the company would pass me around and pet me and exclaim about me, and you could see the pride in the eyes of Sadie and her mother; and when the people wanted to know what made me limp, they looked ashamed and changed the subject, and sometimes when people hunted them this way and that way with questions about it, it looked to me as if they were going to cry.

And this was not all the glory; no, the master's friends came, a whole twenty of the most distinguished people, and

你真让人伤心，我们的——”

我非常感激地叫了一声，打断了她。赛迪紧接着冲过来，跌跌跸跸地冲到黑暗和旧家具堆里，大喊着，告诉家里人：“找到她啦，找到她啦！”

接下来的日子——嘿，太棒了。母亲，赛迪和佣人们——啊，他们简直就是敬奉我。给我铺的床，他们似乎都嫌不够好；给我的食物只要不是野味和未到时令的珍馐，他们就不满意；每天都有朋友和邻居涌进来听我的英雄事迹——“英雄事迹”是他们的叫法，是“农业”[①]的意思。我记得有一次妈妈把这个词带到一个狗窝里，就是那么解释的，但没有说“农业”是什么，只说它与“内部的白热光”同义。那个故事格雷夫人和赛迪每天要向新来的客人讲十几次，说我冒着生命危险救了宝宝，还说我们俩身上有烧伤能够证明。接着人们就会围着我，抚摸我，赞扬我，你还能看到赛迪和她母亲眼中的那份骄傲。但是当人们想知道我的腿是怎么瘸的时候，她们就满脸羞愧，岔开话题。有时，人们翻来覆去地追问这事，我看她们好像都快要哭了。

骄傲的事还不止这些。不，男主人的朋友们来了，足足有二十个，都是最杰出的人物。他们把我带到实验室，讨论我，好像我是个

① agriculture 以及下文中出现的 intramural incandescence 都是“我”的母亲在众狗面前卖弄时随便乱说的解释。在意义上，它们与上文的 heroism 不沾边，但是读音听起来气派。这一做法符合母亲的性格。

had me in the laboratory, and discussed me as if I was a kind of discovery; and some of them said it was wonderful in a dumb beast, the finest exhibition of instinct they could call to mind; but the master said, with vehemence, "It's far above instinct; it's reason, and many a man, privileged to be saved and go with you and me to a better world by right of its possession, has less of it than this poor silly quadruped that's foreordained to perish"; and then he laughed, and said: "Why, look at me—I'm a sarcasm! bless you, with all my grand intelligence, the only think I inferred was that the dog had gone mad and was destroying the child, whereas but for the beast's intelligence—it's reason, I tell you!—the child would have perished!"

They disputed and disputed, and I was the very center and subject of it all, and I wished my mother could know that this grand honor had come to me; it would have made her proud.

Then they discussed optics, as they called it, and whether a certain injury to the brain would produce blindness or not, but they could not agree about it, and said they must test it by experiment by and by; and next they discussed plants, and that interested me, because in the summer Sadie and I had planted seeds—I helped her dig the holes, you know—and after days and days a little shrub or a flower came up there, and it was a wonder how that could happen; but it did, and I wished I could talk—I would have told those people about it and shown them how much I knew, and been all alive with the subject; but I didn't care for the optics; it was dull, and when they came back to it again it bored me, and I went to sleep.

什么发现似的。其中有些人说，这在一个不会说话的动物身上真了不起，说这是他们能够想到的最好的本能的表现。可男主人激动地说："这远远胜过本能，这是理智，许多人因为拥有这个，享受了被拯救的优遇，跟你我一起进入更好的世界，可他们的理智还比不上这条可怜、愚蠢、注定要完蛋的四条腿的动物。"接着他大笑起来，说："嗨，看看我——我就是个讽刺！天哪，借助我的全部聪明才智，我得出的唯一结论是那条狗疯了，要弄死孩子。然而，要不是那畜生的智慧——这是理智，我告诉你们！——孩子早就死了！"

他们争来争去，而我是全部争论的核心和主题。我真希望妈妈能知道我得到的这份殊荣，这一定会让她感到骄傲。

然后，他们讨论起他们所说的光学，讨论对大脑的某种损伤是否会致盲，但是对此他们的观点不一，说以后一定要用实验来证明；接着，他们又讨论起植物。那引起了我的兴趣，因为夏天的时候，我和赛迪播过种子——我帮她刨坑，你知道——一天一天过去了，在那儿长了一小丛灌木，或是开了一朵花，真不知道是怎么发生的，但确实发生了。真希望我会说话——我会把这告诉那些人，让他们知道我懂很多事情，对这个话题很在行。可我对光学不感兴趣，那很乏味，所以当他们又回到这个话题时，我觉得无聊，就睡着了。

Pretty soon it was spring, and sunny and pleasant and lovely, and the sweet mother and the children patted me and the puppy good-by, and went away on a journey and a visit to their kin, and the master wasn't any company for us, but we played together and had good times, and the servants were kind and friendly, so we got along quite happily and counted the days and waited for the family.

And one day those men came again, and said, now for the test, and they took the puppy to the laboratory, and I limped three-leggedly along, too, feeling proud, for any attention shown to the puppy was a pleasure to me, of course. They discussed and experimented, and then suddenly the puppy shrieked, and they set him on the floor, and he went staggering around, with his head all bloody, and the master clapped his hands and shouted:

"There, I've won—confess it! He's as blind as a bat!"

And they all said:

"It's so—you've proved your theory, and suffering humanity owes you a great debt from henceforth," and they crowded around him, and wrung his hand cordially and thankfully, and praised him.

But I hardly saw or heard these things, for I ran at once to my little darling, and snuggled close to it where it lay, and licked the blood, and it put its head against mine, whimpering softly, and I knew in my heart it was a comfort to it in its pain and trouble to feel its mother's touch, though it could not see me. Then it dropped down, presently, and its little velvet nose rested

很快到了春天，阳光明媚，天气宜人。迷人的母亲和孩子们拍了拍我和小狗以示告别，出门走亲戚去了。男主人根本不陪我们，不过我和小狗在一起玩，过得很开心。仆人们也都和善友好，所以我们相处得很愉快，算着日子盼家里人回来。

一天，那群人又来了，还说现在要做实验。他们把小狗带到了实验室，我三条腿一瘸一拐地也跟了进去，感到很骄傲，因为小狗受到的任何关注自然都会令我感到高兴。他们一边讨论一边实验，接着小狗突然尖叫一声。他们把它放到地板上。它满头是血，踉踉跄跄地撞来撞去，男主人拍着手叫道：

"瞧，我赢了——承认了吧！它什么也看不见了！"

他们都跟着说：

"确实——你证明了你的观点，受苦的人们从今往后都会感激你。"然后他们把他围起来，热诚而又感激地紧握着他的手，称赞他。

而我几乎看不见，也听不到这些事。我立刻奔向我的小宝贝，在它身边紧紧地挨着它，舔舐着它的血。它顶着我的头，轻轻地呜咽着。我心里明白，它虽然看不到我，但是在疼痛难受的时候，感觉到妈妈的抚摸就是一种安慰。接着不一会儿，它倒了，软软的小鼻子贴在地上，安安静静，一动也不动。

upon the floor, and it was still, and did not move any more.

Soon the master stopped discussing a moment, and rang in the footman, and said, “Bury it in the far corner of the garden,” and then went on with the discussion, and I trotted after the footman, very happy and grateful, for I knew the puppy was out of its pain now, because it was asleep. We went far down the garden to the farthest end, where the children and the nurse and the puppy and I used to play in the summer in the shade of a great elm, and there the footman dug a hole, and I saw he was going to plant the puppy, and I was glad, because it would grow and come up a fine handsome dog, like Robin Adair, and be a beautiful surprise for the family when they came home; so I tried to help him dig, but my lame leg was no good, being stiff, you know, and you have to have two, or it is no use. When the footman had finished and covered little Robin up, he patted my head, and there were tears in his eyes, and he said: “Poor little doggie, YOU SAVED his child.”

I have watched two whole weeks, and he doesn’t come up! This last week a fright has been stealing upon me. I think there is something terrible about this. I do not know what it is, but the fear makes me sick, and I cannot eat, though the servants bring me the best of food; and they pet me so, and even come in the night, and cry, and say, “Poor doggie—do give it up and come home; don’t break our hearts!” and all this terrifies me the more, and makes me sure something has happened. And I am so weak; since yesterday I cannot stand on my feet anymore. And within this hour the servants, looking toward the sun where it was

不久男主人停了下来，按铃叫来男仆说："把它埋到花园尽头的角落里。"接着继续讨论。我一蹦一跳地跟着男仆，很是高兴和感激，我知道小狗睡着了，所以现在不疼了。我们来到花园尽头。夏天，我、孩子们、保姆和小狗常在那儿的一棵大榆树树荫下玩耍。男仆在那儿挖了个坑，我知道他要把小狗种下去，我很高兴，因为它会长出来，长成一条漂亮英俊的狗，像罗宾·阿代尔一样。等家人回来时，一定会让他们大吃一惊，所以我试图帮他挖。但是你要知道，我那条瘸腿很僵硬，不听使唤，而挖坑你得用两条腿，不然就不管用。男仆挖好坑，把小罗宾埋好，拍了拍我的头，眼中含着泪说："可怜的小狗，你救了他的孩子啊。"

我守了整整两周，可他还不出来！在这最后一周，一股恐惧渐渐袭上了我的心头。我觉得事情有些糟糕。我不知道是怎么回事，只是惶恐不安。尽管仆人给我最好的食物，我也吃不下去。他们抚摸着我，甚至夜里过来，一边哭一边说："可怜的小狗——算了吧，回家吧，别让我们难过了！"这让我更加害怕，使我确信是出事了。我非常虚弱，从昨天开始就站不起来了。在最后这个钟头，仆人们望着太阳落下去的地方，夜晚的寒气渐重，他们说了些事。虽然我听不懂，但是其中却包含着某些让我心寒的东西。

sinking out of sight and the night chill coming on, said things I could not understand, but they carried something cold to my heart.

"Those poor creatures! They do not suspect. They will come home in the morning, and eagerly ask for the little doggie that did the brave deed, and who of us will be strong enough to say the truth to them: 'The humble little friend is gone where go the beasts that perish.' "

“那些可怜的人啊！她们不会想到。明早她们就会到家，就会急切地问到那条见义勇为的小狗，我们谁会忍心告诉她们实话，说：‘那个卑贱的小伙伴去畜生死后该去的地方了。’”

The £1,000,000 Bank-Note
一张百万英镑的钞票

《一张百万英镑的钞票》（The £1,000,000 Bank-Note, 1893）讲述的是一个身无分文的穷青年因意外得到一张百万钞票，从此命运发生了翻天覆地的变化，最终成为一名真正的百万富翁的故事。与马克·吐温同时代蜚声一时的幽默家不乏其人，但他们大都昙花一现，不久便销声匿迹，唯有马克·吐温的幽默与世长存。究其原因，马克·吐温自己曾经说过："仅仅是'幽默的'作家是不可能逾远弥存的，幽默只是一股香气，一些装饰点缀。"充满幽默的喜剧是严肃的内容、非严肃的形式。马克·吐温的喜剧让人读后捧腹大笑，但他的喜剧并不单是为了逗乐，而是想让读者在哈哈大笑之后，能感受到严峻残酷的现实。本篇小说中，餐馆老板对钞票的崇拜、刻薄店员见到钞票后态度180度的大转弯、裁缝店老板跑前跑后的谄媚之态，皆滑稽至极，使人忍俊不禁。钞票给"我"带来一连串的好运，并让"我"与佳人喜结良缘，整篇文章沉浸在一片喜悦的气氛中，但在这些欢声笑语之下却隐藏了"我"贫穷时备受白眼、轻慢和侮辱的事实。"我"其实就生活在一个名利场中，有了钱，便有了名誉、地位、信誉等一切东西；没了钱，便一无是处；人与人之间只剩下了冰冷冷、赤裸裸的金钱关系。读者大笑之后可以感受到小人物的处世艰难以及世态炎凉的沉重心酸。但马克·吐温表现这一切并不是用刻板的说教，而是寓教于乐，使人在轻松诙谐中了解现实，这也正是他作为一个幽默作家的伟大深刻之处。1953年上映的影片《百万英镑》即根据本篇小说改编，由好莱坞传奇影星格里高利·派克（Gregory Peck, 1916—2003）主演。

When I was twenty-seven years old, I was a mining-broker's clerk in San Francisco, and an expert in all the details of stock traffic. I was alone in the world, and had nothing to depend upon but my wits and a clean reputation; but these were setting my feet in the road to eventual fortune, and I was content with the prospect.

My time was my own after the afternoon board, Saturdays, and I was accustomed to put it in on a little sail-boat on the bay. One day I ventured too far, and was carried out to sea. Just at nightfall, when hope was about gone, I was picked up by a small brig which was bound for London. It was a long and stormy voyage, and they made me work my passage without pay, as a common sailor. When I stepped ashore in London my clothes were ragged and shabby, and I had only a dollar in my pocket. This money fed and sheltered me twenty-four hours. During the next twenty-four I went without food and shelter.

About ten o'clock on the following morning, seedy and hungry, I was dragging myself along Portland Place, when a child that was passing, towed by a nurse-maid, tossed a luscious big pear—minus one bite—into the gutter. I stopped, of course, and fastened my desiring eye on that muddy treasure. My mouth watered for it, my stomach craved it, my whole being begged for it. But every time I made a move to get it some passing eye detected my purpose, and of course I straightened up then, and looked indifferent, and pretended that I hadn't been thinking about the pear at all. This same thing kept happening and happening, and I couldn't get the pear. I was just getting desperate enough to

二十七岁那年，我在旧金山的一名矿产经纪人手下做办事员，熟悉证券交易的所有细节。在这世上我孤身一人，除了我的智慧和清白的名声外别无所依，但是凭借这些就能让我踏上最终的成功之路，我对前景感到满意。

星期六下午收盘后，时间便归我自己支配，而我习惯于在海湾上的一只小帆船里度过。有一天我冒险划出去太远，帆船漂到海里去了。傍晚时，我都快绝望了，却被一艘驶往伦敦的小型双桅横帆船给救了起来。航程漫长，颇多风暴，他们让我作为普通的水手工作，这样就可以免掉我的旅费。当我最终在伦敦离船上岸时，身上的衣服破烂不堪，口袋里只有一美元。这点钱够我二十四小时内有吃有住，可在接下来的二十四小时里我只得忍饥挨饿、露宿街头。

第二天早上大约十点钟，我衣衫褴褛、饥肠辘辘，拖着脚步沿波特兰广场溜达。这时，一个被保姆牵着手的小孩从我身边经过，把一只甘美多汁的大梨——仅咬了一口——扔进了水沟里。我当然停了下来，一双渴望的眼睛紧紧地盯着那个沾满烂泥的宝贝。我嘴角开始流口水，肚子开始咕咕叫，全身心地乞求得到它。但每当我动一下准备去拿它时，某个过路人的眼睛就会看穿我的企图，当然这时我就会挺直腰板，使自己看起来毫不在意，装作根本没在想那只梨。这样的事情老是重复发生，使我怎么也拿不到那只梨。当我绝望到快不顾羞耻去抓它时，我身后的一扇窗户推上去了，一位绅士从里面往外喊：

brave all the shame, and to seize it, when a window behind me was raised, and a gentleman spoke out of it, saying:

"Step in here, please."

I was admitted by a gorgeous flunkey, and shown into a sumptuous room where a couple of elderly gentlemen were sitting. They sent away the servant, and made me sit down. They had just finished their breakfast, and the sight of the remains of it almost overpowered me. I could hardly keep my wits together in the presence of that food, but as I was not asked to sample it, I had to bear my trouble as best I could.

Now, something had been happening there a little before, which I did not know anything about until a good many days afterwards, but I will tell you about it now. Those two old brothers had been having a pretty hot argument a couple of days before, and had ended by agreeing to decide it by a bet, which is the English way of settling everything.

You will remember that the Bank of England once issued two notes of a million pounds each, to be used for a special purpose connected with some public transaction with a foreign country. For some reason or other only one of these had been used and canceled; the other still lay in the vaults of the Bank. Well, the brothers, chatting along, happened to get to wondering what might be the fate of a perfectly honest and intelligent stranger who should be turned adrift in London without a friend, and with no money but that million-pound bank-note, and no way to account for his being in possession of it. Brother A said he would starve to death; Brother B said he wouldn't. Brother

“请进来吧。”

一位衣着华丽的仆人迎接我，引我进了一个豪华的房间，那儿坐着两位年长的绅士。他们打发走仆人，让我坐下。他们刚吃完早餐，看到那些剩饭剩菜，我简直难以自制。在那些食物面前，我几乎不能保持理智。但既然人家不是让我来品尝食物的，我就必须尽力忍受住苦恼。

不久前，那儿发生了点事情，对这件事我毫不知情，过了许多天后才知道，但我现在就要告诉你这件事。两天前，那老哥俩进行过一场激烈的争辩，最终决定用打赌①，也就是用英国人解决一切问题的办法，来决定胜负。

可能你还记得，有一次英格兰银行②发行了两张面额均为一百万英镑的钞票，这是为了同某国进行政府间交易这一特殊目的。出于某种原因，只有一张在用过后被注销，另外一张仍躺在银行的保险库里。就这样，兄弟俩闲聊时，忽发奇想：假如一个非常诚实又很聪明的外地人在伦敦流浪，无朋无友，除了那张百万钞票外身无分文，而他又无法解释为什么会拥有那张钞票，那么他的命运将会怎样呢？哥哥说他会饿死，弟弟说他不会，哥哥说他无法在银行或其他方使用，因为他会当场被捕。就这样，他们一直争论下去，

① 英国人特别好赌，在英国各地，人们每年赌马、赌狗、赌足球投下的赌注往往有几十亿英镑之多。英国有60个赌马场。每年有8,000多个赛马日。此外，英国的赛狗场有100多个，聚赌俱乐部有18,000多个。

② 英格兰银行，伦敦城区最重要的机构和建筑物之一。1964年至今作为英国的中央银行，是全世界最大、最繁忙的金融机构。

A said he couldn't offer it at a bank or anywhere else, because he would be arrested on the spot. So they went on disputing till Brother B said he would bet twenty thousand pounds that the man would live thirty days, anyway, on that million, and keep out of jail, too. Brother A took him up. Brother B went down to the Bank and bought that note. Just like an Englishman, you see; pluck to the backbone. Then he dictated a letter, which one of his clerks wrote out in a beautiful round hand, and then the two brothers sat at the window a whole day watching for the right man to give it to.

They saw many honest faces go by that were not intelligent enough; many that were intelligent, but not honest enough; many that were both, but the possessors were not poor enough, or, if poor enough, were not strangers. There was always a defect, until I came along; but they agreed that I filled the bill all around; so they elected me unanimously, and there I was now waiting to know why I was called in. They began to ask me questions about myself, and pretty soon they had my story. Finally they told me I would answer their purpose. I said I was sincerely glad, and asked what it was. Then one of them handed me an envelope, and said I would find the explanation inside. I was going to open it, but he said no; take it to my lodgings, and look it over carefully, and not be hasty or rash. I was puzzled, and wanted to discuss the matter a little further, but they didn't; so I took my leave, feeling hurt and insulted to be made the butt of what was apparently some kind of a practical joke, and yet obliged to put up with it, not being in circumstances to resent

直到弟弟说他愿意出两千英镑，赌那个人无论如何都能靠那张百万英镑生活三十天，并且不会进监狱。哥哥同意了这个提议，于是弟弟就去银行买下了那张钞票。你看，他就像一个英国人那样，浑身是胆。接着他口授了一封信，他的一个职员用漂亮的圆体字写了出来。然后兄弟俩就在窗边坐了一整天，寻觅着合适的人选把信交给他。

他们看见许多诚实的面孔经过，但不够聪明；很多人非常聪明，但不够诚实；或者他们既聪明又诚实，但又不够穷；即使足够穷，却又不是外地人。反正总会有一项不符合，直到我走过来。他们觉得我各方面都符合这张钞票的要求，所以一致选定了我。现在我坐在那儿等着，想知道为什么被叫了进来。他们开始问我问题，打听我的情况，很快就弄清了我的来历。最终他们告诉我，说我符合他们的目的，我说我很乐意，并问需要我做什么。接着他们中间的一位交给我一个信封，说我会在里面得到解释。我正要打开信封，但他阻止了我，要我把它带回住所，从头到尾地仔细读一遍，既不要匆忙也不要草率。我感到困惑不解，想进一步讨论这件事，但他们不愿意，于是我只好告辞，感到受了伤害和侮辱，因为很明显我成了某一恶作剧捉弄的对象，然而我却不得不忍受，因为在当时的情况下，对于有钱有势的人所施加的侮辱，我是不能够表示怨恨的。

affronts from rich and strong folk.

I would have picked up the pear now and eaten it before all the world, but it was gone; so I had lost that by this unlucky business, and the thought of it did not soften my feeling toward those men. As soon as I was out of sight of that house I opened my envelope, and saw that it contained money! My opinion of those people changed, I can tell you! I lost not a moment, but shoved note and money into my vest pocket, and broke for the nearest cheap eating house. Well, how I did eat! When at last I couldn't hold any more, I took out my money and unfolded it, took one glimpse and nearly fainted. Five millions of dollars! Why, it made my head swim.

I must have sat there stunned and blinking at the note as much as a minute before I came rightly to myself again. The first thing I noticed, then, was the landlord. His eye was on the note, and he was petrified. He was worshiping, with all his body and soul, but he looked as if he couldn't stir hand or foot. I took my cue in a moment, and did the only rational thing there was to do. I reached the note towards him, and said, carelessly:

"Give me the change, please."

Then he was restored to his normal condition, and made a thousand apologies for not being able to break the bill, and I couldn't get him to touch it. He wanted to look at it, and keep on looking at it; he couldn't seem to get enough of it to quench the thirst of his eye, but he shrank from touching it as if it had been something too sacred for poor common clay to handle. I said:

"I am sorry if it is an inconvenience, but I must insist.

现在我本该把梨捡起来，当着全世界人的面把它吃掉，但是它不见了，因为这桩倒霉的交易我失去了它，想到这一点，我对那两个人更加没有好感。我一到看不见那座房子的地方就马上把信封打开，发现里面竟装着钱！我可以告诉你，我对那两人的看法改变了！我片刻也没耽搁，把纸条和钱往背心口袋里一塞，便冲进最近的一家廉价餐馆。啊，我可真是大吃了一顿！当最后肚子里实在装不下任何东西时，我便掏出钱展开它，只看了一眼便差点晕过去。五百万美元[①]！天哪，我感到一阵头晕。

我一定是目瞪口呆地坐在那里，对着钞票直眨巴眼睛，足足有一分钟之久才又回过神来。那时，我注意到的第一件事，就是店主。他正盯着钞票，吓得呆住了。他全身心地崇拜它，但看起来好像手脚都动不了了。我很快理出了头绪，并采取了那种情况下唯一合情合理的行动。我把钞票递给他，漫不经心地说：

"请找钱给我。"

接着他恢复了常态，为不能找开钞票向我不停地道歉。我把钞票递给他，但他连碰都不敢碰，他想看它，一直盯着它看，好像怎么看都不足以消除眼中的饥渴似的，但他往后退缩着，不敢碰它一下，好像它太神圣了，可怜的平常人不能摸它一样。我说：

"如果它给你带来了不便，我感到抱歉，但我非请你找开不可，

① 五百万美元，当时一英镑等于五美元。

Please change it; I haven't anything else."

But he said that wasn't any matter; he was quite willing to let the trifle stand over till another time. I said I might not be in his neighborhood again for a good while; but he said it was of no consequence, he could wait, and, moreover, I could have anything I wanted, any time I chose, and let the account run as long as I pleased. He said he hoped he wasn't afraid to trust as rich a gentleman as I was, merely because I was of a merry disposition, and chose to play larks on the public in the matter of dress. By this time another customer was entering, and the landlord hinted to me to put the monster out of sight; then he bowed me all the way to the door, and I started straight for that house and those brothers, to correct the mistake which had been made before the police should hunt me up, and help me do it. I was pretty nervous; in fact, pretty badly frightened, though, of course, I was no way in fault; but I knew men well enough to know that when they find they've given a tramp a million-pound bill when they thought it was a one-pounder, they are in a frantic rage against him instead of quarreling with their own near-sightedness, as they ought. As I approached the house my excitement began to abate, for all was quiet there, which made me feel pretty sure the blunder was not discovered yet. I rang. The same servant appeared. I asked for those gentlemen.

"They are gone." This in the lofty, cold way of that fellow's tribe.

"Gone? Gone where?"

"On a journey."

除此以外我一分钱也没有了。”

但他说这没关系，他很乐意让这笔小账推迟到下次再算。我说我可能很长一段时间都不会再到这一带来了，他说这不要紧，他可以等，并且只要我乐意，可以在任何时间想吃什么就吃什么，账单爱赊多久就赊多久。他说他不希望仅仅因为我性情诙谐，喜欢在衣着方面跟大家开玩笑，就不敢信任一位像我这样富有的绅士。这时另一位顾客进来了，老板示意我将这个怪物收起来，然后一路鞠躬将我送到门外。我立即直奔那栋房屋，去找那两兄弟，在警察开始搜寻我之前，我需要纠正这个已造成的错误，把这件事情处理好。我很紧张，实际上非常害怕，尽管我当然是毫无过错，但我非常了解人们，当他们发现把一张百万英镑的钞票当作一英镑送给一个流浪汉时，他们就会对他恼怒地发狂，而不是像他们应该做的那样抱怨自己的近视。当我走近那所房子时，紧张的心情开始慢慢平静下来，因为那儿一切都静悄悄的，使我确信这个大错还没被发现。我按响了门铃，出来的还是刚才那个仆人，我要求见那两位绅士。

“他们走了。”那家伙用他那类人高傲、冷漠的口气回答我。

“走了？去哪儿了？”

“去旅行了。”

"But whereabouts?"

"To the Continent, I think."

"The Continent?"

"Yes, sir."

"Which way—by what route?"

"I can't say, sir."

"When will they be back?"

"In a month, they said."

"A month! Oh, this is awful! Give me some sort of idea of how to get a word to them. It's of the last importance."

"I can't, indeed. I've no idea where they've gone, sir."

"Then I must see some member of the family."

"Family's away, too; been abroad months—in Egypt and India, I think."

"Man, there's been an immense mistake made. They'll be back before night. Will you tell them I've been here, and that I will keep coming till it's all made right, and they needn't be afraid?"

"I'll tell them, if they come back, but I am not expecting them. They said you would be here in an hour to make inquiries, but I must tell you it's all right, they'll be here on time and expect you."

So I had to give it up and go away. What a riddle it all was! I was like to lose my mind. They would be here "on time." What could that mean? Oh, the letter would explain, maybe. I had forgotten the letter; I got it out and read it. This is what it said:

"You are an intelligent and honest man, as one may see by

“但是去哪儿旅行了呢？”

“我想是去欧洲大陆了。”

“欧洲大陆？”

“是的，先生。”

“朝哪儿走的——走哪条路线？”

“我说不上来，先生。”

“他们什么时候回来？”

“一个月后，他们说的。”

“一个月！啊，这可糟了！帮我想个办法，看怎样能捎句话给他们，这非常重要。”

“我真的做不到。我不知道他们去哪儿了，先生。”

“那么我得见见这家里别的什么人。”

“家里人也都走了，出国几个月了——我想是在埃及和印度。”

“老兄，这儿有一个天大的错误。天黑前他们就会回来。你能不能告诉他们我来过，并且还会再来，直到把这个错误纠正过来，叫他们不必担心？”

“如果他们回来，我会告诉他们的，但我想他们不会回来了。他们说你一小时内就会来询问些事，但我必须告诉你一切正常，他们会准时回来，在这儿等你。”

于是我只好放弃努力，离开了。这一切真叫人百思不得其解啊！我快要疯了。他们会“准时”在这儿，这是什么意思？噢，或许那封信会作出解释。我都把它给忘了。我取出信读了起来，上面是这样写的：

“你是一个聪明正直的人，从你的脸上就可以看出来。我们猜

your face. We conceive you to be poor and a stranger. Enclosed you will find a sum of money. It is lent to you for thirty days, without interest. Report at this house at the end of that time. I have a bet on you. If I win it you shall have any situation that is in my gift—any, that is, that you shall be able to prove yourself familiar with and competent to fill."

No signature, no address, no date.

Well, here was a coil to be in! You are posted on what had preceded all this, but I was not. It was just a deep, dark puzzle to me. I hadn't the least idea what the game was, nor whether harm was meant me or a kindness. I went into a park, and sat down to try to think it out, and to consider what I had best do.

At the end of an hour my reasonings had crystallized into this verdict.

Maybe those men mean me well, maybe they mean me ill; no way to decide that—let it go. They've got a game, or a scheme, or an experiment, of some kind on hand; no way to determine what it is—let it go. There's a bet on me; no way to find out what it is—let it go. That disposes of the indeterminable quantities; the remainder of the matter is tangible, solid, and may be classed and labeled with certainty. If I ask the Bank of England to place this bill to the credit of the man it belongs to, they'll do it, for they know him, although I don't; but they will ask me how I came in possession of it, and if I tell the truth, they'll put me in the asylum, naturally, and a lie will land me in jail. The same result would follow if I tried to bank the bill

想你很穷，而且是个外地人。随信你会发现附有一笔钱，借你三十天，不收利息。期满之日到这间屋子里来汇报。我在你身上打了个赌，如果我赢了，你可以获得任意一个我能授予的职位——也就是你能证明自己熟悉并胜任的任何职位。”

没有签名，没有地址，没有日期。

啊，这是一个圈套！你们了解在这一切之前所发生的事情，但当时我却不知道。对我来说它就是一个深不可测、神秘难解的谜。我全然不知玩的是什么游戏，更无从知晓这对我是福还是祸。我走进一个公园，坐下来想把这事理出个所以然来，考虑一下怎么做才好。

一个小时后，通过推理我得出了这样一个结论。

或许那些人对我是心存善意，也可能是心怀恶意，无法断定是哪一种——不去管它。他们现在有一个游戏，或是一个阴谋，或是一个实验，又或是其他的想法，无法确定是什么东西——不管它。他们在我身上打了一个赌，没法弄清赌的是什么——不管它。除掉那些不确定的因素，这事剩下的部分却是实实在在、可触摸到的，可以说是确定不疑的。如果我要求苏格兰银行，将这张钞票存进它主人的账户，他们会这样做的，因为他们知道钞票的主人，虽然我不知道。但他们会问为什么这张钞票在我手上，如果我说实话，他们自然会将我送进收容所，如果我说谎，他们就会把我关进监狱。如果我想在任何地方把这张钞票存入银行或者凭它借钱的话，也会发生同样的结果。不管愿意与否，我随身都得扛着这个沉重的负担，直到那两人回来。对我来说，它像一把灰那样毫无用处，然而在乞讨

anywhere or to borrow money on it. I have got to carry this immense burden around until those men come back, whether I want to or not. It is useless to me, as useless as a handful of ashes, and yet I must take care of it, and watch over it, while I beg my living. I couldn't give it away, if I should try, for neither honest citizen nor highwayman would accept it or meddle with it for anything. Those brothers are safe. Even if I lose their bill, or burn it, they are still safe, because they can stop payment, and the Bank will make them whole; but meantime I've got to do a month's suffering without wages or profit—unless I help win that bet, whatever it may be, and get that situation that I am promised. I should like to get that; men of their sort have situations in their gift that are worth having.

I got to thinking a good deal about that situation. My hopes began to rise high. Without doubt the salary would be large. It would begin in a month; after that I should be all right. Pretty soon I was feeling first-rate. By this time I was tramping the streets again. The sight of a tailor-shop gave me a sharp longing to shed my rags, and to clothe myself decently once more. Could I afford it? No; I had nothing in the world but a million pounds. So I forced myself to go on by. But soon I was drifting back again. The temptation persecuted me cruelly. I must have passed that shop back and forth six times during that manful struggle. At last I gave in; I had to. I asked if they had a misfit suit that had been thrown on their hands. The fellow I spoke to nodded his head towards another fellow, and gave me no answer. I went to the indicated fellow, and he indicated another

求生的同时，我还得保管好它，小心照看好它。就算我想把它送掉，也不可能送得出去，因为如果我试图这样做，无论是正直的公民还是拦路抢劫的强盗，都不会要它，或跟它有什么牵扯。那两兄弟是没风险的。即使我把钞票弄丢或烧掉，他们也是安然无恙的，因为他们能够挂失，银行可以保护他们毫发无损；可同时我不得不受一个月的折磨，既没工资也没好处——除非我帮他打赢这场赌，不管赌的是什么，然后获得那个允诺给我的职位。我想得到那个职位，像他们那种人，所授予的职位是值得争取的。

我对那个职位做了大量的设想。我的期望开始升高，毫无疑问薪水会很高。一个月后我便可以开始工作，然后一切都会变好，很快我便感觉极佳。这时我又在街上漫步了。当我看到一家裁缝店时，心里有股强烈的渴望，想脱掉这身破衣服，重新换上体面的服装。我能付得起吗？不能，在这世界上，除了那张百万钞票外，我身无分文。所以我强迫自己一直走过去，但不久又遛了回来。这份诱惑残忍地压在我心上，在那场勇敢的搏斗中，我一定在店门前来来回回走了五六次。最终我屈服了。我问他们是否有因不合身而被顾客退回的衣服。我问的那个伙计没有回答我，只是朝另一个伙计点了点头。我走向他点头示意的那个伙计，他也没说话，又朝另一个伙计点了点他的头。我走向那个伙计，他说：

fellow with his head, and no words. I went to him, and he said:

"Tend to you presently."

I waited till he was done with what he was at, then he took me into a back room, and overhauled a pile of rejected suits, and selected the rattiest one for me. I put it on. It didn't fit, and wasn't in any way attractive, but it was new, and I was anxious to have it; so I didn't find any fault, but said, with some diffidence:

"It would be an accommodation to me if you could wait some days for the money. I haven't any small change about me."

The fellow worked up a most sarcastic expression of countenance, and said:

"Oh, you haven't? Well, of course, I didn't expect it. I'd only expect gentlemen like you to carry large change."

I was nettled, and said:

"My friend, you shouldn't judge a stranger always by the clothes he wears. I am quite able to pay for this suit; I simply didn't wish to put you to the trouble of changing a large note."

He modified his style a little at that, and said, though still with something of an air:

"I didn't mean any particular harm, but as long as rebukes are going, I might say it wasn't quite your affair to jump to the conclusion that we couldn't change any note that you might happen to be carrying around. On the contrary, we can."

I handed the note to him, and said:

"Oh, very well; I apologize."

"马上就来。"

我一直等他将手头上的事情做完。接着他把我带到后面的一个房间，解开一大包顾客退回的衣服，选了最差的一件给我。我穿上了它。衣服并不合身，一点也不漂亮，但它是新的，我急切地想买下它，所以我毫不挑剔，只是略带胆怯地说：

"请帮个忙，等过几天我再来付钱，我身上没带零钱。"

那个伙计的脸上浮现出极为讽刺的表情，说：

"噢，你没带零钱？啊，当然喽，我想你也没带。像你这样的绅士，我想只会带大票子。"

我被惹恼了，说：

"我的朋友，你不应该从衣着上来判断一个陌生人。我完全买得起这套衣服，我只是不想为难你找开一张大票子罢了。"

听到这话，他稍微改变了一下态度，但还是带着一点傲慢的神色说：

"我并非有意伤害你，既然你要指责我们，我可以说，你不必急于下结论，说我们找不开你刚好带在身上的钞票，恰恰相反，我们找得开。"

我把钞票递给他，说：

"哦，很好，我向你道歉。"

He received it with a smile, one of those large smiles which goes all around over, and has folds in it, and wrinkles, and spirals, and looks like the place where you have thrown a brick in a pond; and then in the act of his taking a glimpse of the bill this smile froze solid, and turned yellow, and looked like those wavy, wormy spreads of lava which you find hardened on little levels on the side of Vesuvius. I never before saw a smile caught like that, and perpetuated. The man stood there holding the bill, and looking like that, and the proprietor hustled up to see what was the matter, and said, briskly:

"Well, what's up? what's the trouble? what's wanting?"

I said: "There isn't any trouble. I'm waiting for my change."

"Come, come; get him his change, Tod; get him his change."

Tod retorted: "Get him his change! It's easy to say, sir; but look at the bill yourself."

The proprietor took a look, gave a low, eloquent whistle, then made a dive for the pile of rejected clothing, and began to snatch it this way and that, talking all the time excitedly, and as if to himself:

"Sell an eccentric millionaire such an unspeakable suit as that! Tod's a fool—a born fool. Always doing something like this. Drives every millionaire away from this place, because he can't tell a millionaire from a tramp, and never could. Ah, here's the thing I am after. Please get those things off, sir, and

他微笑着接了过去，那是一种遍布全脸的夸张的微笑，里面有褶子、皱纹和螺旋纹，看起来就像池塘里扔进了一块砖头那样；接着他瞟了一眼钞票，脸上的笑容立即凝固了，脸色瞬间变得黄，看起来像维苏威火山①的熔岩冷却后沿山坡形成的火山岩，波浪或蠕虫似的一小层一小层延伸开来。我还从没见过人陷入那样僵住不动的笑容。那个人站在那里拿着钞票，保持着那副表情，老板急忙赶来，看发生了什么事，他急忙问道：

“喂，怎么了？出什么问题了？需要什么？”

我说：“没有什么问题。我在等他找钱。”

“喂，喂，找钱给他，托德；找钱给他。”

托德反驳说：“找钱给他！说得容易，先生，还是请你自己看一下钞票吧。”

老板看了一眼钞票，低声欢快地吹了一下口哨，然后一头扎进了那堆被退回的衣服里，开始这边那边地到处乱抓，还兴奋地讲个不停，好像在自言自语似的：

“卖给一个脾气古怪的百万富翁一套那样糟糕的衣服！托德真是个傻瓜——十足的大傻瓜。他总是干这样的事，把所有的百万富翁都从这儿赶跑了，因为他分不清百万富翁和流浪汉，永远都分不清。啊，这就是我要找的那套衣服。请把身上的东西脱下来吧，先生，把它们扔到火堆里去。请赏光穿上这件衬衣和西服，这才合适，

① 维苏威火山，欧洲大陆唯一的活火山，位于意大利西南部那不勒斯市东南，现在海拔高度1277米。因火山喷发被掩埋的庞贝古城至今仍是意大利著名的游览胜地。

throw them in the fire. Do me the favor to put on this shirt and this suit; it's just the thing, the very thing—plain, rich, modest, and just ducally nobby; made to order for a foreign prince—you may know him, sir, his Serene Highness the Hospodar of Halifax; had to leave it with us and take a mourning-suit because his mother was going to die—which she didn't. But that's all right; we can't always have things the way we—that is, the way they—there! trousers all right, they fit you to a charm, sir; now the waistcoat; aha, right again! now the coat—Lord! look at that, now! Perfect—the whole thing! I never saw such a triumph in all my experience."

I expressed my satisfaction.

"Quite right, sir, quite right; it'll do for a makeshift, I'm bound to say. But wait till you see what we'll get up for you on your own measure. Come, Tod, book and pen; get at it. Length of leg, 32''"—and so on. Before I could get in a word he had measured me, and was giving orders for dress-suits, morning suits, shirts, and all sorts of things. When I got a chance I said:

"But, my dear sir, I can't give these orders, unless you can wait indefinitely, or change the bill."

"Indefinitely! It's a weak word, sir, a weak word. Eternally—that's the word, sir. Tod, rush these things through, and send them to the gentleman's address without any waste of time. Let the minor customers wait. Set down the gentleman's address and—"

"I'm changing my quarters. I will drop in and leave the new address."

就是这件——简洁、精致、庄重，一副真正的公爵派头。这是一个外国王子定做的——或许您认识他，先生，尊贵的哈利法克斯总督殿下，因为他的母亲快要死了，他只好把它留在我们这儿，然后定做了一套丧服——可后来他母亲并没有死。但是这没关系，我们不能总是按我们的方式——也就是说，他们的方式行事——瞧！裤子刚好，先生，穿上去真是合适极了；现在是背心，啊哈，又刚好！现在外套——天哪！您瞧瞧！完美——一切都非常完美！我这辈子还从没缝过这么成功的衣服。”

我也表示很满意。

“没错，先生，一点没错。我必须说，这只是临时替换用的，等着瞧我们为您量身定制的衣服吧。托德，拿本子和笔来。记下来，腿长，32英寸——”等，我还没来得及插上一句话，他已经为我量好了尺寸，并下了燕尾服、晨礼服、衬衫和各种衣服的订单。当我终于有了插嘴的机会，便说：

“但是，老兄，我不能下这些订单，除非你能无限期地等下去，或者找开这张钱。”

“无限期！这个词太没劲，先生，太没劲。永远等——这个词才够带劲，先生。托德，快点把这批货赶出来，然后送到这位先生的府上去，不得耽误片刻。让那些小顾客们等一下吧。记下这位先生的地址并且——”

“我要搬家了，我会顺便来这儿留下我的新地址。”

"Quite right, sir, quite right. One moment—let me show you out, sir. There—good day, sir, good day."

Well, don't you see what was bound to happen? I drifted naturally into buying whatever I wanted, and asking for change. Within a week I was sumptuously equipped with all needful comforts and luxuries, and was housed in an expensive private hotel in Hanover Square. I took my dinners there, but for breakfast I stuck by Harris's humble feeding house, where I had got my first meal on my million-pound bill. I was the making of Harris. The fact had gone all abroad that the foreign crank who carried million-pound bills in his vest pocket was the patron saint of the place. That was enough. From being a poor, struggling, little hand-to-mouth enterprise, it had become celebrated, and overcrowded with customers. Harris was so grateful that he forced loans upon me, and would not be denied; and so, pauper as I was, I had money to spend, and was living like the rich and the great. I judged that there was going to be a crash by and by, but I was in now and must swim across or drown. You see there was just that element of impending disaster to give a serious side, a sober side, yes, a tragic side, to a state of things which would otherwise have been purely ridiculous. In the night, in the dark, the tragedy part was always to the front, and always warning, always threatening; and so I moaned and tossed, and sleep was hard to find. But in the cheerful daylight the tragedy element faded out and disappeared, and I walked on air, and was happy to giddiness, to intoxication, you may say.

And it was natural; for I had become one of the notorieties

“没问题，先生，没问题。等一下——让我送您出去，先生。好啦——再见，先生，再见。”

啊，你知道接下来会发生什么事情吗？很自然地，我会顺手购买所有我想要的东西，然后让人家找钱给我。不到一个星期，我便将所有所需的舒适品和奢侈品都配备齐全，还在汉诺威广场一家昂贵的私人酒店里住了下来。我通常在酒店里用晚餐，但早饭时我却继续在哈里斯那家简陋的小餐馆用餐，就是我用百万钞票吃了第一顿饭的地方。我一手成就了哈里斯。消息到处都传开了，说有一个背心口袋里揣着百万钞票的外国怪人，他是这家餐馆的守护神。这就足够了。刚开始它还是一家档次低、为生计而挣扎、仅能糊口的小餐馆，现在已经变成了一家有名的饭店，宾客爆满。哈里斯对我非常感激，非要借钱给我，毫无回绝的余地。因此，尽管我穷得叮当响，却不缺钱花，过得像有钱的大人物一样。我知道不久事情就会败露，但我现在已经下了水，必须游过去，否则就会淹死。本来这只是个荒诞不经的故事，但是你知道，即将到来的灾难却使这件事显出它严肃、清醒、甚至悲剧性的一面。到了晚上，在黑暗中，悲剧性的一面总是在前面警告我、威胁我，所以我呻吟着，翻来覆去，无法入睡。但是在快乐的白天，那些悲剧性的因素淡化了，消失得无影无踪，于是我洋洋得意，可以说是快活得头晕目眩，陶醉其中。

这很自然，因为在这个世界性的大都市里，我已经变成了著名

of the metropolis of the world, and it turned my head, not just a little, but a good deal. You could not take up a newspaper, English, Scotch, or Irish, without finding in it one or more references to the "vest-pocket million-pounder" and his latest doings and saying. At first, in these mentions, I was at the bottom of the personal-gossip column; next, I was listed above the knights, next above the baronets, next above the barons, and so on, and so on, climbing steadily, as my notoriety augmented, until I reached the highest altitude possible, and there I remained, taking precedence of all dukes not royal, and of all ecclesiastics except the primate of all England. But mind, this was not fame; as yet I had achieved only notoriety. Then came the climaxing stroke—the accolade, so to speak—which in a single instant transmuted the perishable dross of notoriety into the enduring gold of fame: Punch caricatured me! Yes, I was a made man now; my place was established. I might be joked about still, but reverently, not hilariously, not rudely; I could be smiled at, but not laughed at. The time for that had gone by. Punch pictured me all a-flutter with rags, dickering with a beef-eater for the Tower of London. Well, you can imagine how it was with a young fellow who had never been taken notice of before, and now all of a sudden couldn't say a thing that wasn't taken up and repeated everywhere; couldn't stir abroad without constantly overhearing the remark flying from lip to lip, "There he goes; that's him!" couldn't take his breakfast without a crowd to look on; couldn't appear in an opera-box without concentrating there the fire of a thousand lorgnettes. Why, I just

人物之一，这使我不仅有点头脑发热，而且飘飘然起来了。你随意拿起一份报纸，不管它是英格兰、苏格兰还是爱尔兰的，都会发现一处或多处提及“背心口袋里装着百万钞票的人”和他最近的言行。起初我只是在“人物杂谈”专栏的最底端被提及；接着，我的名字排到了爵士的上面，然后超过了准男爵，后来又超过了男爵，就这样，随着我的名气越来越大，我的位置也在稳步攀升，直到可能达到的最高位置，然后就稳定在那儿，排在所有的非王室公爵之上，排在了除全英首主教①外所有的神职人员之前。但是请注意，目前我只是名声大噪，这并不代表声誉。接着便是具有决定性的一举——可以说，就像骑士受勋似的——它顷刻间便将昙花一现的残渣似的烂名声变成黄金似的不朽声誉：《笨拙周刊》②将我画进了漫画！啊，我现在是个名人了，地位已经被确认。人们还是可以拿我开玩笑，但玩笑中带着敬意，既不滑稽，也不粗鲁。人们可以对我微笑，但不能嘲笑。那样做的时代已经过去了。《笨拙周刊》把我画得一身破衣服碎片随风飘扬，正和伦敦塔③的一个卫士为一笔小生意讨价还价。啊，你可以想象得出那种感觉，一个年轻人，以前从未有人注意，忽然之间，现在每说一句话便会有人记下来，到处传播；每次外出，都会听到人们飞速地传递这样的话：“他在那儿，就是他！”每次吃早饭时都会有人围观，每次出现在歌剧院包厢时，总会发现有一千个热切的望远镜对着他。嗨，我每天都沉浸在荣耀中——总的来说就是这样。

① 首主教，指一国或一省内地位高于所有其他主教的主教或大主教。the primate of all England，全英首主教，即坎特伯雷大主教。
② 《笨拙周刊》，伦敦一种适合中产阶级趣味的幽默刊物，于2002年停刊。
③ 伦敦塔，英国著名古迹。位于伦敦泰晤士河北岸。1066年威廉一世为保卫和控制伦敦城开始营建。有宫殿、天文台、教堂、监狱等建筑。伦敦塔的卫兵，依然穿着传统的制服，头戴高高的黑色熊皮帽，是维持秩序和供游人参观、摄影的对象。

swam in glory all day long—that is the amount of it.

You know, I even kept my old suit of rags, and every now and then appeared in them, so as to have the old pleasure of buying trifles, and being insulted, and then shooting the scoffer dead with the million-pound bill. But I couldn't keep that up. The illustrated papers made the outfit so familiar that when I went out in it I was at once recognized and followed by a crowd, and if I attempted a purchase the man would offer me his whole shop on credit before I could pull my note on him.

About the tenth day of my fame I went to fulfill my duty to my flag by paying my respects to the American minister. He received me with the enthusiasm proper in my case, upbraided me for being so tardy in my duty, and said that there was only one way to get his forgiveness, and that was to take the seat at his dinner-party that night made vacant by the illness of one of his guests. I said I would, and we got to talking. It turned out that he and my father had been schoolmates in boyhood, Yale students together later, and always warm friends up to my father's death. So then he required me to put in at his house all the odd time I might have to spare, and I was very willing, of course.

In fact, I was more than willing; I was glad. When the crash should come, he might somehow be able to save me from total destruction; I didn't know how, but he might think of a way, maybe. I couldn't venture to unbosom myself to him at this late date, a thing which I would have been quick to do

你知道，我还保留着原来那套破衣服，不时地穿着它外出，为的是享受一下以前买小东西时的乐趣，先是让人侮辱，然后拿出那张百万钞票将嘲笑我的人吓个半死。但是现在我享受不到这样的乐趣了。画报把我那身行头弄得尽人皆知，每次我穿上它外出时便立即被认出，然后就有一大群人跟随。如果我想买件东西，不等我拿出那张钞票，老板就愿意将整个店赊欠给我。

大约在我出名的第十天，我去向美国公使致意，借以履行我对祖国的义务。公使以与我身份相称的热情接待了我，责备我过了这么久才来履行义务，说只有一种方法才能获得他的原谅，那就是代替一位因病缺席的客人，参加当晚在他家举行的宴会。我说我会去的，然后我们就聊了起来。结果发现他和我父亲从小就是校友，后来一起就读于耶鲁大学[①]，直到我父亲去世，他们一直都是很好的朋友。因此他要求我一有空就去他家坐坐，我当然很乐意去。

实际上，我不仅乐意，还很高兴去。万一事情败露，他可能会有什么法子来救我，使我免遭彻底的毁灭。我不知道该怎么办，但他或许能为我想出一个办法。我不敢冒险对他吐露实情，如果是我在伦敦刚碰到这桩倒霉事情的时候，我会马上告诉他。但现在我不敢冒这个险，我已陷得太深，也就是说，深到不敢冒险把这件事告诉

① 美国耶鲁大学，成立于1701年，是一所私立大学，与哈佛大学、普林斯顿大学齐名。

in the beginning of this awful career of mine in London. No, I couldn't venture it now; I was in too deep; that is, too deep for me to be risking revelations to so new a friend, though not clear beyond my depth, as I looked at it. Because, you see, with all my borrowing, I was carefully keeping within my means—I mean within my salary. Of course, I couldn't know what my salary was going to be, but I had a good enough basis for an estimate in the fact, that if I won the bet I was to have choice of any situation in that rich old gentleman's gift provided I was competent—and I should certainly prove competent; I hadn't any doubt about that. And as to the bet, I wasn't worrying about that; I had always been lucky. Now my estimate of the salary was six hundred to a thousand a year; say, six hundred for the first year, and so on up year by year, till I struck the upper figure by proved merit. At present I was only in debt for my first year's salary. Everybody had been trying to lend me money, but I had fought off the most of them on one pretext or another; so this indebtedness represented only £300 borrowed money, the other £300 represented my keep and my purchases. I believed my second year's salary would carry me through the rest of the month if I went on being cautious and economical, and I intended to look sharply out for that. My month ended, my employer back from his journey, I should be all right once more, for I should at once divide the two years' salary among my creditors by assignment, and get right down to my work.

It was a lovely dinner-party of fourteen. The Duke and

一个刚结交的朋友，尽管在我看来，它还不至于将我彻底毁灭。因为，你瞧，尽管我借了很多钱，但我总是小心地使它不超出我的收入——我指的是我的薪水。当然，我不知道我的薪水将有多少，但是我能预测出来，因为我有充分的依据，那就是如果我赌赢了，那位富有的老先生就会让我挑选一个他能授予的职位，一个我能胜任的职位——我当然会胜任，对此我毫不怀疑。对于那个赌我也不担心，因为我一直都很幸运。现在我估计一年的薪水将会是六百到一千英镑，也就是说，第一年是六百英镑，然后逐年增加，直到靠公认的业绩达到那个最高额。目前我只欠第一年的薪水。每个人都想借钱给我，但我用各种各样的借口谢绝了绝大部分的人。所以目前我借的现金只有三百英镑，所欠的另外三百英镑则是我食宿和购物的花销。我想如果我继续小心节俭，第二年的薪水将帮我度过这个月剩下的日子，所以我打算在这点上仔细留意一下。当月底我的雇主旅行回来时，一切都会重新好起来，因为我会立即将我两年的薪水分配给我的债主们，然后马上开始工作。

Duchess of Shoreditch[①], and their daughter the Lady Anne-Grace-Eleanor-Celeste-and-so-forth-and-so-forth-de-Bohun, the Earl and Countess of Newgate[②], Viscount Cheapside[③], Lord and Lady Blatherskite[④], some untitled people of both sexes, the minister and his wife and daughter, and his daughter's visiting friend, an English girl of twenty-two, named Portia Langham, whom I fell in love with in two minutes, and she with me—I could see it without glasses. There was still another guest, an American—but I am a little ahead of my story. While the people were still in the drawing-room, whetting up for dinner, and coldly inspecting the late comers, the servant announced:

"Mr. Lloyd Hastings."

The moment the usual civilities were over, Hastings caught sight of me, and came straight with cordially outstretched hand; then stopped short when about to shake, and said, with an embarrassed look:

"I beg your pardon, sir, I thought I knew you."

"Why, you do know me, old fellow."

"No. Are you the—the—"

"Vest-pocket monster? I am, indeed. Don't be afraid to call me by my nickname; I'm used to it."

"Well, well, well, this is a surprise. Once or twice I've seen your own name coupled with the nickname, but it never

① Shoreditch: 原意为海边的水沟，此处是马克·吐温对道貌岸然的公爵的讽刺。
② Newgate: 纽盖特监狱，伦敦的一所著名监狱，1902年被拆除，此处讽刺伯爵实际上和罪犯一样。
③ Cheapside: 原意为便宜货，此处讽刺子爵其实是个不入流的货色。
④ Blatherskite: 原意为喋喋不休、废话连篇的人，此处讽刺勋爵只是个废话多、惹人厌的家伙。

这是一个愉快的宴会，有十四个人参加，有肖尔迪希公爵[1]、公爵夫人和他们的女儿安妮—格蕾丝—埃莉诺—塞莱斯特—等等等等—德·博亨夫人，纽盖特伯爵和伯爵夫人，奇普赛德子爵，布莱泽斯凯特勋爵及勋爵夫人，一些没有头衔的男女来宾，公使及其夫人和女儿，还有一位二十二岁的英国姑娘，她是公使女儿的一位密友，名叫鲍西娅·朗汉姆。不到两分钟我便爱上她了，她也爱上了我——不戴眼镜我也能看出来。那儿还有一位美国人——我把故事讲得有点提前了。当客人们还在客厅里一边刺激食欲准备用餐，一边冷眼观看迟来的客人时，仆人宣布：

“劳埃德·黑斯廷斯先生到了。”

惯例的寒暄刚完，黑斯廷斯就看到了我，他朝我径直走过来，热情地伸出手，握手前略微迟疑了一下，局促不安地说：

“请您原谅，先生，我还以为我认识您呢。”

“嗨，你当然认识我，老伙计。”

“不会吧，你是不是那个——那个——”

“背心口袋装钞票的怪物？就是我，没错。尽管叫我的绰号，别顾忌，我已经习惯了。”

“哦，哦，哦，这太出乎意料了。有那么一两次我看到你的名字和绰号放在一起，但我从未想到你就是人们指的亨利·亚当斯。啊，六个月前你还是旧金山布莱克·霍普金斯手下的一名办事员，挣点薪水，为获得额外津贴而加夜班，帮我整理、核对古尔德和柯里发展

① 英国爵位排行依次为：公 (Duke)、侯 (Marquess)、伯 (Earl)、子 (Viscount)、男 (Baron)。公爵、侯爵、伯爵、子爵和男爵都可以称为 Lord 勋爵，是对男性英国贵族的一种敬称。

occurred to me that you could be the Henry Adams referred to. Why, it isn't six months since you were clerking away for Blake Hopkins in Frisco on a salary, and sitting up nights on an extra allowance, helping me arrange and verify the Gould and Curry Extension papers and statistics. The idea of your being in London, and a vast millionaire, and a colossal celebrity! Why, it's the Arabian Nights come again. Man, I can't take it in at all; can't realize it; give me time to settle the whirl in my head."

"The fact is, Lloyd, you are no worse off than I am. I can't realize it myself."

"Dear me, it is stunning, now isn't it? Why, it's just three months today since we went to the Miners' restaurant—"

"No; the What Cheer."

"Right, it was the What Cheer; went there at two in the morning, and had a chop and coffee after a hard six-hours grind over those Extension papers, and I tried to persuade you to come to London with me, and offered to get leave of absence for you and pay all your expenses, and give you something over if I succeeded in making the sale; and you wouldn't listen to me, said I wouldn't succeed, and you couldn't afford to lose the run of business and be no end of time getting the hang of things again when you got back home. And yet here you are. How odd it all is! How did you happen to come, and whatever did give you this incredible start?"

"Oh, just an accident. It's a long story—a romance, a body may say. I'll tell you all about it, but not now."

"When?"

矿山的文件和数据。没想到你来了伦敦，成了一个百万大富翁、名声大振的社会名流！天哪，这简直就是天方夜谭[①]的再现。老兄，我根本就无法接受，也弄不明白这件事。给我点时间，让我混乱的思绪安定下来。”

“劳埃德，事实上，我跟你一样，也搞不清楚这件事。”

“哎呀，这真让人感到震惊，不是吗？哦，那天我们还去了矿工餐馆，离现在才刚三个月——”

“不，是好心情。”

“对，是好心情餐馆。我们凌晨两点钟去的那儿，在对着那些发展矿山的文件苦干了六个小时后，吃了一份排骨，喝了一杯咖啡。我想说服你和我一起来伦敦，我会帮你请假，承担你的一切费用，如果交易成功的话，还给你点别的好处。但你并不听我的劝，说我不会成功，还说若让你丢掉手头上的工作，回来就会发现，想要重新熟悉这行业简直是遥遥无期，这你可负担不起。可现在你却在这儿，这一切是多么神奇！你怎么碰巧来这儿了，究竟是什么让你飞黄腾达起来的？”

“噢，这只是一个巧合。说来话长——可以说是个传奇。我会全部告诉你的，但不是现在。”

“什么时候？”

① 天方夜谭，即阿拉伯民间故事《一千零一夜》，通常指荒诞离奇的事情或不可思议的奇迹。

"The end of this month."

"That's more than a fortnight yet. It's too much of a strain on a person's curiosity. Make it a week."

"I can't. You'll know why, by and by. But how's the trade getting along?"

His cheerfulness vanished like a breath, and he said with a sigh:

"You were a true prophet, Hal, a true prophet. I wish I hadn't come. I don't want to talk about it."

"But you must. You must come and stop with me to-night, when we leave here, and tell me all about it."

"Oh, may I? Are you in earnest?" and the water showed in his eyes.

"Yes; I want to hear the whole story, every word."

"I'm so grateful! Just to find a human interest once more, in some voice and in some eye, in me and affairs of mine, after what I've been through here—lord! I could go down on my knees for it!"

He gripped my hand hard, and braced up, and was all right and lively after that for the dinner—which didn't come off. No; the usual thing happened, the thing that is always happening under that vicious and aggravating English system—the matter of precedence couldn't be settled, and so there was no dinner. Englishmen always eat dinner before they go out to dinner, because they know the risks they are running; but nobody ever warns the stranger, and so he walks placidly into trap. Of course, nobody was hurt this time, because we had all been to

"这个月底。"

"那还要等两个多星期。这太考验一个人的好奇心了。缩到一个星期吧。"

"我不能，不久你就会知道原因了，生意干得怎样？"

他的喜悦瞬间消失了，叹了口气说：

"你是个真正的预言家，哈尔，一个真真正正的预言家。我希望我没有来过，我都不想谈这事。"

"但是你必须谈。我们离开这儿时，你必须和我一起走，今晚就住我那儿，告诉我一切。"

"啊，我可以吗？你是认真的吗？"他的眼睛湿润了。

"是的，我想听整个故事，一字不漏。"

"我真是太感激了！在这儿经历了一切之后，终于在别人的声音和眼睛里，发现又有人对我感兴趣了，问候我并关注我的事情——天哪！为了它我都可以跪下！"

他紧紧地握住我的手，重新振作起来了，从那之后就快快乐乐地等着用餐——可晚餐并没有开始。不行，老问题又出现了，这种事在可恶的、使人恼火的英国制度下总是发生——座次没决定，晚餐就没法开始。英国人总是先吃好饭再外出赴宴，因为他们知道将要冒的风险，但从没有人会警告陌生人，所以他就会毫无察觉地走进陷阱里。当然这一次没有人受苦，我们都参加过宴会，只有黑斯廷斯一个人是新手，而他在受邀时便被告知，为了尊重英国的习俗，公使并没有准备酒席。每位客人手挽着一位女士，列队进入餐室，因为照例要装装样子走下过场，但争论却由此而起。肖尔迪希公爵

dinner, none of us being novices excepting Hastings, and he having been informed by the minister at the time that he invited him that in deference to the English custom he had not provided any dinner. Everybody took a lady and processioned down to the dining-room, because it is usual to go through the motions; but there the dispute began. The Duke of Shoreditch wanted to take precedence, and sit at the head of the table, holding that he outranked a minister who represented merely a nation and not a monarch; but I stood for my rights, and refused to yield. In the gossip column I ranked all dukes not royal, and said so, and claimed precedence of this one. It couldn't be settled, of course, struggle as we might and did, he finally (and injudiciously) trying to play birth and antiquity, and I "seeing" his Conqueror and "raising" him with Adam, whose direct posterity I was, as shown by my name, while he was of a collateral branch, as shown by his, and by his recent Norman origin; so we all processioned back to the drawing-room again and had a perpendicular lunch—plate of sardines and a strawberry, and you group yourself and stand up and eat it. Here the religion of precedence is not so strenuous; the two persons of highest rank chuck up a shilling, the one that wins has first go at his strawberry, and the loser gets the shilling. The next two chuck up, then the next two, and so on. After refreshment, tables were brought, and we all played cribbage, sixpence a game. The English never play any game for amusement. If they can't make something or lose something—they don't care which—they won't play.

认为他的地位比公使高，因为公使只代表了一个国家而不是王国，所以他应该走在前面，坐在桌子的首位，但是我坚持我的权利，拒绝让步。我说，在人物杂谈栏里，我位于所有的非王室公爵之上，所以有权坐在他前面。尽管我们争执了半天，但是当然，问题并没有解决。他最终（有失公允地）试图玩出身和祖宗的把戏，我"看穿"了他的老祖宗就是征服王[①]，于是搬出亚当把他"抬上去"，说我是亚当的直系后裔，从我的姓就可以看出来，而他只是旁系后裔，从他的姓和最近的诺曼血统就可以看出来。于是我们重新列队回到了客厅站着吃饭——一碟沙丁鱼，一盘草莓，人们各自结伴站着吃。在这儿座位的次序没那么重要，先是两个地位最高的人往上抛一先令的硬币来猜，赢的人先吃草莓，输的人得到那一先令。接着是下一对抛，然后再下一对，一直按顺序排下去。吃过茶点，桌子搬来了，我们便都玩起了克里比奇牌[②]，六便士一局。英国人从不为娱乐玩游戏。如果说他们既不赢东西也不输东西——他们也倒不在乎输赢——他们就不玩。

① 征服王，指1066年-1070年征服英国的法国诺曼底公爵，史称威廉一世。诺曼征服整个改变了英格兰的文化，甚至是其语言。
② 克里比奇，一种纸牌游戏，适合于两人对打，其中15点得两分，对子得两分，顺子三张以上每张牌得一分，总分得到121分即获胜。下文中"我"和朗汉姆小姐对打时，因两人爱慕对方，皆心不在焉，总是算不对分，所以谁也没赢过。

We had a lovely time; certainly two of us had, Miss Langham and I. I was so bewitched with her that I couldn't count my hands if they went above a double sequence; and when I struck home I never discovered it, and started up the outside row again, and would have lost the game every time, only the girl did the same, she being in just my condition, you see; and consequently neither of us ever got out, or cared to wonder why we didn't; we only just knew we were happy, and didn't wish to know anything else, and didn't want to be interrupted. And I told her—I did, indeed—told her I loved her; and she—well, she blushed till her hair turned red, but she liked it; she said she did. Oh, there was never such an evening! Every time I pegged I put on a postscript; every time she pegged she acknowledged receipt of it, counting the hands the same. Why, I couldn't even say "Two for his heels" without adding, "My, how sweet you do look!" and she would say, "Fifteen two, fifteen four, fifteen six, and a pair are eight, and eight are sixteen—do you think so?"—peeping out aslant from under her lashes, you know, so sweet and cunning. Oh, it was just too-too!

Well, I was perfectly honest and square with her; told her I hadn't a cent in the world but just the million-pound note she'd heard so much talk about, and it didn't belong to me, and that started her curiosity; and then I talked low, and told her the whole history right from the start, and it nearly killed her laughing. What in the nation she could find to laugh about I couldn't see, but there it was; every half-minute some new detail would fetch her, and I would have to stop as much as a

我们玩得很愉快，当然是指我和朗汉姆小姐。我完全被她迷住了，手里的同花顺子超过两组的话，我就数不清楚，该得分时却觉察不到。两人又重新从外面一排开始打，本来该局局都输的，还好那个女孩打得和我一样，跟我状态相同，也打得稀里糊涂的，你明白吧。结果我们俩老打个没完没了，谁也没输谁也没赢，也根本不去想为什么会这样，我们只知道我们玩得很高兴，别的什么也不想知道，也不想被打搅。我告诉她——我真的这样做了——告诉她我爱她，而她——啊，脸都快红到发梢了，但是她喜欢这句话，她说她喜欢。哎呀，从没有过这么美妙的夜晚！每次记分我都会加上一句附言，每次她记分都会计算手中的牌点数，确认收到我的附言。啊，我每说一句“再加两分”后都要紧接着加上一句“天哪，你看起来真漂亮！”她就会说：“十五点得两分，十五点得四分，十五点得六分，加一对是八分，再加八分是十六分——你真这么想吗？”——从眼睫毛下往外偷偷斜视，你知道，她是那么可爱、狡黠，哦，这简直太美妙了！

喔，我对她绝对诚实无欺，告诉她在这世上除了那张她听到了太多传闻的百万钞票，我身无分文，然而它却不属于我，这激起了她的好奇心，接着我就低声告诉她这件事的来龙去脉，她听完都快笑死了。我不明白，究竟有什么让她感到可笑，但她就是感到好笑。每过半分钟就会有某个新的细节使她笑个不停，我只好停下一分半钟，好让她有时间重新平静下来。天哪，她都快笑出毛病了——她真的笑出毛病了，我从没见过有人笑成那样。我的意思是，我以前从没见过一个令人痛苦的故事——一个关于一个人的麻烦、担忧和

minute and a half to give her a chance to settle down again. Why, she laughed herself lame—she did, indeed; I never saw anything like it. I mean I never saw a painful story—a story of a person's troubles and worries and fears—produce just that kind of effect before. So I loved her all the more, seeing she could be so cheerful when there wasn't anything to be cheerful about; for I might soon need that kind of wife, you know, the way things looked. Of course, I told her we should have to wait a couple of years, till I could catch up on my salary; but she didn't mind that, only she hoped I would be as careful as possible in the matter of expenses, and not let them run the least risk of trenching on our third year's pay. Then she began to get a little worried, and wondered if we were making any mistake, and starting the salary on a higher figure for the first year than I would get. This was good sense, and it made me feel a little less confident than I had been feeling before; but it gave me a good business idea, and I brought it frankly out.

"Portia, dear, would you mind going with me that day, when I confront those old gentlemen?"

She shrank a little, but said:

"N—o; if my being with you would help hearten you. But—would it be quite proper, do you think?"

"No, I don't know that it would—in fact, I'm afraid it wouldn't; but, you see, there's so much dependent upon it that—"

"Then I'll go anyway, proper or improper," she said, with a beautiful and generous enthusiasm. "Oh, I shall be so happy to

害怕的故事——竟会产生那种效果。看到她在没什么可开心时，感到那么开心，我就更加爱她了。因为你知道，照目前的形势来看，不久后我可能就需要那样的一位妻子。当然，我告诉她我们还要等两年，一直等到我用薪水还完债务。但她对此毫不介意，只是希望我在花销方面尽可能小心些，不要冒丝毫的风险，影响我们第三年的收入。接着，她开始有点担心，怀疑我们是否估算错误，把第一年的薪水定得高出了我所应得的。这话很有道理，让我感到没以前那么自信了，但这让我想到了一个很好的商业点子，我坦率地说了出来。

“鲍西亚，亲爱的，等那天我去见那两位老先生时，你愿意陪我一起去吗？”

她有点退缩，但是说：

“好——吧，如果在你身边能鼓励你，但是——你觉得这样做很合适吗？”

“不，我不知道它合不合适——实际上，我担心它不合适。但是，你瞧，你去的话能决定很多事情——”

“那么无论如何我都会去的，不管合不合适，”她慷慨热情地说，看起来漂亮极了，“噢，想想能帮上忙我感到真高兴。”

think I'm helping!"

"Helping, dear? Why, you'll be doing it all. You're so beautiful and so lovely and so winning, that with you there I can pile our salary up till I break those good old fellows, and they'll never have the heart to struggle."

Sho! you should have seen the rich blood mount, and her happy eyes shine!

"You wicked flatterer! There isn't a word of truth in what you say, but still I'll go with you. Maybe it will teach you not to expect other people to look with your eyes."

Were my doubts dissipated? Was my confidence restored? You may judge by this fact: privately I raised my salary to twelve hundred the first year on the spot. But I didn't tell her; I saved it for a surprise.

All the way home I was in the clouds, Hastings talking, I not hearing a word. When he and I entered my parlor, he brought me to myself with his fervent appreciations of my manifold comforts and luxuries.

"Let me just stand here a little and look my fill. Dear me! it's a palace—it's just a palace! And in it everything a body could desire, including cozy coal fire and supper standing ready. Henry, it doesn't merely make me realize how rich you are; it makes me realize, to the bone, to the marrow, how poor I am—how poor I am, and how miserable, how defeated, routed, annihilated!"

Plague take it! this language gave me the cold shudders. It scared me broad awake, and made me comprehend that I was

“仅仅是帮上忙吗，亲爱的？啊，你会把一切都办好的，你这么漂亮、这么可爱、这么讨人喜欢，有你在那儿我会把我们的薪水一直往上加，直到那两位好心的老家伙破了产也不好意思跟我们讲价。”

嗨！你真该看看，她的脸涨得通红，眼睛快活得闪闪发亮！

“你这个可恶的马屁精！你说的话没有一句是真的，但我还是会和你一起去，或许它能教会你，叫你别指望别人的眼光和你的一样。”

我的怀疑消失了吗？我的自信恢复了吗？你可以从这样一个事实来判断：我立马就暗自将我第一年的薪水提高到一千两百英镑。但是我没有告诉她，我留着给她一个惊喜。

回去的路上我好像一直飘在云端上，黑斯廷斯一直在说话，但我一个字也没听进去。我们走进客厅，他开始热烈地赞美我房内各式各样的舒适物和奢侈品，我这才清醒过来。

“让我在这儿站一会儿，看看就心满意足了。天哪！这是一座宫殿啊——简直就是一座宫殿！人们能想到的东西，这儿都应有尽有，包括温暖的炭火和备好的晚餐。亨利，这不仅使我意识到你是多么富有，还使我刻骨铭心地意识到我太穷了——我是多么贫穷、多么悲惨、多么失败，一败涂地，我完了！”

真该死！他的话让我打起了冷战。它把我完全吓醒了，使我意识到我正站在一个火山口上，脚下的地壳只有半英寸厚。我不知道

standing on a half inch crust, with a crater underneath. I didn't know I had been dreaming—that is, I hadn't been allowing myself to know it for a while back; but now—oh, dear! Deep in debt, not a cent in the world, a lovely girl's happiness or woe in my hands, and nothing in front of me but a salary which might never—oh, would never—materialize! Oh, oh, oh! I am ruined past hope! nothing can save me!

"Henry, the mere unconsidered drippings of your daily income would—"

"Oh, my daily income! Here, down with this hot Scotch, and cheer up your soul. Here's with you! Or, no—you're hungry; sit down and—"

"Not a bite for me; I'm past it. I can't eat, these days; but I'll drink with you till I drop. Come!"

"Barrel for barrel, I'm with you! Ready? Here we go! Now, then, Lloyd, unreel your story while I brew."

"Unreel it? What, again?"

"Again? What do you mean by that?"

"Why, I mean do you want to hear it over again?"

"Do I want to hear it over again? This is a puzzler. Wait; don't take any more of that liquid. You don't need it."

"Look here, Henry, you alarm me. Didn't I tell you the whole story on the way here?"

"You?"

"Yes, I."

"I'll be hanged if I heard a word of it."

"Henry, this is a serious thing. It troubles me. What did you

我一直在做梦——也就是说刚才我一直都没有让自己认识到这一点，但是现在——哦，天哪！一个可爱女孩的幸福或痛苦就掌握在我的手上，而我却负债累累，身无分文，面前除了那份薪水外一无所有，这薪水或许永远都不会——啊，恐怕永远都不会——兑现！啊，啊，啊！我完了，没希望了！什么也救不了我！

"亨利，只要你每天的收入漏一点给我就——"

"哦，我每天的收入！来，喝下这杯带劲的苏格兰酒，振作起来。咱们干杯！噢，不——你饿了，坐下来——"

"我一口也吃不下，我饿过头了，这些天我都吃不下，但是我会陪你喝下去，咱们一醉方休，来吧！"

"你喝多少我喝多少！准备好了吗？来吧！那么，劳埃德，趁我现在调酒，讲一下你的故事吧。"

"讲我的故事？什么，再讲一遍吗？"

"再讲一遍？你这话什么意思？"

"喔，我指的是你想再重复听一遍吗？"

"我想再重复听一遍？这真令人费解。等一下，不要再喝这种酒了，你不必喝这个。"

"听着，亨利，你吓到我了。来这的路上我不是把整个故事都告诉你了吗？"

"你讲过了？"

"是的，我讲过了。"

"如果听到了一个字我就不得好死。"

"亨利，这可是件严肃的事情。这真让我苦恼，在公使家你干什

take up yonder at the minister's?"

Then it all flashed on me, and I owned up like a man.

"I took the dearest girl in this world—prisoner!"

So then he came with a rush, and we shook, and shook, and shook till our hands ached; and he didn't blame me for not having heard a word of a story which had lasted while we walked three miles. He just sat down then, like the patient, good fellow he was, and told it all over again. Synopsized, it amounted to this: He had come to England with what he thought was a grand opportunity; he had an "option" to sell the Gould and Curry Extension for the "locators" of it, and keep all he could get over a million dollars. He had worked hard, had pulled every wire he knew of, had left no honest expedient untried, had spent nearly all the money he had in the world, had not been able to get a solitary capitalist to listen to him, and his option would run out at the end of the month. In a word, he was ruined. Then he jumped up and cried out:

"Henry, you can save me! You can save me, and you're the only man in the universe that can. Will you do it? Won't you do it?"

"Tell me how. Speak out, my boy."

"Give me a million and my passage home for my 'option'! Don't, don't refuse!"

I was in a kind of agony. I was right on the point of coming out with the words, "Lloyd, I'm a pauper myself—absolutely penniless, and in debt!" But a white-hot idea came flaming through my head, and I gripped my jaws together, and calmed myself down till I was as cold as a capitalist. Then I said, in a

么去了？”

然后我一切都想起来了，像个男子汉那样爽快地承认了。

“我把世界上最可爱的女孩——追到手了！”

然后他冲了过来，和我握手，我们握了又握，直到握得手都疼了。在走回来的三英里路上，他一直在讲他的故事，我却一个字也没听到，他也没有责备我。像他这样有耐心的好人此时只是坐了下来，从头到尾又讲了一遍。概括起来大致是这样的：他来到了英格兰，以为得到了一个发大财的机会；在古尔德和柯里的矿山发展业务中，他搞到一个为“勘测者们”出售股票的“期权[①]”，所售金额超过一百万美元的部分全都归他所有。他工作得非常努力，每一个知道的线索他都不放过，所有正当的方法都试过了，所有的积蓄都快花光了，但没有一个投资者肯听从他的建议，而他的出售权月底就要到期了。一句话，他破产了。接着他跳起来喊道：

“亨利，你能救我！你是这世上唯一能救我的人。你会救我吗？还是不会救我？”

“尽管直说，告诉我怎么办，我的朋友。”

“给我一百万美元和回家的路费，我就把‘期权’转让给你。不要，不要拒绝！”

我感到有点儿苦恼。我正要说出这样的话：“劳埃德，我自己也是个穷光蛋——确实是一贫如洗，还欠了债。”但是我脑中灵光一闪，浮现出一个大胆的想法，于是我闭紧嘴巴，镇静下来，一直冷静

① 期权，选择权。期权合约赋予购买者在一个协议日或协议日以前（执行期），以特定的价格购买或出售基础工具的权利（但非义务）。购买者向出售者支付权酬以获取这个权利。

commercial and self-possessed way:

"I will save you, Lloyd—"

"Then I'm already saved! God be merciful to you forever! If ever I—"

"Let me finish, Lloyd. I will save you, but not in that way; for that would not be fair to you, after your hard work, and the risks you've run. I don't need to buy mines; I can keep my capital moving, in a commercial center like London, without that; it's what I'm at, all the time; but here is what I'll do. I know all about that mine, of course; I know its immense value, and can swear to it if anybody wishes it. You shall sell out inside of the fortnight for three millions cash, using my name freely, and we'll divide, share and share alike."

Do you know, he would have danced the furniture to kindling-wood in his insane joy, and broken everything on the place, if I hadn't tripped him up and tied him.

Then he lay there, perfectly happy, saying:

"I may use your name! Your name—think of it! Man, they'll flock in droves, these rich Londoners; they'll fight for that stock! I'm a made man, I'm a made man forever, and I'll never forget you as long as I live!"

In less than twenty-four hours London was abuzz! I hadn't anything to do, day after day, but sit at home, and say to all comers:

"Yes; I told him to refer to me. I know the man, and I know the mine. His character is above reproach, and the mine is worth far more than he asks for it."

到像个资本家时才开口，接着，我以一种商人的沉着口吻说道：

“我会救你的，劳埃德——”

“那么我已经得救了！愿上帝永远保佑你！假如有一天我能——”

“让我说完，劳埃德。我会救你，但不是用那种方式，因为那样对你不公平，你工作得这么努力，还冒了这么大的风险。我不需要购买矿山，在伦敦这样的金融中心，不用那样做，我也可以让我的资本周转下去，我一直都是这样做的，但这才是我接下来要做的。我当然了解那座矿山，也知道它的巨大价值，谁要想让我对它发誓都行。你尽管用我的名义兜售，在两星期内就可以卖到三百万美元，然后赚的钱我们对半分。”

你知道吗？他高兴得快疯了，狂蹦乱跳，如果我不把他绊倒绑起来，他会把所有的家具踢成柴火，把屋子里所有的东西毁掉。

然后他躺在那儿，快活极了，说：

“我可以使用你的名义！你的名义——想想吧！伙计，那些有钱的伦敦佬会成群地涌来，争着买股份！我成功了，我永远是一个成功的人了，只要我活着，就决不会忘记你！”

不到二十四个小时，伦敦就沸腾了！每天我不用干别的事情，只需要坐在家里，对所有的来访者说：

“是的，我告诉他使用我的名义。我知道这个人，也知道这座矿山。他的人品无可挑剔，而那座矿山的价值也远远大于他的要价。”

Meantime I spent all my evenings at the minister's with Portia. I didn't say a word to her about the mine; I saved it for a surprise. We talked salary; never anything but salary and love; sometimes love, sometimes salary, sometimes love and salary together. And my! the interest the minister's wife and daughter took in our little affair, and the endless ingenuities they invented to save us from interruption, and to keep the minister in the dark and unsuspicious—well, it was just lovely of them!

When the month was up at last, I had a million dollars to my credit in the London and County Bank, and Hastings was fixed in the same way. Dressed at my level best, I drove by the house in Portland Place, judged by the look of things that my birds were home again, went on towards the minister's and got my precious, and we started back, talking salary with all our might. She was so excited and anxious that it made her just intolerably beautiful. I said:

"Dearie, the way you're looking it's a crime to strike for a salary a single penny under three thousand a year."

"Henry, Henry, you'll ruin us!"

"Don't you be afraid. Just keep up those looks, and trust to me. It'll all come out right."

So, as it turned out, I had to keep bolstering up her courage all the way. She kept pleading with me, and saying:

"Oh, please remember that if we ask for too much we may get no salary at all; and then what will become of us, with no way in the world to earn our living?"

We were ushered in by that same servant, and there they

同时，每天傍晚我都在公使家和鲍西娅一起度过。关于矿山，我对她只字未提，我要留着，给她一个惊喜。我们谈薪水，除了薪水和爱情，什么也不谈，有时是爱情，有时是薪水，有时是爱情和薪水一起谈。喔，公使的妻子和女儿对我们的恋爱小事很关心，她们不断地想方设法使我们不受打搅，让公使蒙在鼓里，一点也不起疑心——啊，她们太可爱了！

终于到了月底，我在伦敦银行的账户上已经有了一百万美元，黑斯廷斯也是一样。我穿上了我最好的衣服，驱车经过波特兰广场的那所房子时，我从外面的情形看出，那两位老先生已经回来了。接着，我去公使家，接上我心爱的人，然后我们就往回走，路上一个劲儿地讨论薪水。她既兴奋又担心，这使她看起来美丽极了。我说：

"亲爱的，你现在看起来这么漂亮，我一定力争要到每年三千英镑，少一个便士都是罪过。"

"亨利，亨利，你会把我们毁了的！"

"不要害怕，你就保持现在的样子，相信我，一切都会没问题的。"

所以，结果就是这一路上我只得不断地给她打气。她不断地请求我说：

"啊，请记住，如果我们要求太过分，就根本不会得到任何薪水，然后在这世上无法谋生，我们将会怎样？"

还是上次那个仆人把我们带了进去，那两位年老的绅士果然

were, the two old gentlemen. Of course, they were surprised to see that wonderful creature with me, but I said:

"It's all right, gentlemen; she is my future stay and helpmate."

And I introduced them to her, and called them by name. It didn't surprise them; they knew I would know enough to consult the directory. They seated us, and were very polite to me, and very solicitous to relieve her from embarrassment, and put her as much at her ease as they could. Then I said:

"Gentlemen, I am ready to report."

"We are glad to hear it," said my man, "for now we can decide the bet which my brother Abel and I made. If you have won for me, you shall have any situation in my gift. Have you the million-pound note?"

"Here it is, sir," and I handed it to him.

"I've won!" he shouted, and slapped Abel on the back. "Now what do you say, brother?"

"I say he did survive, and I've lost twenty thousand pounds. I never would have believed it."

"I've a further report to make," I said, "and a pretty long one. I want you to let me come soon, and detail my whole month's history; and I promise you it's worth hearing. Meantime, take a look at that."

"What, man! Certificate of deposit for £200,000. Is it yours?"

"Mine. I earned it by thirty days' judicious use of that little loan you let me have. And the only use I made of it was to buy trifles and offer the bill in change."

都在，他们看见跟我一起的那位美人儿时，当然感到很惊讶，但是我说：

“没什么，先生们，她是我未来的伴侣和贤内助。”

我把他们介绍给她，并且直呼他们的姓名。他们并不感到惊讶，因为他们明白我懂得去查人名地址簿。他们让我们坐下，对我很客气，极为热心地想解除她的不安，尽可能地让她感到放松。接着我说：

“先生们，我已经准备好报告了。”

“我们很乐意听，”我的那位先生说道，“现在我们可以决定我哥哥亚伯和我打的那个赌的胜者了。如果你帮我打赢了赌，你可以在我委任权内任选一个职位，那张百万英镑的钞票带来了吗？”

“在这儿，先生。”我把钞票递给他。

“我赢了！”他叫道，拍了一下亚伯的背，“现在你怎么说，老兄？”

“我承认他的确挺过来了，我输掉了两万英镑，我本来是怎么也不会相信这件事的。”

“我还有些事要报告，”我说，“这个报告很长，我希望不久后还可以再来，详细地报告这一个月来的经历，我保证它值得一听。同时，请看一下这个。”

“天哪，伙计！二十万英镑的存单，这是你的吗？”

“是我的，是我在三十天内审慎地运用你们借给我的那一小笔贷款挣来的，我只是用它来买一些小东西，然后让他们找钱给我。”

"Come, this is astonishing! It's incredible, man!"

"Never mind, I'll prove it. Don't take my word unsupported."

But now Portia's turn was come to be surprised. Her eyes were spread wide, and she said:

"Henry, is that really your money? Have you been fibbing to me?"

"I have, indeed, dearie. But you'll forgive me, I know."

She put up an arch pout, and said:

"Don't you be so sure. You are a naughty thing to deceive me so!"

"Oh, you'll get over it, sweetheart, you'll get over it; it was only fun, you know. Come, let's be going."

"But wait, wait! The situation, you know. I want to give you the situation," said my man.

"Well," I said, "I'm just as grateful as I can be, but really I don't want one."

"But you can have the very choicest one in my gift."

"Thanks again, with all my heart; but I don't even want that one."

"Henry, I'm ashamed of you. You don't half thank the good gentleman. May I do it for you?"

"Indeed, you shall, dear, if you can improve it. Let us see you try."

She walked to my man, got up in his lap, put her arm round his neck, and kissed him right on the mouth. Then the two old gentlemen shouted with laughter, but I was dumfounded, just petrified, as you may say. Portia said:

"喂，这真让人吃惊！简直不可思议，伙计！"

"不要紧，我会证明这是真的，不要以为我的话没有根据。"

但是现在轮到鲍西娅吃惊了，她的眼睛睁得大大的，说：

"亨利，这真是你的钱吗？你一直都在对我说谎吗？"

"我确实是的，亲爱的。但是你会原谅我的，我知道。"

她撅起了小嘴，说：

"不要这么肯定，你真是太淘气了，竟敢这样欺骗我。"

"哦，你会原谅我的，甜心，会原谅的。你知道的，这只是个玩笑，来，我们走吧。"

"但是等等，等等！那个职位，你知道的，我想给你一个职位。"我的那位先生说道。

"啊，"我说，"我实在是万分感激，可我真的不想要了。"

"但是你可以任选一个最好的职位。"

"我再次衷心地感谢你，但是甚至那样好的职位我也不想要了。"

"亨利，我真为你感到羞愧，你一点都不感谢这位好心的先生，我可以替你感谢他吗？"

"亲爱的，如果能感谢得更好，你当然可以的。你试试看吧。"

她朝那位老先生走去，坐在他的膝上，胳膊搂住他的脖子，刚好亲在他嘴上。然后两位老先生大笑起来，而我却目瞪口呆，可以说僵住了。鲍西娅说：

"Papa, he has said you haven't a situation in your gift that he'd take; and I feel just as hurt as—"

"My darling, is that your papa?"

"Yes; he's my step-papa, and the dearest one that ever was. You understand now, don't you, why I was able to laugh when you told me at the minister's, not knowing my relationships, what trouble and worry papa's and Uncle Abel's scheme was giving you?"

Of course, I spoke right up now, without any fooling, and went straight to the point.

"Oh, my dearest dear sir, I want to take back what I said. You have got a situation open that I want."

"Name it."

"Son-in-law."

"Well, well, well! But you know, if you haven't ever served in that capacity, you, of course, can't furnish recommendations of a sort to satisfy the conditions of the contract, and so—"

"Try me—oh, do, I beg of you! Only just try me thirty or forty years, and if—"

"Oh, well, all right; it's but a little thing to ask, take her along."

Happy, we two? There are not words enough in the unabridged to describe it. And when London got the whole history, a day or two later, of my month's adventures with that bank-note, and how they ended, did London talk, and have a good time? Yes.

My Portia's papa took that friendly and hospitable bill back

“爸爸，他说你的职位他一个也不想要，我感到受到了伤害，就像——”

“亲爱的，他是你爸爸？”

“是的，他是我的继父，是这世上最亲的人。那天在公使家，你不了解我和他们之间的关系，告诉我爸爸和亚伯叔叔的计划让你苦恼和焦虑时，我居然会笑起来，现在你明白为什么了，对吗？”

当然我马上说了出来，不再开玩笑，直奔主题。

“噢，我最亲爱的先生，我想收回刚才说过的话。你所提供的职位有一个是我想要的。”

“说吧。”

“女婿。”

“好啦，好啦，好啦！但是你知道，你从没干过那个职位，当然也就无法提供这方面的推荐信，证明你满足合同的要求，所以——”

“让我试一下吧——喔，我求你了！只要让我试个三四十年，如果——”

“哦，好吧，可以；这只是个小小的要求，把她带走吧。”

我们俩幸福吗？用足本大词典也无法形容它。一两天后，伦敦人知道了整个故事，也就是我同那张百万钞票一个月来的历险内容及结局。他们是否谈论了这件事，是否感到很快乐？是的。

我的鲍西娅的爸爸将那张友好、热情的钞票拿回了英格兰银

to the Bank of England and cashed it; then the Bank canceled it and made him a present of it, and he gave it to us at our wedding, and it has always hung in its frame in the sacredest place in our home ever since. For it gave me my Portia. But for it I could not have remained in London, would not have appeared at the minister's, never should have met her. And so I always say, "Yes, it's a million-pounder, as you see; but it never made but one purchase in its life, and then got the article for only about a tenth part of its value."

行，将它兑成现金，然后银行将它注销并作为礼物送给了他，而他在我们的婚礼上又将它送给了我们。从那之后，我们将它镶框装裱好，挂在我们家最神圣的地方，因为它给我带来了我的鲍西娅。如果没有它，我就不会留在伦敦，不会出现在公使家，也永远不会遇见她。所以我总是说："是的，你看，它是一张百万英镑的钞票，但是它一生仅被使用过一次，然后它买到了价值比它大十倍的东西。"

Is He Living or Is He Dead?

他是生是死？

《他是生是死？》（Is He Living or Is He Dead?，1893）讲述了一群穷困潦倒的画家为生计所迫，通过导演一场精心设计的骗局，最终出名并且发财的故事。

故事中，米勒的朋友们仅仅用了六周的时间就将米勒从一个无人知晓的乡村画家塑造成为红遍全球的艺术大师。这是因为他们深知人们的心理，充分利用报纸媒介制造社会舆论；他们紧紧抓住人们爱慕虚荣的弱点为米勒宣传造势。

世人追逐的是艺术家的名气，而不是艺术本身的价值。作者在故事中刻画了两个不同形象的米勒：一个默默无闻，为生活所困，在众目睽睽之下抬着自己的灵柩，在人世间孤苦伶仃地度过残年；而另一个人尽皆知，光彩耀人，躺在棺材里受人景仰，作为艺术大师永远活在人们心中。前者虽然是真正的艺术家，却无人欣赏；后者尽管只是一个抽象称谓，却成为世人追逐的偶像。此外，米勒作品的售价也发生了戏剧性的变化。同样一幅《晚祷》，起初一文不值，换不到一棵白菜；后来却卖到了两千二百法郎；在画家“死”后，居然拍出了五十五万法郎的天价，这一巨大变化反映了世人趋名附利的虚荣。

小说用一则寓意深刻的童话贯穿始终，引人深思：善鸣的鸟儿活着时受尽冷遇，最终被饥渴夺去了生命；死后却换来了豪华的葬礼和人们悲痛的眼泪。这一强烈的反差既表达出作者对有着相似命运的艺术家的同情，也讽刺了世人附庸风雅，盲目崇拜虚名，忽视艺术本身价值的现象。

I was spending the month of March, 1892, at Mentone, in the Riviera. At this retired spot one has all the advantages, privately, which are to be had at Monte Carlo and Nice, a few miles farther along, publicly. That is to say, one has the flooding sunshine, the balmy air and the brilliant blue sea, without the marring additions of human powwow and fuss and feathers and display. Mentone is quiet, simple, restful, unpretentious; the rich and the gaudy do not come there. As a rule, I mean, the rich do not come there. Now and then a rich man comes, and I presently got acquainted with one of these. Partially to disguise him I will call him Smith. One day, in the Hôtel des Anglais, at the second breakfast, he exclaimed:

"Quick! Cast your eye on the man going out at the door. Take in every detail of him."

"Why?"

"Do you know who he is?"

"Yes. He spent several days here before you came. He is an old, retired, and very rich silk manufacturer from Lyons, they say, and I guess he is alone in the world, for he always looks sad and dreamy, and doesn't talk with anybody. His name is Théophile Magnan."

I supposed that Smith would now proceed to justify the large interest which he had shown in Monsieur Magnan; but instead he dropped into a brown study, and was apparently lost to me and to the rest of the world during some minutes. Now and then he passed his fingers through his flossy white hair, to

1892年，我在里维埃拉[①]地区的门托尼[②]度过了三月份。在这个僻静的地方，你会独自享有全部的有利条件，而这在数英里之外的蒙特卡洛和尼斯[③]，却得和大家一起分享。也就是说，你享有充足的阳光，宜人的空气和明亮湛蓝的大海，而不会被人们的聚会、夸夸其谈和炫耀所破坏。门托尼宁静、质朴、悠闲、自然；富贵和浮华之人都不去那里。我是说，通常富贵之人都不去那里。偶尔也来个有钱人，我很快就认识了其中的一位。部分为了掩饰他的身份，我就叫他史密斯吧。有一天，在英格兰饭店喝早茶[④]的时候，他突然喊道：

“快！看门口那个要出去的人，看仔细了。”

“为什么？”

“你知道他是谁吗？”

“知道。你来之前，他在这儿待过几天。据说他是里昂[⑤]一个很有钱的丝绸厂厂主，年纪大了，退了休。我猜他在这世上是孤零零一个人，因为他看起来总是郁郁寡欢、神情恍惚的，不和任何人说话。他叫西奥菲尔·马格南。”

我以为史密斯先生接着马上会解释对马格南先生表现出巨大兴趣的缘由，但是他却陷入了沉思，显然，一时间将我和世上的其他

① 里维埃拉，法国东南部和意大利西北部的地中海沿海地区，从法国戛纳一直延伸到意大利的拉斯佩齐亚，被称作蓝岸，因其风景和宜人的气候而闻名，是欧洲主要旅游胜地之一。

② 门托尼，法国阿尔卑斯省的一个镇，位于地中海沿岸，在摩纳哥与意大利之间。

③ 蒙特卡洛，位于法国的东南方的摩纳哥公国；尼斯，法国南部城市。两座城市都濒临地中海岸，是著名的度假胜地。

④ 欧洲某些国家的习俗，介于早饭和午饭之间的一餐，通常在上午十点半左右，喝点咖啡，吃些点心之类的简单食物。

⑤ 里昂，法国中东部大城市，曾经是西方丝织业中心。

assist his thinking, and meantime he allowed his breakfast to go on cooling. At last he said:

"No, it's gone; I can't call it back."

"Can't call what back?"

"It's one of Hans Andersen's beautiful little stories. But it's gone from me. Part of it is like this: A child has a caged bird, which it loves, but thoughtlessly neglects. The bird pours out its song unheard and unheeded; but in time, hunger and thirst assail the creature, and its song grows plaintive and feeble and finally ceases—the bird dies. The child comes, and is smitten to the heart with remorse; then, with bitter tears and lamentations, it calls its mates, and they bury the bird with elaborate pomp and the tenderest grief, without knowing, poor things, that it isn't children only who starve poets to death and then spend enough on their funerals and monuments to have kept them alive and made them easy and comfortable. Now—"

But here we were interrupted. About ten that evening I ran across Smith, and he asked me up to his parlor to help him smoke and drink hot Scotch. It was a cozy place, with its comfortable chairs, its cheerful lamps, and its friendly open fire of seasoned olive-wood. To make everything perfect, there was the muffled booming of the surf outside. After the second Scotch and much lazy and contented chat, Smith said:

"Now we are properly primed[1]—I to tell a curious history, and you to listen to it. It has been a secret for many years—a secret between me and three others; but I am going to break the

① primed: 原意为事先准备好的，此处指主人公喝完酒、准备好讲故事的状态。

事情忘到了一边。他偶尔搔搔轻柔的白发以助思考，同时任凭早餐凉掉。最后他说：

“不行，忘了，想不起来了。”

“想不起来什么？”

“就是汉斯·安徒生[①]笔下的一个美丽的小故事，可是我忘了。有一部分内容好像是这样：一个孩子有只圈在笼子里的鸟，他喜欢它，却疏忽大意，不去照顾它。鸟儿倾其歌声，却没人理睬，没人注意。终于饥饿和干渴侵袭了这个生命，它的歌声变得凄凉和微弱，最后停止了——鸟儿死了。孩子来了，心中痛悔不已；然后含着伤心的眼泪，怀着悲痛的心情，叫来了他的伙伴。他们悲痛万分，以隆重的仪式安葬了那只鸟。而这些可怜的人并不知道，把诗人饿死，然后为了让他们永存，为了使他们安心和舒服，在葬礼和纪念碑上面大把花钱的人何止孩子。现在——”

但这时我们的谈话被打断了。那天晚上十点钟，我碰见了史密斯，他请我上楼去他的房间陪他抽抽烟，喝加热的苏格兰威士忌酒[②]。这是个惬意的地方，有舒适的椅子，欢快明亮的灯光，还有晒干的橄榄木燃烧发出的怡人火焰。外面是海浪低沉的隆隆声，让一切达到了完美。两杯威士忌下肚，我们慵懒闲适、心满意足地闲聊了许久之后，史密斯说：

“现在我们喝得差不多了——我来讲段离奇的故事，你要听好。多少年来，这一直是个秘密——我和另外三个人之间的秘密；但是

① 汉斯·安徒生（1805—1875），19世纪丹麦著名的童话作家，著有《丑小鸭》《卖火柴的小女孩》等脍炙人口的童话作品。
② 苏格兰威士忌，仅产于苏格兰地区的一种烈性酒。

seal[1] now. Are you comfortable?"

"Perfectly. Go on."

Here follows what he told me:

A long time ago I was a young artist—a very young artist, in fact—and I wandered about the country parts of France, sketching here and sketching there, and was presently joined by a couple of darling young Frenchmen who were at the same kind of thing that I was doing. We were as happy as we were poor, or as poor as we were happy—phrase it to suit yourself. Claude Frère and Carl Boulanger—these are the names of those boys; dear, dear fellows, and the sunniest spirits that ever laughed at poverty and had a noble good time in all weathers.

At last we ran hard aground in a Breton village, and an artist as poor as ourselves took us in and literally saved us from starving—François Millet—

"What! the great François Millet?"

Great? He wasn't any greater than we were, then. He hadn't any fame, even in his own village; and he was so poor that he hadn't anything to feed us on but turnips, and even the turnips failed us sometimes. We four became fast friends, doting friends, inseparables. We painted away together with all our might, piling up stock, piling up stock, but very seldom getting rid of any of it. We had lovely times together; but, O my soul! how we were pinched now and then!

For a little over two years this went on. At last, one day,

① break the seal: 原意为打开机密文件的封口物，此处指打破保密的约定。

现在我要打破这个约定。你觉得舒服吗？”

“好极了，开始吧。”

下面就是他讲给我的故事：

很久以前，我曾是个年轻的画家——实际上，是个非常年轻的画家——我在法国的乡村四处漂泊，在这儿画画，在那儿画画。不久有了两个迷人的法国青年做伴，他们和我一样画画。我们有多穷就有多快活，或者说有多快活就多穷——随便你怎么说吧。克劳德·弗里尔和卡尔·布朗热——这是那两个小伙儿的名字；他们是非常非常可爱的人，性格极其乐观，对贫困向来是一笑置之，无论遇到什么事，总是乐呵呵的。

最后，我们在布列塔尼[①]的一个村子里被困住了。一位穷得跟我们一样的画家收留了我们，简直是救了我们的命，才没让我们饿死——弗朗索瓦·米勒[②]——

“什么！伟大的法朗斯瓦·米勒？”

伟大？他那时并不比我们伟大。甚至在他自己的村子里，他也没有什么名望；他穷困潦倒，以至于除了大头菜，他再也拿不出别的什么东西给我们吃了，有时候连大头菜也吃不上。我们四个人成为了相互交心、相互倾爱的朋友，形影不离的伙伴。我们一块儿出去，全力以赴地画画，作品越堆越多，越堆越多，却极少能甩出一件。我们在一起过得很开心；但是，天啊！有的时候我们真够苦的！

这样过了两年有余。终于有一天，克劳德说：

① 布列塔尼地区，位于法国西北部的布列塔尼半岛。

② 让·弗朗索瓦·米勒(Jean François Millet, 1814—1875)，19世纪法国最杰出的现实主义画家，一生贫困潦倒，以乡村风俗画中感人的人性闻名于法国画坛，代表作有《播种者》(The Sower, 1850)、《拾穗》(The Gleaners, 1857)、《晚祷》(The Angelus,1859) 等。本文所讲述的有关此画家的大多数内容属作者杜撰。

Claude said:

"Boys, we've come to the end. Do you understand that?—absolutely to the end. Everybody has struck—there's a league formed against us. I've been all around the village and it's just as I tell you. They refuse to credit us for another centime until all the odds and ends are paid up."

This struck us cold. Every face was blank with dismay. We realized that our circumstances were desperate, now. There was a long silence. Finally, Millet said with a sigh:

"Nothing occurs to me—nothing. Suggest something, lads."

There was no response, unless a mournful silence may be called a response. Carl got up, and walked nervously up and down awhile, then said:

"It's a shame! Look at these canvases: stacks and stacks of as good pictures as anybody in Europe paints—I don't care who he is. Yes, and plenty of lounging strangers have said the same—or nearly that, anyway."

"But didn't buy," Millet said.

"No matter, they said it; and it's true, too. Look at your 'Angelus' there! Will anybody tell me—"

"Pah, Carl—My 'Angelus'! I was offered five francs for it."

"When?"

"Who offered it?"

"Where is he?"

“伙计们，我们走投无路了，明白吗？——彻底走投无路了。任何人都不肯赊了——他们联合起来对付我们。我在村子里整整转了一圈，事情正如我所告诉你们的。在所有零零碎碎的欠账还清之前，他们拒绝再借给我们一生丁[①]。”

这给了我们当头一棒。每张脸上都是一片茫然，神情沮丧。现在我们认识到，我们的处境糟糕透了。很长一段时间都鸦雀无声。最后，米勒叹了口气，说：

“我没辙了——没了。兄弟们，出点儿主意。”

没人回应，除非悲伤的沉默能算是回应。卡尔站起来，焦急地来回走了一会儿，然后说道：

“真不像话！看看这些画：一堆一堆的，不比欧洲的任何人画得差——我才不管他是谁呢。是的，很多闲逛的陌生人也说过一样的话——或者，反正大致是那个意思。”

“可都没买。”米勒说。

“无所谓，他们说过；而且说得也对。看看那边你的那幅《晚祷》[②]！谁会告诉我——”

“哼，卡尔——我的那幅《晚祷》！有人曾出五法郎要买它。”

“什么时候？”

“谁要买？”

“他在哪儿？”

---

① 生丁，法国货币单位，100生丁=1法郎。这里用来形容极少的钱。

② 《晚祷》(The Angelus,1859)，让·弗朗索瓦·米勒的代表作之一，此画描绘了一对在田间默默祈祷的农民夫妇。米勒去世后，此画几经易手，后被一位法国人以80万法郎购得，并捐献给法国政府。

"Why didn't you take it?"

"Come—don't all speak at once. I thought he would give more—I was sure of it—he looked it—so I asked him eight."

"Well—and then?"

"He said he would call again."

"Thunder and lightning! Why, François—"

"Oh, I know—I know! It was a mistake, and I was a fool. Boys, I meant for the best; you'll grant me that, and I—"

"Why, certainly, we know that, bless your dear heart; but don't you be a fool again."

"I? I wish somebody would come along and offer us a cabbage for it— you'd see!"

"A cabbage! Oh, don't name it—it makes my mouth water. Talk of things less trying."

"Boys," said Carl, "do these pictures lack merit? Answer me that."

"No!"

"Aren't they of very great and high merit? Answer me that."

"Yes."

"Of such great and high merit that, if an illustrious name were attached to them they would sell at splendid prices. Isn't it so?"

"Certainly it is. Nobody doubts that."

"But—I'm not joking—isn't it so?"

"Why, of course it's so—and we are not joking. But what of it? What of it? How does that concern us?"

"In this way, comrades—we'll attach an illustrious name to

"你怎么没答应？"

"好啦——别都一起说。我原以为他会出更多的钱——我对这很有把握——他盯着那幅画——于是我要了他八法郎。"

"那么——后来呢？"

"他说他会再来的。"

"见鬼！唉，弗朗索瓦——"

"噢，我知道——我知道！这是我的错，我是个傻瓜。伙计们，我原是好意；你们要相信我，而且我——"

"啊，当然了，我们知道，天哪；但是以后你别再犯傻了。"

"我吗？我真希望有人来用棵白菜跟我们换那幅画——你们瞧吧！"

"白菜！噢，别说它了——它让我口水都流出来了。说些不那么让人难受的吧。"

"伙计们，"卡尔说，"难道这些画没多少价值吗？回答我。"

"不是！"

"难道它们不算卓越非凡吗？回答我。"

"算。"

"如此卓越非凡的作品，若是贴上个名人的名字，它们一定会卖出高价的，不是这样吗？"

"当然是了，毫无疑问。"

"不过——我不是在开玩笑——难道不是这样吗？"

"噢，当然是这样——我们也不是在开玩笑。可是那又怎么样呢？那又怎么样呢？那跟我们有什么关系？"

"这样的话，朋友们——我们就给那些作品贴上个名人的名

them!”

The lively conversation stopped. The faces were turned inquiringly upon Carl. What sort of riddle might this be? Where was an illustrious name to be borrowed? And who was to borrow it?

Carl sat down, and said:

“Now, I have a perfectly serious thing to propose. I think it is the only way to keep us out of the almshouse, and I believe it to be a perfectly sure way. I base this opinion upon certain multitudinous and long-established facts in human history. I believe my project will make us all rich.”

“Rich! You’ve lost your mind.”

“No, I haven’t.”

“Yes, you have—you’ve lost your mind. What do you call rich?”

“A hundred thousand francs apiece.”

“He has lost his mind. I knew it.”

“Yes, he has. Carl, privation has been too much for you, and—”

“Carl, you want to take a pill and get right to bed.”

“Bandage him first—bandage his head, and then—”

“No, bandage his heels; his brains have been settling for weeks—I’ve noticed it.”

“Shut up!” said Millet, with ostensible severity, “and let the boy say his say. Now, then—come out with your project, Carl. What is it?”

“Well, then, by way of preamble I will ask you to note this

字！”

热闹的对话停了下来。一张张脸转向卡尔，露出探问的神色。他究竟卖的什么关子啊？到哪儿去借个名人的名字？而且谁去借呢？

卡尔坐下来，说：

“现在，我有一件非常重要的事情要说。我想，这是不让我们进救济院的唯一办法。而且我相信，这个办法绝对靠得住。我的这个想法基于人类历史上长期存在的诸多事实。我相信我的计划会让大家都发财。”

“发财！你疯了。”

“不，我没有。”

“是的，你疯了——你疯了。你说的发财指的是多少呢？”

“每人十万法郎。”

“他已经疯了，我就知道。”

“是的，他疯了。卡尔，穷困潦倒实在让你忍受不下去了，而且——”

“卡尔，你应该吃片药，然后立即上床睡觉。”

“先用绷带绑住他——绑住他的头，再——”

“不，绑住他的脚后跟；几周来他的脑袋一直往下面沉——我看出来了。”

“住口！”米勒貌似严肃地说，“先让他把话说完。好啦，下面——说说你的计划吧，卡尔。是什么？”

“好吧，那么作为开场白，我请大家注意人类历史上的这么一个

fact in human history: that the merit of many a great artist has never been acknowledged until after he was starved and dead. This has happened so often that I make bold to found a law upon it. This law: that the merit of every great unknown and neglected artist must and will be recognized and his pictures climb to high prices after his death. My project is this: we must cast lots—one of us must die."

The remark fell so calmly and so unexpectedly that we almost forgot to jump. Then there was a wild chorus of advice again—medical advice—for the help of Carl's brain; but he waited patiently for the hilarity to calm down, and then went on again with his project:

"Yes, one of us must die, to save the others—and himself. We will cast lots. The one chosen shall be illustrious, all of us shall be rich. Hold still, now—hold still; don't interrupt—I tell you I know what I am talking about. Here is the idea. During the next three months the one who is to die shall paint with all his might, enlarge his stock all he can—not pictures, no! skeleton sketches, studies, parts of studies, fragments of studies, a dozen dabs of the brush on each—meaningless, of course, but his with his cipher on them; turn out fifty a day, each to contain some peculiarity or mannerism, easily detectable as his—they're the things that sell you know, and are collected at fabulous prices for the world's museums, after the great man is gone; we'll have a ton of them ready—a ton! And all that time the rest of us will be busy supporting the moribund, and working Paris and the dealers—preparations for the coming event, you know; and

事实：很多伟大画家的价值直到他们饿死之后才被认可。这种事情屡屡发生，从中我可以大胆地得出一条规律。这条规律就是：每一位不为人知和被忽视的伟大画家，他的价值一定会被而且总有一天会被人认可。等他死后，他的画会卖上很高的价钱。我的计划是这样的：我们得抓阄——我们中的一个人得死。”

话说得非常平静，非常出人意料，我们惊得几乎都忘了跳起来。接着，又是七嘴八舌的一通建议——治疗建议——帮助治疗卡尔的大脑。但他却耐心地等着喧闹声平静下来，然后又继续说他的计划：

“不错，我们中的一个人得死，为了救其他人——还有他自己。我们抓阄。选中的人将会出名，我们所有人都会发财。现在静一静——静一静，不要插嘴——告诉你们，我知道自己在说什么。我是这么打算的。接下来的三个月里，要死的那个人必须全力以赴地作画，尽力增加他作品的数量——不是规规矩矩的画作，不是！轮廓草图、习作、残缺的习作、习作片段都行，每幅画寥寥十来笔——当然是随意的，但必须是他的，上面要有他的花押[①]；一天出五十幅，每幅带些特色和风格，让人容易认出是他的作品——要知道，这个伟大的人死了以后，它们是用来卖的，是让世界上的博物馆出大价钱收藏的；我们要准备大量作品——大量！在那段时间里，我们其余的人要全力支持这个快死的人，到巴黎和交易商当中去活动——要知道，这是为将来的事做准备；当一切进行得如火如荼、恰好合适的时候，我们就突然向他们公布死讯，并且举办一场让世人瞩目的葬礼。你们明白了吗？”

① 花押，代替签名的一种签署样式，常见于书画作品上。

when everything is hot and just right, we'll spring the death on them and have the notorious funeral. You get the idea?"

"N—o; at least, not qu—"

"Not quite? Don't you see? The man doesn't really die; he changes his name and vanishes; we bury a dummy, and cry over it, with all the world to help. And I—"

But he wasn't allowed to finish. Everybody broke out into a rousing hurrah of applause; and all jumped up and capered about the room and fell on each other's necks in transports of gratitude and joy. For hours we talked over the great plan, without ever feeling hungry; and at last, when all the details had been arranged satisfactorily, we cast lots and Millet was elected—elected to die, as we called it. Then we scraped together those things which one never parts with until he is betting them against future wealth—keepsake trinkets and such like—and these we pawned for enough to furnish us a frugal farewell supper and breakfast, and leave us a few francs over for travel, and a stake of turnips and such for Millet to live on for a few days.

Next morning, early, the three of us cleared out, straightway after breakfast—on foot, of course. Each of us carried a dozen of Millet's small pictures, purposing to market them. Carl struck for Paris, where he would start the work of building up Millet's fame against the coming great day. Claude and I were to separate, and scatter abroad over France.

Now, it will surprise you to know what an easy and comfortable thing we had. I walked two days before I began

“不，至少不太——”

“不太明白？难道你们还不清楚吗？那个人并没真死；他改姓换名，销声匿迹；我们埋个假人，再和全世界的人一起为它大哭一场。而且我——”

可是还没等他把话说完，大家就报以热烈的掌声表示赞同，所有人都跳起来，在屋子里面雀跃，彼此搂住脖子，感激不已，喜不自胜。关于这个伟大的计划我们谈论了数个小时，丝毫没有感觉到饿；最后，全部的细节都安排妥当之后，我们抓阄，结果米勒抽中——抽中了我们所谓的死签。然后，我们凑了些东西，若不是到了为将来的富贵赌一把的时候，谁也不会卖掉它们——纪念品之类的小玩意儿——我们当了这些东西，足够支付一顿简单的告别晚餐和一顿早餐，还给我们剩下几个法郎做路费，给米勒留下一些大头菜之类的东西，供他维持几天的生活。

次日一早，我们三人刚吃过早餐就马上匆匆离开了——当然是徒步行走。我们每人带了十来幅米勒的小画，打算把它们卖出去。卡尔前往巴黎，他将开始在那儿树立起米勒的名望，为即将到来的伟大日子做准备。克劳德和我要分头前往法国各地。

接下来，我们过得那么轻松、那么惬意，你知道了准会大吃一惊。我走了两天才开始办正事。当时，我在一个大城市的郊外，给

business. Then I began to sketch a villa in the outskirts of a big town—because I saw the proprietor standing on an upper veranda. He came down to look on—I thought he would. I worked swiftly, intending to keep him interested. Occasionally he fired off a little ejaculation of approbation, and by and by he spoke up with enthusiasm, and said I was a master!

I put down my brush, reached into my satchel, fetched out a Millet, and pointed to the cipher in the corner. I said, proudly:

"I suppose you recognize that? Well, he taught me! I should think I ought to know my trade!"

The man looked guiltily embarrassed, and was silent. I said, sorrowfully:

"You don't mean to intimate that you don't know the cipher of François Millet!"

Of course he didn't know that cipher; but he was the gratefulest man you ever saw, just the same, for being let out of an uncomfortable place on such easy terms. He said:

"No! Why, it is Millet's, sure enough! I don't know what I could have been thinking of. Of course I recognize it now."

Next, he wanted to buy it; but I said that although I wasn't rich I wasn't that poor. However, at last, I let him have it for eight hundred francs.

"Eight hundred!"

Yes. Millet would have sold it for a pork chop. Yes, I got eight hundred francs for that little thing. I wish I could get it back for eighty thousand. But that time's gone by. I made a very nice picture of that man's house, and I wanted to offer it to him

一栋别墅画起了素描——因为我看到房主正站在楼上的阳台上面。他走下来在一旁看着——我就料到他会的。我快速地画着，有意引起他的兴趣。他偶尔冒出几句赞赏的话，很快就热情洋溢地说起来，还说我是位大师！

我放下画笔，手伸进我的包里，拿出了一幅米勒的画，并且指着角上的花押，骄傲地说：

“我想您认识这个吧？嗯，他教的我！我想我应当懂我这一行！”

那人看上去像是做错了什么事，显得很难为情，一言不发。我遗憾地说：

“您不是要说您不认识弗朗索瓦·米勒的花押吧！”

他当然不认识那个花押；可他就跟你见过的最感激的人一样，因为这么一句简单的话就让他摆脱了难堪的境地。他说：

“哪里！哎呀，这是米勒的，千真万确！真不知道刚才我在想什么。可不是，现在我认出来了。”

然后，他要买那幅画；但是我说，虽然我并不宽裕，但是也并没穷成那样。不过，最终我八百法郎卖给了他。

“八百法郎！”

是啊，米勒原本会卖了它换块儿排骨。是啊，那幅小东西我卖了八百法郎。我真希望能用八万法郎把它买回来。但是那个时候已经过去了。我为那个人的房子作了幅很不错的画，并想十法郎卖给他，可是那说不过去，要知道我可是这么一位大师的弟子，于是就

for ten francs, but that wouldn't answer, seeing I was the pupil of such a master, so I sold it to him for a hundred. I sent the eight hundred francs straight back to Millet from that town and struck out again next day.

But I didn't walk—no. I rode. I have ridden ever since. I sold one picture every day, and never tried to sell two. I always said to my customer:

"I am a fool to sell a picture of François Millet's at all, for that man is not going to live three months, and when he dies his pictures can't be had for love or money."

I took care to spread that little fact as far as I could, and prepare the world for the event.

I take credit to myself for our plan of selling the pictures—it was mine. I suggested it that last evening when we were laying out our campaign, and all three of us agreed to give it a good fair trial before giving it up for some other. It succeeded with all of us. I walked only two days, Claude walked two—both of us afraid to make Millet celebrated too close to home—but Carl walked only half a day, the bright, conscienceless rascal, and after that he travelled like a duke.

Every now and then we got in with a country editor and started an item around through the press; not an item announcing that a new painter had been discovered, but an item which let on that everybody knew François Millet; not an item praising him in any way, but merely a word concerning the present condition of the "master"—sometimes hopeful, sometimes despondent, but always tinged with fears for the worst. We always marked

一百法郎卖给了他。我在那座城市直接把八百法郎汇给了米勒，接着第二天又出发了。

我可没再走路——不。我坐上了车。从此我就一直坐车。我每天卖一幅画，从不卖两幅。我总是对我的买主说：

“我真是个傻瓜，卖了弗朗索瓦·米勒的画。因为那个人活不过三个月，等他死了，无论多喜欢，多有钱也得不到他的画了。”

我尽可能地向外散布这一消息，好让世人为这事做好准备。

我们卖画的计划可是我的功劳——那是我的主意。最后那天晚上，我们在布置行动的时候，我提出来的，而且我们三人都同意先好好试一试，不行再想别的办法。我们全都成功了。我只走了两天，克莱德走了两天——我们俩都担心米勒出名的地方离家太近——但是卡尔只走了半天，那个头脑灵活、没有良心的家伙，从那以后他就像个公爵似的一路游逛。

我们经常结识地方编辑，借助报纸散布新闻。不是宣布发现了一名画家新秀那样的新闻，而是装作每个人都知道弗朗索瓦·米勒。不是以任何方式赞扬他的新闻，而仅是一句话提提该“大师”当前的病情——时而有望好转，时而不容乐观，但总带着几分对最坏情况的担忧。我们总是标出这些段落，把报纸寄给所有买过我们画的人。

these paragraphs, and sent the papers to all the people who had bought pictures of us.

Carl was soon in Paris and he worked things with a high hand. He made friends with the correspondents, and got Millet's condition reported to England and all over the continent, and America, and everywhere.

At the end of six weeks from the start, we three met in Paris and called a halt, and stopped sending back to Millet for additional pictures. The boom was so high, and everything so ripe, that we saw that it would be a mistake not to strike now, right away, without waiting any longer. So we wrote Millet to go to bed and begin to waste away pretty fast, for we should like him to die in ten days if he could get ready.

Then we figured up and found that among us we had sold eighty-five small pictures and studies, and had sixty-nine thousand francs to show for it. Carl had made the last sale and the most brilliant one of all. He sold the "Angelus" for twenty-two hundred francs. How we did glorify him!— not foreseeing that a day was coming by and by when France would struggle to own it and a stranger would capture it for five hundred and fifty thousand, cash.

We had a wind-up champagne supper that night, and next day Claude and I packed up and went off to nurse Millet through his last days and keep busybodies out of the house and send daily bulletins to Carl in Paris for publication in the papers of several continents for the information of a waiting world. The sad end came at last, and Carl was there in time to help in the

卡尔很快到了巴黎，然后就自个儿行动了起来。他结交记者朋友，并向英国、整个欧洲大陆、美国及世界各地报道米勒的病情。

从最开始算起，六周快要过去了。我们三人在巴黎见面，停止了行动，不再写信向米勒另要画作。形势如此高涨，诸事如此成熟，我们明白要是现在不行动，必将是个错误，要马上，刻不容缓。于是，我们写信要米勒躺在床上，并且要尽快消瘦下去，因为他要是准备好了，我们想让他在十天之后死去。

当时我们计算了一下，发现一共卖出了八十五幅小画和习作，得了六万九千法郎。卡尔做成了最后一笔买卖，也是最漂亮的一笔。他以两千二百法郎卖掉了那幅《晚祷》。我们把他好好地称赞了一番！——谁也没想到不久会有一天，法国千方百计地想要得到它，而且有个陌生人愿意出五十五万法郎争夺那幅画，还是现金支付。

那天晚上，我们吃了一顿香槟晚餐作为收场。第二天，我和克莱德便收拾行装出发，去照顾米勒走完他最后的日子，将好事者挡在门外，并且给在巴黎的卡尔寄去每天的病情报告，供各大洲的报纸发表，向等候的世人提供信息。悲痛的一天终于到来了，卡尔及时赶到那里，帮忙办理最后的哀悼仪式。

final mournful rites.

You remember that great funeral, and what a stir it made all over the globe, and how the illustrious of two worlds came to attend it and testify their sorrow. We four—still inseparable—carried the coffin, and would allow none to help. And we were right about that, because it hadn't anything in it but a wax figure, and any other coffin-bearers would have found fault with the weight. Yes, we same old four, who had lovingly shared privation together in the old hard times now gone forever, carried the cof—

"Which four?"

"We four—for Millet helped to carry his own coffin. In disguise, you know. Disguised as a relative—distant relative."

"Astonishing!"

"But true just the same. Well, you remember how the pictures went up. Money? We didn't know what to do with it. There's a man in Paris to-day who owns seventy Millet pictures. He paid us two million francs for them. And as for the bushels of sketches and studies which Millet shoveled out during the six weeks that we were on the road, well, it would astonish you to know the figure we sell them at nowadays—that is, when we consent to let one go!"

"It is a wonderful history, perfectly wonderful!"

"Yes—it amounts to that."

"Whatever became of Millet?"

"Can you keep a secret?"

你记得那场隆重的葬礼吧，它在全球引起了多么大的轰动啊，新老世界[1]多少声名显赫的人都来参加，表示他们的哀痛。我们四个人——仍旧形影不离——抬着棺材，不让任何人帮忙。我们那样做是对的，因为里面除了个蜡人什么也没有，别的谁抬棺材都会在重量上发现破绽。是的，还是我们老哥儿四个，我们在过去艰苦的岁月里情深义厚，一起分担困苦，而今一去不复返了，抬着棺——

"哪四个？"

"我们四个——因为米勒帮着抬他自己的棺材。你知道，乔装打扮，扮作一个亲戚——远房亲戚。"

"不可思议！"

"但是千真万确。好啦，你还记得那些画升值得有多快。钱？我们真不知道怎么花。现在巴黎有个人拥有七十幅米勒的画。为此他支付给我们二百万法郎。至于我们在外面的六周里，米勒胡乱画的那些成堆的草图和习作，喔，你要是知道我们现在卖的价钱一定会吓一跳的——就是说，也得我们愿意卖才行！"

"真是个奇妙的故事，奇妙绝伦！"

"是的——可以那么说。"

"米勒后来怎么样了？"

"你能保密吗？"

① 这里指美洲大陆和欧洲大陆。

"I can."

"Do you remember the man I called your attention to in the dining-room today? That was François Millet."

"Great—"

"Scott[①]! Yes. For once they didn't starve a genius to death and then put into other pockets the rewards he should have had himself. This songbird was not allowed to pipe out its heart unheard and then be paid with the cold pomp of a big funeral. We looked out for that."

① Great scott! (表示吃惊)天哪!

“能。”

“你还记得今天在餐厅里我叫你注意的那个人吗？那就是弗朗索瓦·米勒。”

“啊——”

“天哪！是的，只有这一次他们没有把一位天才饿死，之后把本该属于他的报酬装到别人的口袋里。这只唱歌的鸟不会听任倾诉的歌声无人理睬，只是得到隆重葬礼的凄凉盛况作为回报。我们提防着那种事呐。”

Was It Heaven? Or Hell?

上天堂？还是下地狱？

《上天堂？还是下地狱？》（Was It Heaven? Or Hell?, 1902）讲述的是两位年迈的姑妈照顾一对生病的年轻母女的故事。姑妈们从不撒谎，但为了安慰生病的母亲，免得她担心女儿，她们被迫说出善意的谎言，然后逐步“堕落”为撒谎的能手。马克·吐温在这篇小说中借鉴了弥尔顿《失乐园》的框架结构，故事沿着“引诱—堕落—失去伊甸园”的线索发展。

初看《上天堂？还是下地狱？》的小说名字，我们就会想起人类始祖徜徉在伊甸园，及至后来痛失乐园的神话传说。不难看出，本文中医生的原型是引诱人类堕落的撒旦，两位姑妈的原型是纯洁的亚当、夏娃，而善意的谎言则象征了伊甸园中的智慧之果。医生的面貌酷似狮子，他有基督般博大的胸怀，对病人仁慈地救赎；另一方面，他藐视一切世俗传统，又有撒旦的反叛精神以及让人感到畏惧的王者风范。但在传统卫道士的眼里，他是魔鬼的化身，正是他促成了姑妈们的堕落。姑妈们代表了纯洁的亚当、夏娃，她们正直、善良，但受传统文明的束缚，茫然无知，不能明辨是非。为了自己死后能够上天堂，她们把残酷的事实告诉生病的母亲，不顾病人的安危，且振振有词——“一切谎言都是禁止的！”直到在医生的教导下，她们才学会了撒谎，也就等于吃了智慧之果后，眼前才能豁然开朗，明白真理。痛失乐园对她们来讲是一种幸运，因为从此告别了混混沌沌的生活，真正开始了作为“人”的存在。

文章结尾她们拒绝忏悔，声明如果再次处于那样的情况下，她们还会再次撒谎。为了病人的幸福，她们还会一如既往地说善意的谎言，宁愿自己下地狱。如同哈克贝里·费恩为了挽救黑人吉姆宁愿选择下地狱一样，她们的选择也意味着良心的胜利和对习俗的战胜，姑妈们的“堕落”犹如凤凰涅槃，摆脱了不合理旧传统的束缚，也意味着彻底的重生。结尾处，作者对姑妈们将会上天堂还是下地狱的发问给读者留下了悬念，增加了文章的张力，体现了马克·吐温对人类生存现状的关怀。

1

"You told a lie?"

"You confess it—you actually confess it—you told a lie!"

2

The family consisted of four persons: Margaret Lester, widow, aged thirty six; Helen Lester, her daughter, aged sixteen; Mrs. Lester's maiden aunts, Hannah and Hester Gray, twins, aged sixty-seven. Waking and sleeping, the three women spent their days and nights in adoring the young girl; in watching the movements of her sweet spirit in the mirror of her face; in refreshing their souls with the vision of her bloom and beauty; in listening to the music of her voice; in gratefully recognizing how rich and fair for them was the world with this presence in it; in shuddering to think how desolate it would be with this light gone out of it.

By nature—and inside—the aged aunts were utterly dear and lovable and good, but in the matter of morals and conduct their training had been so uncompromisingly strict that it had made them exteriorly austere, not to say stern. Their influence was effective in the house; so effective that the mother and the daughter conformed to its moral and religious requirements cheerfully, contentedly, happily, unquestionably. To do this was become second nature to them. And so in this peaceful heaven there were no clashings, no irritations, no fault-findings, no

一

“你说谎了？”

“你承认了——事实上你承认了——你说谎了！”

二

这家共有四位成员：守寡的玛格丽特·莱斯特，三十六岁；她的女儿海伦·莱斯特，十六岁；莱斯特夫人的两位单身姑妈，汉娜·格雷和海丝特·格雷，一对双胞胎，六十七岁。无论醒着还是睡着，白天还是黑夜，三个女人将这个年轻女孩像神明一样供奉着，总是注视着从她镜子般的脸上映出的可爱心灵的动向，总是看着她青春焕发的美貌而倍感欣慰，总是听着她那音乐般美妙的声音，充满感激之情地意识到有了她的存在，这世界对她们是多么慷慨、公平，总是一想到这束光逝去时世界会多么荒凉，就会不寒而栗。

从本性上——以及内心来说——这对年老的姑妈绝对亲切、可爱、善良，但在道德和行为方面，她们的训练非常严格，毫不妥协，这使她们从外表看来很严肃，如果算不上严厉的话。在这个家里她们的影响力很大，以至于那对母女由衷地、满意地、高兴地、不容置疑地遵从她们在道德和宗教上的要求。这样做成了她们的第二天性。所以在这平静的天堂[1]里，没有冲突，没有烦恼，没有人找碴挑刺，没有人心怀不满。

① 天堂，根据基督教传统，这是唯一神祇与众天使、圣人居住之地。一般人类若怀有敬虔之信仰心、一生无罪无垢即有可能进入此地。

heart-burnings.

In it a lie had no place. In it a lie was unthinkable. In it speech was restricted to absolute truth, iron-bound truth, implacable and uncompromising truth, let the resulting consequences be what they might. At last, one day, under stress of circumstances, the darling of the house sullied her lips with a lie—and confessed it, with tears and self-upbraidings. There are not any words that can paint the consternation of the aunts. It was as if the sky had crumpled up and collapsed and the earth had tumbled to ruin with a crash. They sat side by side, white and stern, gazing speechless upon the culprit, who was on her knees before them with her face buried first in one lap and then the other, moaning and sobbing, and appealing for sympathy and forgiveness and getting no response, humbly kissing the hand of the one, then of the other, only to see it withdrawn as suffering defilement by those soiled lips.

Twice, at intervals, Aunt Hester said, in frozen amazement:

"You told a lie?"

Twice, at intervals, Aunt Hannah followed with the muttered and amazed ejaculation:

"You confess it—you actually confess it—you told a lie!"

It was all they could say. The situation was new, unheard of, incredible; they could not understand it, they did not know how to take hold of it, it approximately paralyzed speech.

At length it was decided that the erring child must be taken to her mother, who was ill, and who ought to know what had happened. Helen begged, besought, implored that she might be

在这儿，谎言没有立足之地。在这儿，谎言是无法想象的。在这儿，言论被限定为绝对的真实，苛刻的真实，不容更改的、毫不妥协的真实，结果如何且不去管它[1]。终于，有一天，由于形势所逼，这个屋子里的宝贝用一个谎言玷污了她的嘴唇——并在流着泪水的自责中承认了。没有哪个词能描述两位姑妈的惊恐。好像天空都扭曲了、坍塌了，大地开始猛然翻转，然后轰的一声变成了一片废墟，毁掉了。她们肩并肩地坐在一起，脸色苍白、严厉，盯着犯人说不出话来。她正跪在她们面前，把脸先埋在一只膝盖上，然后又埋在另外一只膝盖上，呜咽啜泣着，请求同情和原谅，但没得到任何回答。她谦恭地亲吻一个人的手，然后再亲另外一个人的手，却只看到它们抽了回去，好像怕被这肮脏的嘴唇给玷污了似的。

期间，有两次，吓呆了的海丝特姑妈惊愕地说：

“你说谎了？”

期间，有两次，汉娜姑妈突然喃喃地、呆呆地跟着叫道：

“你承认了——事实上你承认了——你说谎了！”

她们只能说出这些话。这种情况以前从未有过，从未听说过，令人难以置信；她们不能理解，不知道该怎么处理，这几乎使她们丧失了语言能力。

最终她们决定，必须将犯错的孩子带到她母亲那儿去，虽然她

① 结果如何且不去管它。指姑妈们机械地执行说真话的训诫，却从不考虑后果的严重，及这样做是否正确。

spared this further disgrace, and that her mother might be spared the grief and pain of it; but this could not be: duty required this sacrifice, duty takes precedence of all things, nothing can absolve one from a duty, with a duty no compromise is possible.

Helen still begged, and said the sin was her own, her mother had had no hand in it—why must she be made to suffer for it?

But the aunts were obdurate in their righteousness, and said the law that visited the sins of the parent upon the child was by all right and reason reversible; and therefore it was but just that the innocent mother of a sinning child should suffer her rightful share of the grief and pain and shame which were the allotted wages of the sin.

The three moved toward the sick-room.

At this time the doctor was approaching the house. He was still a good distance away, however. He was a good doctor and a good man, and he had a good heart, but one had to know him a year to get over hating him, two years to learn to endure him, three to learn to like him, and four and five to learn to live him. It was a slow and trying education, but it paid. He was of great stature; he had a leonine head, a leonine face, a rough voice, and an eye which was sometimes a pirate's and sometimes a woman's, according to the mood. He knew nothing about etiquette, and cared nothing about it; in speech, manner, carriage, and conduct he was the reverse of conventional. He was frank, to the limit; he had opinions on all subjects; they were always on tap and ready for delivery, and he cared not a

母亲正在生病，但应该知道发生的事情。海伦乞求着，哀求免除接下来的耻辱，这样她母亲就可以不必因此而痛苦悲伤，但这是不可能的，天职需要做此牺牲，天职高于一切，没有什么可以免除一个人的天职，在天职面前是不容让步的。

海伦还在乞求，说这是她一个人的罪过，她母亲并没有参与进来——为什么非要让她承受这一切呢？

但姑妈们倔强地坚持她们的正义，说律法因父母造孽而降罪于子女，反过来也是完全正当合理的，因此对一个无辜的母亲来说，如果她的孩子犯了罪，那么作为罪恶应得的报应，她理应承受属于她的那份悲伤、痛苦与羞辱，这么做是公正的。

三个人朝病房走去。

这时医生正朝这幢房子走来，但还有很长一段距离。他是一个好医生，也是个好人，有一颗善良的心，然而你要在认识他一年后才能不再讨厌他，两年后才学会忍受他，三年后才学会喜欢他，四五年后才学会爱上他。这是一个缓慢难挨的经历，不过它很划算。他身材高大，有狮子般的脑袋，狮子般的脸庞，嗓音粗哑，一双眼睛有时像强悍的海盗，有时像温柔的妇人，因心情而异。他一点也不懂得礼节，对此也毫不在意，言行举止完全不合习俗。他坦率至极，对任何事情都有自己的看法，并且随时都有，可以马上开始高谈阔论，至于听众喜欢与否，他一点也不在乎。

farthing whether his listener liked them or didn't. Whom he loved he loved, and manifested it; whom he didn't love he hated, and published it from the housetops. In his young days he had been a sailor, and the salt-airs of all the seas blew from him yet. He was a sturdy and loyal Christian, and believed he was the best one in the land, and the only one whose Christianity was perfectly sound, healthy, full-charged with common sense, and had no decayed places in it. People who had an ax to grind, or people who for any reason wanted to get on the soft side of him, called him The Christian—a phrase whose delicate flattery was music to his ears, and whose capital T was such an enchanting and vivid object to him that he could see it when it fell out of a person's mouth even in the dark. Many who were fond of him stood on their consciences with both feet and brazenly called him by that large title habitually, because it was a pleasure to them to do anything that would please him; and with eager and cordial malice his extensive and diligently cultivated crop of enemies gilded it, beflowered it, expanded it to "The only Christian." Of these two titles, the latter had the wider currency; the enemy, being greatly in the majority, attended to that. Whatever the doctor believed, he believed with all his heart, and would fight for it whenever he got the chance; and if the intervals between chances grew to be irksomely wide, he would invent ways of shortening them himself. He was severely conscientious, according to his rather independent lights, and whatever he took to be a duty he performed, no matter whether the judgment of the professional moralists agreed with his

他爱他所爱的人，并且表现出来；他讨厌他所不爱的人，并会爬上屋顶告诉大家。年轻时他做过水手，现在还能从他身上闻到海面上的咸腥味。他是个坚定、虔诚的基督徒，并且认为他是世界上最优秀的基督徒，只有他的基督教才是完全明智、健康、充满常识的，没有任何腐朽之处。存有私心的人，或者出于什么原因想看到他温和一面的人，称他为基督徒——词中那微妙的奉承，在他听来就像音乐一般动听，那大写的 T 在他看来是那么令人陶醉、栩栩如生，即使在黑暗中，也能看到它从人们的嘴角滑落。很多喜欢他的人双脚踩在良心上，习惯于厚着脸皮喊他那大名鼎鼎的称号，因为任何使他感到高兴的事情，他们都乐于去做。他那人数众多而又勤勉文雅的敌人们，带着一丝热切和貌似热情的恶毒，把这个词镀上金、装饰华丽、扩展为"唯一的基督徒[1]"。就这两个头衔来说，后者流传更为广泛，因为数量占绝对优势的敌人致力于传播它。不管医生相信什么，他都会全身心地相信它，并且一有机会便会为它奋斗。如果两次机会的间隔时间太长，让人心烦，他就想方设法把间隔缩短。他严格地按良心办事，从他那相当独立的眼光出发，无论什么，只要他觉得是项职责，就会去完成，不管专业的道德家对他的观点同意与否。

① 唯一的基督徒，这是敌人们形容医生的反语，意思是唯一一个不正统的基督徒。

own or not. At sea, in his young days, he had used profanity freely, but as soon as he was converted he made a rule, which he rigidly stuck to ever afterward, never to use it except on the rarest occasions, and then only when duty commanded. He had been a hard drinker at sea, but after his conversion he became a firm and outspoken teetotaler, in order to be an example to the young, and from that time forth he seldom drank; never, indeed, except when it seemed to him to be a duty—a condition which sometimes occurred a couple of times a year, but never as many as five times.

Necessarily, such a man is impressionable, impulsive, emotional. This one was, and had no gift at hiding his feelings; or if he had it he took no trouble to exercise it. He carried his soul's prevailing weather in his face, and when he entered a room the parasols or the umbrellas went up—figuratively speaking—according to the indications. When the soft light was in his eye it meant approval, and delivered a benediction; when he came with a frown he lowered the temperature ten degrees. He was a well-beloved man in the house of his friends, but sometimes a dreaded one.

He had a deep affection for the Lester household, and its several members returned this feeling with interest. They mourned over his kind of Christianity, and he frankly scoffed at theirs; but both parties went on loving each other just the same.

He was approaching the house—out of the distance; the aunts and the culprit were moving toward the sick-chamber.

年轻时在海上当水手，他经常说出亵渎神灵[1]的话，但皈依之后，他马上给自己定了一条规矩，从此以后严格地执行它，从不逾规，只有当职责所需时除外，当然这样的场合是很少的。在海上他酗酒很厉害，但皈依之后，为了给年轻人树立一个好榜样，他成了一个坚定的、坦率的、绝对戒酒的人，从那以后他很少喝酒，真的从不喝酒，除非对他来说是项职责时——这种情况一年出现几次，但从没达到五次。

这样一个人必定敏感、好冲动、易动感情。此人便是如此，他没有隐藏感情的天赋，或者即使有，也懒得去用。他心里所涌动的阴晴全表现在脸上，打个比方，当他走进一间屋子时，就会有太阳伞或雨伞撑起来——根据不同的迹象而定。当他的眼中显出柔和的光芒，那就表示赞许，送出一个祝福；当他进来时皱着眉，温度就会下降十度。他在朋友家备受爱戴，但有时让人感到畏惧。

他对莱斯特家怀有深厚的感情，这家的成员们也乐意回报他同样的情感。她们哀叹他那种基督教，他则坦率地嘲笑她们的基督教，但双方仍一如既往地爱着彼此。

他正朝房子走来——快到了；姑妈们和犯人正朝病房走去。

---

① 亵渎神灵，是指对别人或自身宗教信仰的神灵作出诽谤的言论或冒犯的行为。

3

The three last named stood by the bed; the aunts austere, the transgressor softly sobbing. The mother turned her head on the pillow; her tired eyes flamed up instantly with sympathy and passionate mother-love when they fell upon her child, and she opened the refuge and shelter of her arms.

"Wait!" said Aunt Hannah, and put out her hand and stayed the girl from leaping into them.

"Helen," said the other aunt, impressively, "tell your mother all. Purge your soul; leave nothing unconfessed."

Standing stricken and forlorn before her judges, the young girl mourned her sorrowful tale through the end, then in a passion of appeal cried out:

"Oh, mother, can't you forgive me? won't you forgive me? —I am so desolate!"

"Forgive you, my darling? Oh, come to my arms! —there, lay your head upon my breast, and be at peace. If you had told a thousand lies—"

There was a sound—a warning—the clearing of a throat. The aunts glanced up, and withered in their clothes—there stood the doctor, his face a thunder-cloud. Mother and child knew nothing of his presence; they lay locked together, heart to heart, steeped in immeasurable content, dead to all things else. The physician stood many moments glaring and glooming upon the scene before him; studying it, analyzing it, searching out its genesis; then he put up his hand and beckoned to the aunts.

三

刚才提到的三位站在床边，姑妈们表情严厉，犯规者轻声啜泣着。母亲枕着枕头转过头来，当目光落在孩子身上时，疲惫的眼神立即燃起了同情与强烈的母爱，她伸出双臂，向女孩敞开了避难所。

“等等！”汉娜姑妈说道，她伸出一只手，阻止女孩扑进母亲的怀抱。

“海伦，”另一个姑妈严厉地说，“告诉你妈妈一切，净化你的灵魂，毫无保留地承认一切！”

女孩愁眉苦脸地、孤零零地站在审判者面前，悲哀地把这个伤心的故事从头到尾讲述了一遍，接着放声大哭，哀求道：

“啊，妈妈，你不能原谅我吗？你不会原谅我吗？——我真的好难过！”

“原谅你，我的宝贝？啊，到我怀里来吧！——好啦，把头靠在我胸口，放心吧，就算你说了一千个谎——”

有一个声音响起——一声警告——清嗓子的声音。姑妈们抬头一看，头便缩进衣服里去了——医生站在那儿，脸上阴云密布。母亲和孩子丝毫没有觉察他的到来，她们牢牢地靠在一起，心贴着心，沉浸在无限的满足中，对周围的一切浑然不觉。医生站了很久，阴着脸盯着眼前的情景，研究它、分析它、查出了它的原因，接着他举起手，向姑妈们打了个手势。她们哆哆嗦嗦地走向他，恭顺地站在他面前，等待着。他弯下腰低声说：

They came trembling to him, and stood humbly before him and waited. He bent down and whispered:

"Didn't I tell you this patient must be protected from all excitement? What the hell have you been doing? Clear out of the place!"

They obeyed. Half an hour later he appeared in the parlor, serene, cheery, clothed in sunshine, conducting Helen, with his arm about her waist, petting her, and saying gentle and playful things to her; and she also was her sunny and happy self again.

"Now, then," he said, "good-by, dear. Go to your room, and keep away from your mother, and behave yourself. But wait—put out your tongue. There, that will do—you're as sound as a nut!" He patted her cheek and added, "Run along now; I want to talk to these aunts."

She went from the presence. His face clouded over again at once; and as he sat down he said:

"You two have been doing a lot of damage—and maybe some good. Some good, yes—such as it is. That woman's disease is typhoid! You've brought it to a show-up, I think, with your insanities, and that's a service—such as it is. I hadn't been able to determine what it was before."

With one impulse the old ladies sprang to their feet, quaking with terror.

"Sit down! What are you proposing to do?"

"Do? We must fly to her. We—"

"You'll do nothing of the kind; you've done enough harm for one day. Do you want to squander all your capital of crimes

“我不是告诉过你们，病人绝对不能受到任何刺激吗？你们究竟在干什么？都出去！”

她们顺从地离开了。半小时后他出现在客厅里，平和、愉悦、笼罩在阳光里，他手揽着海伦的腰，带她走了过来，爱抚着她，对她讲些轻松、有趣的事，她也变回从前那个阳光快乐的海伦了。

“那么，”他说，“再见，亲爱的，到你房间去，不要去找你妈妈，做个乖孩子。但是等一下——伸出你的舌头。噢，这样就可以了——你像坚果一样强壮！”他拍了拍她的脸颊，又加了句：“现在回去吧，我想和姑妈们谈一谈。”

她离开了。医生的脸马上又阴沉下来，他坐下来说：

“你们俩造成了很大的破坏——或许有点好处。有点好处，是的——虽然只是帮了这点忙。那个女人得的是伤寒[①]！我想，由于你们疯狂的举动，使它显现出来了，这就是帮的忙——虽然不是什么大忙。以前我无法确定它是什么病。”

两位姑妈冲动地跳起来，恐惧得发抖。

“坐下！你们打算干什么？”

“干什么？我们必须飞到她身边。我们——”

“你们绝对不能那样做，今天你们已经坏了不少事。你们想把

① 伤寒：伤寒杆菌 (Salmonella typhi) 造成之伤寒病，常称“伤寒热”(typhoid fever)，传染性很强。今天，伤寒可用抗生素治愈。

and follies on a single deal? Sit down, I tell you. I have arranged for her to sleep; she needs it; if you disturb her without my orders, I'll brain you—if you've got the materials for it."

They sat down, distressed and indignant, but obedient, under compulsion. He proceeded:

"Now, then, I want this case explained. They wanted to explain it to me—as if there hadn't been emotion or excitement enough already. You knew my orders; how did you dare to go in there and get up that riot?"

Hester looked appealing at Hannah; Hannah returned a beseeching look at Hester—neither wanted to dance to this unsympathetic orchestra. The doctor came to their help. He said:

"Begin, Hester."

Fingering at the fringes of her shawl, and with lowered eyes, Hester said, timidly:

"We should not have disobeyed for any ordinary cause, but this was vital. This was a duty. With a duty one has no choice; one must put all lighter considerations aside and perform it. We were obliged to arraign her before her mother. She had told a lie."

The doctor glowered upon the woman a moment, and seemed to be trying to work up in his mind an understanding of a wholly incomprehensible proposition; then he stormed out:

"She told a lie! Did she? God bless my soul! I tell a million a day! And so does every doctor. And so does everybody—including you—for that matter. And that was the important thing that authorized you to venture to disobey my orders and imperil that woman's life! Look here, Hester Gray, this is pure lunacy;

自己所有的罪恶和愚蠢的资本一次就挥霍完吗？坐下，我告诉你们，我已经安排她睡下了，她需要睡眠。如果你们没有我的命令去打扰她，我会敲破你们的脑袋——如果你们脑子里有材料的话。”

她们坐了下来，既苦恼又气愤，但是被迫乖乖地坐下，他接着说道：

“好了，我想听听对这件事的解释。这些迹象想要向我表明——好像激动和兴奋还不够多似的。你们知道我的命令，怎么还敢去那儿引起一场骚乱？”

海丝特求助地望了汉娜一眼，汉娜又哀求地回望了海丝特一眼——两人都不想跟着这个没有同情心的乐队跳舞。医生帮了她们的忙，说：

“你先说，海丝特。”

海丝特手指拨弄着披肩的流苏，眼睛向下看着，怯怯地说：

“一般情况下我们是不会违反命令的，但这次是至关重要的。这是天职，在天职面前人们别无选择，必须把无足轻重的顾虑放在一边，去完成天职。我们不得不在她母亲面前提审她。她撒谎了。”

医生瞪眼怒视了她一会儿，好像要努力理解一件根本不可理喻的事情，接着便暴跳如雷：

“她撒谎了！是吗？上帝保佑我的灵魂！我一天撒一百万个谎！每个医生都这样做。每个人——包括你们——也都这样做。而那就是使你们胆敢违反我的命令，将那位妇人的生命置于危险境地的重要事情！听着，海丝特·格雷，这纯粹是疯狂愚蠢的行为，那女孩不可能去撒谎有意伤害别人。这是不可能的——绝对不可能。

that girl couldn't tell a lie that was intended to injure a person. The thing is impossible—absolutely impossible. You know it yourselves—both of you; you know it perfectly well."

Hannah came to her sister's rescue:

"Hester didn't mean that it was that kind of a lie, and it wasn't. But it was a lie."

"Well, upon my word, I never heard such nonsense! Haven't you got sense enough to discriminate between lies! Don't you know the difference between a lie that helps and a lie that hurts?"

"All lies are sinful," said Hannah, setting her lips together like a vise; "all lies are forbidden."

The Only Christian fidgeted impatiently in his chair. He went to attack this proposition, but he did not quite know how or where to begin. Finally he made a venture:

"Hester, wouldn't you tell a lie to shield a person from an undeserved injury or shame?"

"No."

"Not even a friend?"

"No."

"Not even your dearest friend?"

"No. I would not."

The doctor struggled in silence awhile with this situation; then he asked:

"Not even to save him from bitter pain and misery and grief?"

"No. Not even to save his life."

你们自己明白这一点——你们俩都知道，你们对这一点很清楚。”

汉娜来给她妹妹解围：

“海丝特的意思不是说它是那种谎言，它不是。但它是一个谎言。”

“啊，说真的，我从未听过这种蠢话！难道你们没有足够的理智去区别谎言吗？难道你们不知道一个帮人的谎言和一个害人的谎言的区别吗？”

“所有的谎言都是有罪的，”汉娜说，两片嘴唇像铁钳一样合在一起，“所有的谎言都是被禁止的。”

“唯一的基督徒”在椅子里烦躁不安地动弹。他想攻击这一主张，却又不是很清楚怎样或从哪儿开始。最终他做了一下尝试：

“海丝特，为了保护一个人免受不应有的伤害或耻辱，你会不会撒谎？”

“不会。”

“即使为了朋友也不会？”

“是的。”

“即使是你最挚爱的朋友也不会？”

“是的，我不会。”

医生沉默了片刻，考虑着如何应付目前的形势，他接着问：

“甚至是为了保护他不受到剧烈的伤痛、不幸和悲伤也不会？”

“是的，甚至为了挽救他的生命也不会。”

Another pause. Then:

"Nor his soul?"

There was a hush—a silence which endured a measurable interval—then Hester answered, in a low voice, but with decision:

"Nor his soul?"

No one spoke for a while; then the doctor said:

"Is it with you the same, Hannah?"

"Yes," she answered.

"I ask you both—why?"

"Because to tell such a lie, or any lie, is a sin, and could cost us the loss of our own souls—would, indeed, if we died without time to repent."

"Strange ... strange ... it is past belief." Then he asked, roughly: "Is such a soul as that worth saving?" He rose up, mumbling and grumbling, and started for the door, stumping vigorously along. At the threshold he turned and rasped out an admonition: "Reform! Drop this mean and sordid and selfish devotion to the saving of your shabby little souls, and hunt up something to do that's got some dignity to it! Risk your souls! risk them in good causes; then if you lose them, why should you care? Reform!"

The good old gentlewomen sat paralyzed, pulverized, outraged, insulted, and brooded in bitterness and indignation over these blasphemies. They were hurt to the heart, poor old ladies, and said they could never forgive these injuries.

"Reform!"

又一阵沉默，他接着问：

"他的灵魂也不救吗？"

房间里一片寂静——在沉默了不久后——海丝特低声却坚决地回答：

"他的灵魂也不救。"

好长时间没有人说话，然后医生说：

"你也一样吗，汉娜？"

"是的。"她回答道。

"我问你们俩——为什么？"

"因为撒这样一个谎，或是撒任何一个谎，都是有罪的，都会使我们失去自己的灵魂——如果我们没来得及忏悔[1]就死的话，真会的。"

"奇怪……奇怪……这是过时的观念。"接着他粗鲁地问，"这样一个灵魂值得拯救吗？"他站了起来，迈着沉重有力的步子，朝门走去，嘴里含糊不清地抱怨着。走到门槛前他转过身，厉声发出一声告诫："改造吧！不要再热衷于拯救你们那肮脏渺小的灵魂，丢掉那些卑鄙、龌龊、自私的想法吧。去找一些有尊严的事情做吧！让你们的灵魂冒一次险！让它们为了做好事而冒险，那么即使失去它们，又有什么好在意的呢？改造吧！"

两位好心的老妇人瘫坐在那里，一败涂地，怒气冲冲，感觉受到了侮辱。她们痛苦不堪而又愤愤不平地思忖着这些渎神的话。可怜的老妇人，她们伤透了心，说永远都不会原谅这些伤害。

"改造吧！"

① 忏悔，《圣经》约翰一书1章9节说："我们若认自己的罪，神是信实的，是公义的，必要赦免我们的罪，洗净我们一切的不义。"但姑妈们担心死时若没时间忏悔会下地狱，所以无论如何也不撒谎。

They kept repeating that word resentfully. "Reform—and learn to tell lies!"

Time slipped along, and in due course a change came over their spirits. They had completed the human being's first duty—which is to think about himself until he has exhausted the subject, then he is in a condition to take up minor interests and think of other people. This changes the complexion of his spirits—generally wholesomely. The minds of the two old ladies reverted to their beloved niece and the fearful disease which had smitten her; instantly they forgot the hurts their self-love had received, and a passionate desire rose in their hearts to go to the help of the sufferer and comfort her with their love, and minister to her, and labor for her the best they could with their weak hands, and joyfully and affectionately wear out their poor old bodies in her dear service if only they might have the privilege.

"And we shall have it!" said Hester, with the tears running down her face. "There are no nurses comparable to us, for there are no others that will stand their watch by that bed till they drop and die, and God knows we would do that."

"Amen," said Hannah, smiling approval and endorsement through the mist of moisture that blurred her glasses. "The doctor knows us, and knows we will not disobey again; and he will call no others. He will not dare!"

"Dare?" said Hester, with temper, and dashing the water from her eyes; "he will dare anything—that Christian devil! But it will do no good for him to try it this time—but, laws! Hannah! after all's said and done, he is gifted and wise and good, and

她们气愤地重复这个词："改造吧——然后学会撒谎！"

时间悄悄地溜走，这时她们的思想发生了变化。她们已经完成了人类的第一项职责——那就是先反省一下自己，直到把这个问题研究透彻，接着才能拾起次要的事情，并想到别人。这会改变他的精神状态——通常是完全改变。两位老妇人的心思转到了她们心爱的侄女和折磨她的可怕病魔上；顷刻之间，她们忘了自怜自爱时所受到的伤害，心中升起一个强烈的愿望——去帮助那个病人，用她们的爱去安慰她，照顾她，用这双虚弱的手尽其所能地为她劳作，只要她们有幸能为她效劳，就会高兴地、爱怜地为她而拖垮这把可怜的老骨头。

"我们会有这项荣幸的！"海丝特泪流满面地说，"没有哪个护士能比得上我们，因为没有人会一直站在床边看护，直到病人倒下死去为止，上帝知道我们能做到。"

"阿门！"透过被雾水弄花了的眼镜片，汉娜微笑着表示赞同和支持，"医生了解我们，知道我们不会再违背命令。他不会再叫别人来。他不敢！"

"他不敢？"海丝特气冲冲地说，眼中又涌出了泪水，"他什么都敢做——那个恶魔般的基督徒！但是这次他要试图这样做的话，对他可没好处——但是，天哪！汉娜！不管他说了什么，做了什么，他还是那么有天赋、聪明、善良，所以他不会去想这样一件事……现

he would not think of such a thing. . . . It is surely time for one of us to go to that room. What is keeping him? Why doesn't he come and say so?"

They caught the sound of his approaching step. He entered, sat down, and began to talk.

"Margaret is a sick woman," he said. "She is still sleeping, but she will wake presently; then one of you must go to her. She will be worse before she is better. Pretty soon a night-and-day watch must be set. How much of it can you two undertake?"

"All of it!" burst from both ladies at once.

The doctor's eyes flashed, and he said, with energy:

"You do ring true, you brave old relics! And you shall do all of the nursing you can, for there's none to match you in that divine office in this town; but you can't do all of it, and it would be a crime to let you." It was grand praise, golden praise, coming from such a source, and it took nearly all the resentment out of the aged twin's hearts. "Your Tilly and my old Nancy shall do the rest—good nurses both, white souls with black skins, watchful, loving, tender—just perfect nurses! —and competent liars from the cradle. ... Look you! keep a little watch on Helen; she is sick, and is going to be sicker."

The ladies looked a little surprised, and not credulous; and Hester said: "How is that? It isn't an hour since you said she was as sound as a nut."

The doctor answered, tranquilly:

在该我们中的一个去病房了。他在忙什么？为什么不来叫我们过去？”

她们听到了他走近的脚步声。他走进来坐下，开口说话。

“玛格丽特已经病倒了，”他说，“她还在睡觉，不过马上就会醒过来，那时你们中的一位就要到她那边去。她的病在好转前只会变得更严重。很快就必须日夜看护。你们俩能承担多少任务？”

“所有看护！”两位老妇人马上喊道。

医生眼睛一亮，带劲地说：

“你们听起来的确说对了，勇敢的老古董们！你们可以尽你们所能，因为镇上的医院里没人能比得上你们俩，但是你们不能负责所有的看护，让你们这样做那就是犯罪。”从这个人嘴里说出这样的话，就是一场盛赞，无比荣耀的称赞，它几乎使这对年老双胞胎心里的怨恨一扫而空。“你们家的蒂莉和我家的老南希将会负责其余的事情——两人都是很好的护士，黑色的皮肤里包着一颗洁白的心，机警、富有爱心、温柔——正是完美的护士！——并且还在摇篮时便是撒谎的能手……你们注意了！留神点海伦，她生病了，并且会病得更严重。”

女士们看起来有点惊讶，不肯轻易相信它，海丝特问：“怎么会这样？一小时前，你不是还说她像坚果一样强壮吗？”

医生平静地[1]回答：

① 说明医生把撒谎当做是理所当然的。这在姑妈们看来简直不可理喻，所以下文中她们才会愤怒。

"It was a lie."

The ladies turned upon him indignantly, and Hannah said:

"How can you make an odious confession like that, in so indifferent a tone, when you know how we feel about all forms of—"

"Hush! You are as ignorant as cats, both of you, and you don't know what you are talking about. You are like all the rest of the moral moles; you lie from morning till night, but because you don't do it with your mouths, but only with your lying eyes, your lying inflections, your deceptively misplaced emphasis, and your misleading gestures, you turn up your complacent noses and parade before God and the world as saintly and unsmirched Truth-Speakers, in whose cold-storage souls a lie would freeze to death if it got there! Why will you humbug yourselves with that foolish notion that no lie is a lie except a spoken one? What is the difference between lying with your eyes and lying with your mouth? There is none; and if you would reflect a moment you would see that it is so. There isn't a human being that doesn't tell a gross of lies every day of his life; and you—why, between you, you tell thirty thousand; yet you flare up here in a lurid hypocritical horror because I tell that child a benevolent and sinless lie to protect her from her imagination, which would get to work and warm up her blood to a fever in an hour, if I were disloyal enough to my duty to let it. Which I should probably do if I were interested in saving my soul by such disreputable means."

"Come, let us reason together. Let us examine details.

"那是一个谎言。"

女士们愤怒地一齐朝他开火，汉娜说：

"你怎么就这么可恶地承认了，还以一种漫不经心的口气，你知道我们如何看待一切形式的——"

"安静！你们俩像猫一样无知，都不知道自己在说些什么。你们和其他讲道德的鼹鼠[1]一样，从早到晚地撒谎，只是你们不用嘴巴撒谎，只用你们的眼睛撒谎，在说话语调上撒谎，故意放错重点撒谎，用误导性的动作撒谎，你们沾沾自喜地鼻孔朝天，在上帝和世人面前大摇大摆地走过，自认为是一个神圣清白的真理发言人，以为在你们那颗冰冷的灵魂里，谎言到了那儿都会被冻死！为什么你们有这种自欺欺人的愚蠢想法，认为没有说出口的谎言便不是谎言？用眼睛撒谎和用嘴巴撒谎有什么区别？没有任何区别。你们想一下就会明白，就是这样。任何人在世的时候，每天都会撒大量的谎，还有你们——啊，你们俩会撒三千个不为人知的谎，然而在这儿你们却突然爆发出一阵假惺惺的恐惧，脸都吓白了，就因为我向那个孩子撒了个善意无害的谎，免得她胡思乱想，因为它马上就会起作用，让她的血液变热，一小时后就会发高烧。如果我对我的职责不够忠诚，我就会让这样的事情发生，如果我热衷于拯救我的灵魂，我很可能就这么不光彩地去做了。"

"来吧，让我们一起来讨论一下，检查一下细节。当你们在病房惹起那场骚乱时，假如你们知道我快到了，会怎样做？"

① 鼹鼠成年后，眼睛深陷在皮肤下面，视力完全退化。此处医生讽刺传统卫道士们像鼹鼠一样目光短浅。

When you two were in the sick-room raising that riot, what would you have done if you had known I was coming?"

"Well, what?"

"You would have slipped out and carried Helen with you—wouldn't you?"

The ladies were silent.

"What would be your object and intention?"

"Well, what?"

"To keep me from finding out your guilt; to beguile me to infer that Margaret's excitement proceeded from some cause not known to you. In a word, to tell me a lie—a silent lie. Moreover, a possibly harmful one."

The twins colored, but did not speak.

"You not only tell myriads of silent lies, but you tell lies with your mouths—you two."

"That is not so!"

"It is so. But only harmless ones. You never dream of uttering a harmful one. Do you know that that is a concession—and a confession?"

"How do you mean?"

"It is an unconscious concession that harmless lies are not criminal; it is a confession that you constantly make that discrimination. For instance, you declined old Mrs. Foster's invitation last week to meet those odious Higbies at supper—in a polite note in which you expressed regret and said you were very sorry you could not go. It was a lie. It was as unmitigated a lie as was ever uttered. Deny it, Hester—with another lie."

"嗯，怎样做？"

"你们会带着海伦悄悄溜走——对不对？"

女士们沉默了。

"你们的目的和意图是什么呢？"

"嗯，是什么？"

"不止我发现你们的罪过，诱骗我去推断玛格丽特的兴奋是由一些你们不知道的原因引起的。一句话，向我撒了个无声的谎。而且，可能还是个有害的谎。"

双胞胎们的脸红了，但是没有说话。

"你们不仅撒了无数个无声的谎，嘴上还说了很多谎话——你们俩。"

"不是那样的。"

"是这样的，但仅仅是无害的谎言。你们做梦都没想过撒有害的谎。你们知道那就是让步——和认可吗？"

"你是什么意思？"

"认为无害的谎言不是犯罪，是无意识的让步，一直做出有罪无罪的区分，那就是认可。例如，上周你们拒绝了年迈的福斯特夫人的邀请，不想在晚餐时去见那些可恶的海格比家人——用的是一封措辞礼貌的信，表达了你们的歉意，说你们很抱歉不能去。这是一个谎言。这是人们所能说出的最彻底的谎言。否认它吧，海丝特——用另外一个谎言。"

Hester replied with a toss of her head.

"That will not do. Answer. Was it a lie, or wasn't it?"

The color stole into the cheeks of both women, and with a struggle and an effort they got out their confession:

"It was a lie."

"Good—the reform is beginning; there is hope for you yet; you will not tell a lie to save your dearest friend's soul, but you will spew out one without a scruple to save yourself the discomfort of telling an unpleasant truth."

He rose. Hester, speaking for both, said, coldly:

"We have lied; we perceive it; it will occur no more. To lie is a sin. We shall never tell another one of any kind whatsoever, even lies of courtesy or benevolence, to save any one a pang or a sorrow decreed for him by God."

"Ah, how soon you will fall! In fact, you have fallen already; for what you have just uttered is a lie. Good-by. Reform! One of you go to the sick-room now."

4

Twelve days later.

Mother and child were lingering in the grip of the hideous disease. Of hope for either there was little. The aged sisters looked white and worn, but they would not give up their posts. Their hearts were breaking, poor old things, but their grit was steadfast and indestructible. All the twelve days the mother had pined for the child, and the child for the mother, but both

海丝特的回答是摇了一下头。

“这没用。回答问题。这是个谎言，还是不是？”

血色悄悄地爬上两位女士的脸颊，她们挣扎着努力了半天，最终承认了：

“这是个谎言。”

“很好。——改造已经开始了，你们还有希望，你们不会为了挽救最挚爱朋友的灵魂而撒谎，但为了不因说出令人不快的事实而难过，你们会毫不犹豫地撒谎。”

他站了起来，海丝特冷冷地替她俩辩解：

“我们撒过谎，已经觉察到了，这种事不会再发生了。撒谎是有罪的。无论如何我们都不会撒另外一个谎，不管它是什么样的，即使是礼节上所需，或善意的谎言——为了挽救一个人免遭上天注定的打击或痛苦。”

“啊，你们将会堕落得多快！事实上你们已经堕落了，因为你刚才说的就是一个谎言。再见，改造吧！你们中的一位现在要去病房。”

四

十二天后。

母亲和孩子在可怕疾病的掌控下苟延残喘。两个人的希望都很渺茫。年老的姐妹看起来脸色苍白、疲惫不堪，但她们不会放弃她们的职责。可怜的老东西，她们的心都碎了，但她们的勇气是坚不可摧的。十二天来，母亲一直渴望见到孩子，孩子也渴望见到母亲，但双方都知道，对这些渴望的祈求是不会得到批准的。当母亲被告知——在第一天——她得的是伤寒时，就很害怕，问海伦是否

knew that the prayer of these longings could not be granted. When the mother was told—on the first day—that her disease was typhoid, she was frightened, and asked if there was danger that Helen could have contracted it the day before, when she was in the sick-chamber on that confession visit. Hester told her the doctor had poo-pooed the idea. It troubled Hester to say it, although it was true, for she had not believed the doctor; but when she saw the mother's joy in the news, the pain in her conscience lost something of its force—a result which made her ashamed of the constructive deception which she had practised, though not ashamed enough to make her distinctly and definitely wish she had refrained from it. From that moment the sick woman understood that her daughter must remain away, and she said she would reconcile herself to the separation the best she could, for she would rather suffer death than have her child's health imperiled. That afternoon Helen had to take to her bed, ill. She grew worse during the night. In the morning her mother asked after her:

"Is she well?"

Hester turned cold; she opened her lips, but the words refused to come. The mother lay languidly looking, musing, waiting; suddenly she turned white and gasped out:

"Oh, my God! what is it? is she sick?"

Then the poor aunt's tortured heart rose in rebellion, and words came:

"No—be comforted; she is well."

The sick woman put all her happy heart in her gratitude:

有感染上它的危险，因为前天她来过病房坦白过错。海丝特告诉她医生已经否定了这个想法。这样说让海丝特感到苦恼，因为她不相信医生，尽管这是真的。但当她看到母亲听到消息后的喜悦时，良心上的不安稍微减轻——她为练习撒这个建设性的谎言感到羞耻，尽管她没有明确地希望阻止这个谎言，但对此并不感到非常羞愧。从那时起，生病的妇人就明白必须让女儿远离她，她说她会尽力调整好自己，适应分离的状况，因为她宁愿死去也不愿孩子的健康受到损害。那天下午海伦病了，不得不躺在床上。到了夜里病情越发严重。早上母亲问起孩子的情况：

“她身体还好吗？”

海丝特浑身发冷，她张开了嘴，但却说不出话来。母亲虚弱地躺在床上，看着她，默想着，等待着，忽然她脸色变白，喘息着说：

“噢，天哪！怎么回事？她生病了吗？”

这时可怜的姑妈那颗备受折磨的心开始造反了，并说出了这样的话：

“没有——放心吧，她很健康。”

生病的妇人满心欢喜，非常感激：

"Thank God for those dear words! Kiss me. How I worship you for saying them!"

Hester told this incident to Hannah, who received it with a rebuking look, and said, coldly:

"Sister, it was a lie."

Hester's lips trembled piteously; she choked down a sob, and said:

"Oh, Hannah, it was a sin, but I could not help it. I could not endure the fright and the misery that were in her face."

"No matter. It was a lie. God will hold you to account for it."

"Oh, I know it, I know it," cried Hester, wringing her hands, "but even if it were now, I could not help it. I know I should do it again."

"Then take my place with Helen in the morning. I will make the report myself."

Hester clung to her sister, begging and imploring.

"Don't, Hannah, oh, don't—you will kill her."

"I will at least speak the truth."

In the morning she had a cruel report to bear to the mother, and she braced herself for the trial. When she returned from her mission, Hester was waiting, pale and trembling, in the hall. She whispered:

"Oh, how did she take it—that poor, desolate mother?"

Hannah's eyes were swimming in tears. She said:

"God forgive me, I told her the child was well!"

Hester gathered her to her heart, with a grateful "God bless you, Hannah!" and poured out her thankfulness in an inundation

"感谢上帝让我听到这句宝贵的话！亲亲我吧，因为你说这些话，我多么崇拜你啊！"

海丝特把这件事告诉了汉娜，后者却露出责备的神情看着她，冷冷地说：

"妹妹，这是撒谎。"

海丝特的嘴唇可怜地颤抖着，抽噎了一下，说：

"啊，汉娜，这是有罪的，但我没办法不那样做，我受不了她脸上恐惧和痛苦的表情。"

"没用的。这是一个谎言，上帝会逮住你，让你对它作出解释。"

"噢，我知道，我知道，"海丝特绞着双手，哭着说，"即使是现在，我也没办法。我知道我还会这样做的。"

"那么明天早上你替我照顾海伦。我会亲自去汇报。"

海丝特拉着她姐姐，苦苦哀求：

"不要，汉娜，啊，不要——你会杀了她的。"

"至少我会说真话。"

早上她带着一个残忍的报告前往母亲那里，并支撑着她自己接受这场试炼。当她完成使命返回时，海丝特正在大厅里等她，脸色苍白、颤抖着，轻声问：

"啊，她反应怎样——那个可怜的、孤独的母亲？"

汉娜眼里饱含着泪水，说：

"上帝宽恕我，我告诉她孩子很健康！"

海丝特一把抱住她，感激地说了声"上帝保佑你，汉娜！"然后洪水泛滥般的崇拜赞美之词倾泻而出，以表她的感激之情。

of worshiping praises.

After that, the two knew the limit of their strength, and accepted their fate. They surrendered humbly, and abandoned themselves to the hard requirements of the situation. Daily they told the morning lie, and confessed their sin in prayer; not asking forgiveness, as not being worthy of it, but only wishing to make record that they realized their wickedness and were not desiring to hide it or excuse it.

Daily, as the fair young idol of the house sank lower and lower, the sorrowful old aunts painted her glowing bloom and her fresh young beauty to the wan mother, and winced under the stabs her ecstasies of joy and gratitude gave them.

In the first days, while the child had strength to hold a pencil, she wrote fond little love-notes to her mother, in which she concealed her illness; and these the mother read and reread through happy eyes wet with thankful tears, and kissed them over and over again, and treasured them as precious things under her pillow.

Then came a day when the strength was gone from the hand, and the mind wandered, and the tongue babbled pathetic incoherences. this was a sore dilemma for the poor aunts. There were no love-notes for the mother. They did not know what to do. Hester began a carefully studied and plausible explanation, but lost the track of it and grew confused; suspicion began to show in the mother's face, then alarm. Hester saw it, recognized the imminence of the danger, and descended to the emergency, pulling herself resolutely together and plucking victory from the

自那之后，两人知道了她们的力量有限，只好认命了。她们谦恭地缴械投降了，服从形势的苛刻要求。她们每天早晨说谎，然后就在祷告中坦白她们的罪过，并不是请求宽恕，因为这根本就不值得宽恕，只是希望记下她们知道了自己的罪恶，并没有想藏起它或为它找借口。

每天，家里美丽宠儿的病情每况愈下，悲伤的老姑妈们则向生病的母亲描述她如何容光焕发，如何年轻漂亮、充满活力，然后就在她的狂喜和对她们的感激下，心如刀割，抽搐不已。

开始那些天，当孩子还有力气握住铅笔时，她写给母亲一些深情的爱的短笺，信里隐瞒了自己的病情，母亲幸福的眼里饱含感激的泪水，她一遍遍地读，一次次地亲吻短笺，然后把它们当作宝贝收藏在枕头下面。

然后有一天，她手上的力气消失了，精神变得恍惚，嘴里可悲地说出一些模糊不清、语无伦次的话。可怜的姑妈们被痛苦地困住了，进退两难。没有爱的短笺送给母亲，她们不知道该怎么办。海丝特开始做一个精心计划好的、貌似有理的解释，但不知道说到哪儿去了，越讲越乱。母亲脸上出现了先是怀疑、然后警觉的神色。海丝特看在眼里，意识到危险的迫近，立即采取紧急措施，她果断地振作起来，从张开着的失败的嘴巴里摘取胜利的果实，以一种沉着的、令人信服的口气说：

open jaws of defeat. In a placid and convincing voice she said:

"I thought it might distress you to know it, but Helen spent the night at the Sloanes'. There was a little party there, and, although she did not want to go, and you so sick, we persuaded her, she being young and needing the innocent pastimes of youth, and we believing you would approve. Be sure she will write the moment she comes."

"How good you are, and how dear and thoughtful for us both! Approve? Why, I thank you with all my heart. My poor little exile! Tell her I want her to have every pleasure she can—I would not rob her of one. Only let her keep her health, that is all I ask. Don't let that suffer; I could not bear it. How thankful I am that she escaped this infection—and what a narrow risk she ran, Aunt Hester! Think of that lovely face all dulled and burned with fever. I can't bear the thought of it. Keep her health. Keep her bloom! I can see her now, the dainty creature—with the big, blue, earnest eyes; and sweet, oh, so sweet and gentle and winning! Is she as beautiful as ever, dear Aunt Hester?"

"Oh, more beautiful and bright and charming than ever she was before, if such a thing can be" —and Hester turned away and fumbled with the medicine-bottles, to hide her shame and grief.

5

After a little, both aunts were laboring upon a difficult and baffling work in Helen's chamber. Patiently and earnestly, with

“我想你知道的话会伤心，但是海伦昨晚待在斯隆家。那儿有一个小型聚会。尽管她不想去，况且你又生着病，但我们还是说服了她，她还年轻，需要年轻人那种无害的娱乐，并且我们认为你会同意。她肯定一回来就会写信的。”

“你们真是太好了，对我们俩多么疼爱、多么考虑周到！同意？啊，我衷心地感谢你们。我那可怜的小流浪儿！告诉她，我希望她拥有所能得到的一切快乐——我不会从她那儿掠走一个。只要她保持健康，这就是我全部的要求。不要让她的健康受损，我受不了。我多么庆幸她躲过了感染——真是太险了，海丝特姑妈！想一想那张可爱的脸没精打采，发着滚烫的高烧。我想想就受不了。让她保持健康，保持容光焕发！我现在能看到她了，那个美丽的可人儿——有着一双大大的、蓝蓝的、真诚的眼睛，并且甜甜的，噢，那么甜美、温柔、讨人喜欢！她还像以前那么漂亮吗，亲爱的海丝特姑妈？”

“哦，比以前更漂亮、开朗、充满魅力，没有哪个孩子像她那样美丽。”——海丝特把脸转过去，摆弄着药瓶，以便掩盖她的羞愧和悲伤。

五

不久之后，在海伦的房间里，两位姑妈费力地做起一项既困难重重又令人困惑的工作。她们用关节僵硬的老手指，耐心、认真地

their stiff old fingers, they were trying to forge the required note. They made failure after failure, but they improved little by little all the time. The pity of it all, the pathetic humor of it, there was none to see; they themselves were unconscious of it. Often their tears fell upon the notes and spoiled them; sometimes a single misformed word made a note risky which could have been ventured but for that; but at last Hannah produced one whose script was a good enough imitation of Helen's to pass any but a suspicious eye, and bountifully enriched it with the petting phrases and loving nicknames that had been familiar on the child's lips from her nursery days. She carried it to the mother, who took it with avidity, and kissed it, and fondled it, reading its precious words over and over again, and dwelling with deep contentment upon its closing paragraph:

"Mousie darling, if I could only see you, and kiss your eyes, and feel your arms about me! I am so glad my practicing does not disturb you. Get well soon. Everybody is good to me, but I am so lonesome without you, dear mamma."

"The poor child, I know just how she feels. She cannot be quite happy without me; and I—oh, I live in the light of her eyes! Tell her she must practice all she pleases; and, Aunt Hannah—tell her I can't hear the piano this far, nor her dear voice when she sings: God knows I wish I could. No one knows how sweet that voice is to me; and to think—some day it will be silent! What are you crying for?"

"Only because—because—it was just a memory. When I came away she was singing, 'Loch Lomond.' The pathos of it!

试图伪造一封短信。她们经历了一次又一次的失败，但总是一点一点地逐步改进。这令人同情的一切、其中可悲的滑稽之处，并没有人看见，她们自己对此也浑然不觉。经常有几滴眼泪落在信上，便毁了它。有时一个字写得不像，就使本来可以试着呈上去的信有风险。但是汉娜最终伪造了一封信，模仿得极像海伦的笔迹，只要看信的人不起疑心就可以蒙混过关。信中用孩子幼时常挂在嘴边的昵称和爱称，极大地丰富了信的内容。她把信送给母亲，母亲急切地拿过去，又是亲吻，又是抚弄，一遍又一遍地读那些珍贵的话语，结尾那段使她长久地沉浸在深深的满足之中：

“亲爱的小老鼠，如果我能看到你，亲吻你的眼睛，让你的双臂搂着我，那该多好啊！我很高兴我的练习没有打扰你。快点好起来吧。每个人对我都很好。但是没有你，亲爱的妈妈，我感到好孤独。”

“可怜的孩子，我了解她的感受。没有我她不会很开心，而我——啊，我就生活在她那明亮的双眸里！告诉她，她必须练习她喜欢的一切东西，还有，汉娜姑妈——告诉她隔了这么远我听不到钢琴声，也听不到她唱歌时那美妙的歌声，上帝知道我多么希望能听到。没有人知道，那声音对我来说是多么甜美，并且想想——有一天它会寂静下来！你为什么哭了？”

“只是因为——因为——想起了刚才的事。我过来时她正在唱

It always moves me so when she sings that."

"And me, too. How heartbreakingly beautiful it is when some youthful sorrow is brooding in her breast and she sings it for the mystic healing it brings. ... Aunt Hannah?"

"Dear Margaret?"

"I am very ill. Sometimes it comes over me that I shall never hear that dear voice again."

"Oh, don't—don't, Margaret! I can't bear it!"

Margaret was moved and distressed, and said, gently:

"There—there—let me put my arms around you. Don't cry. There—put your cheek to mine. Be comforted. I wish to live. I will live if I can. Ah, what could she do without me! ... Does she often speak of me? —but I know she does."

"Oh, all the time—all the time!"

"My sweet child! She wrote the note the moment she came home?"

"Yes—the first moment. She would not wait to take off her things."

"I knew it. It is her dear, impulsive, affectionate way. I knew it without asking, but I wanted to hear you say it. The petted wife knows she is loved, but she makes her husband tell her so every day, just for the joy of hearing it. ... She used the pen this time. That is better; the pencil-marks could rub out, and I should grieve for that. Did you suggest that she use the pen?"

"Y—no—she—it was her own idea."

The mother looked her pleasure, and said:

‘洛蒙德湖’[①]，每当她唱起它时，里面的哀婉之情总让我感动！”

“我也一样。当一些年轻人的忧伤在她胸中酝酿时，当她歌唱带来神奇疗效时，总是美好得令人心碎……汉娜姑妈？”

“亲爱的玛格丽特？”

“我病得很重。有时我会想，可能再也听不到那可爱的声音了。”

“啊，不要——不要，玛格丽特！这让我受不了！”

玛格丽特被感动了，感到伤心，温和地说：

“好啦——好啦——让我用胳膊搂住你。不要哭。好啦——把你的脸颊贴在我脸上，不要伤心。我希望活着，如果能够的话我会活下去。啊，没了我她该怎么办！……她经常提起我吗？——但是我知道她会的。”

“哦，总是——总是在提你！”

“我那可爱的孩子！她一到家就写信了吗？”

“是的——一到家就写，都来不及放下东西。”

“我知道的。这就是她可爱、冲动、充满爱意的方式。即使不问我也知道，但我想听你这样说。被宠的妻子知道她是被爱着的，但是让丈夫每天都这样告诉她，只是因为听着开心……这次她是用钢笔写的。这样更好，铅笔字有时会被擦掉，我会为此感到痛苦。是你建议她用钢笔写的吗？”

“是——不是——她——这是她自己的主意。”

母亲看起来很高兴，说：

① 洛蒙德湖是苏格兰的第二长湖。《洛蒙德湖》是古代一位骑士在洛蒙德湖边送给他爱人的情歌。

"I was hoping you would say that. There was never such a dear and thoughtful child! ... Aunt Hannah?"

"Dear Margaret?"

"Go and tell her I think of her all the time, and worship her. Why—you are crying again. Don't be so worried about me, dear; I think there is nothing to fear, yet."

The grieving messenger carried her message, and piously delivered it to unheeding ears. The girl babbled on unaware; looking up at her with wondering and startled eyes flaming with fever, eyes in which was no light of recognition:

"Are you—no, you are not my mother. I want her—oh, I want her! She was here a minute ago—I did not see her go. Will she come? will she come quickly? will she come now? ... There are so many houses ... and they oppress me so ... and everything whirls and turns and whirls ... oh, my head, my head!" —and so she wandered on and on, in her pain, flitting from one torturing fancy to another, and tossing her arms about in a weary and ceaseless persecution of unrest.

Poor old Hannah wetted the parched lips and softly stroked the hot brow, murmuring endearing and pitying words, and thanking the Father of all that the mother was happy and did not know.

6

Daily the child sank lower and steadily lower towards the grave, and daily the sorrowing old watchers carried gilded

"我正希望你这样说，从来没有像她那样可爱、细心的孩子！……汉娜姑妈？"

"亲爱的玛格丽特？"

"去告诉她我一直在想念她、深爱着她。怎么——你又哭了。亲爱的，不要为我太担心，我想现在没有什么好害怕的。"

悲哀的信使带来了消息，虔诚地把它传到听不到的耳朵里去。女孩无意识地说着模糊不清的话，眼睛因发高烧变得通红，朝上看着她，既疑惑又害怕，她已经认不出人了：

"你是不——不，你不是我妈妈。我需要她——啊，我需要她！她刚才还在这儿——我没看见她走开。她会来吗？她很快就来吗？她现在就来吗？……好多的房子……它们就这样朝我压来……每件东西都在转，转来转去，转个不停……啊，我的头，我的头！"——就这样，在痛苦中，她不停地胡言乱语，眼前掠过一个个痛苦的幻影，无休止的压迫让她焦躁不安，双臂无力地四处乱挥着。

可怜的汉娜姑妈润湿了一下她那干燥的嘴唇，轻抚着女孩滚烫的额头，喃喃地说着一些钟爱、怜悯的话，感谢天父母亲很快乐，并不知晓实情。

六

孩子的病情日渐恶化，朝坟墓迫近，每天，悲伤的老看护们把镀过金的消息送给快乐的母亲，说她非常健康、容光焕发、甜美可

tidings of her radiant health and loveliness to the happy mother, whose pilgrimage was also now nearing its end. And daily they forged loving and cheery notes in the child's hand, and stood by with remorseful consciences and bleeding hearts, and wept to see the grateful mother devour them and adore them and treasure them away as things beyond price, because of their sweet source, and sacred because her child's hand had touched them.

At last came that kindly friend who brings healing and peace to all. The lights were burning low. In the solemn hush which precedes the dawn vague figures flitted soundless along the dim hall and gathered silent and awed in Helen's chamber, and grouped themselves about her bed, for a warning had gone forth, and they knew. The dying girl lay with closed lids, and unconscious, the drapery upon her breast faintly rising and falling as her wasting life ebbed away. At intervals a sigh or a muffled sob broke upon the stillness. The same haunting thought was in all minds there: the pity of this death, the going out into the great darkness, and the mother not here to help and hearten and bless.

Helen stirred; her hands began to grope wistfully about as if they sought something—she had been blind some hours. The end was come; all knew it. With a great sob Hester gathered her to her breast, crying, "Oh, my child, my darling!" A rapturous light broke in the dying girl's face, for it was mercifully vouchsafed her to mistake those sheltering arms for another's; and she went to her rest murmuring, "Oh, mamma, I am so happy—I so longed for you—now I can die."

爱，而母亲的朝圣旅程现在也快走到尽头了。每天她们模仿孩子的笔迹伪造深情、欢快的短笺，然后怀着一颗忏悔和滴血的心站在一边，哭着看感激的母亲贪婪地读完，赞不绝口，然后把它们作为无价之宝珍藏起来，因为孩子的手触摸过它，这些信笺是甜美、神圣的源泉。

最终那位友好的朋友[①]为所有人愈合了伤痛，带来了平静。烛光低低地燃烧着。破晓前肃穆的寂静中，模糊的身影沿着昏暗的大厅无声地掠过，大家怀着敬畏之心，安静地聚集在海伦的房间里，围在她床边，因为事先被警告过，她们都知情。奄奄一息的女孩躺在那儿，双眼紧闭，毫无意识，盖在她胸口上的被单随着她那渐渐逝去的残余生命微弱地上下起伏。不时有叹息声或者低沉的呜咽打破寂静。每个人的脑海里都笼罩着这样的想法：死者好可怜，她即将进入无边的黑暗之中，而母亲却没在这儿帮助、鼓励、祝福孩子。

海伦动了一下，她的手开始渴望地到处摸索着，好像在寻找什么——她已经失明好几个小时了。最后的时刻到来了，大家都知道。海丝特深深地抽噎了一下，把她抱在怀里，哭喊着："啊，我的孩子，我的心肝宝贝！"一阵狂喜的神色绽放在垂死女孩的脸上，因为对于这个慈悲的恩赐，她误以为这保护的双臂来自另一个人，她继续最后的喃喃之语："啊，妈妈，我好高兴——我好想你——现在我可以死了。"

① 此处指死神。

Two hours later Hester made her report. The mother asked:

"How is it with the child?"

"She is well."

7

A sheaf of white crape and black was hung upon the door of the house, and there it swayed and rustled in the wind and whispered its tidings. At noon the preparation of the dead was finished, and in the coffin lay the fair young form, beautiful, and in the sweet face a great peace. Two mourners sat by it, grieving and worshipping—Hannah and the black woman Tilly. Hester came, and she was trembling, for a great trouble was upon her spirit. She said:

"She asks for a note."

Hannah's face blanched. She had not thought of this; it had seemed that that pathetic service was ended. But she realized now that that could not be. For a little while the two women stood looking into each other's face, with vacant eyes; then Hannah said:

"There is no way out of it—she must have it; she will suspect, else."

"And she would find out."

"Yes. It would break her heart." She looked at the dead face, and her eyes filled. "I will write it," she said.

Hester carried it. The closing line said:

"Darling Mousie, dear sweet mother, we shall soon be

两小时后，海丝特去汇报，母亲问：

"孩子怎么样？"

"她很好。"

七

一束黑白混合的纱布挂在屋子的门上，随风摇摆、沙沙作响，低声诉说着噩耗。中午时，对死者的善后事宜完成了，棺材里躺着年轻女孩那窈窕的身躯，她依然美丽，甜甜的脸非常平静。两个哀悼者——汉娜和黑妇人蒂莉，坐在旁边，悲伤地敬奉着死者。海丝特来了，她在发抖，有一个大麻烦正压在她心头，她说：

"她要看信。"

汉娜的脸变得煞白。她没有想到这一点，在她看来那项悲哀的服务已经结束了，但现在意识到这是不可能的。有那么一会儿，两位老妇人就站在那儿，目光茫然地望着彼此的脸，然后汉娜说：

"没办法——她必须得到信，否则她会起疑心的。"

"并且她会发现实情。"

"是的，这会让她心碎。"她看着死者的脸，眼中又盈满泪水。"我去写信。"她说。

海丝特把信拿过去，结尾那句写道：

"亲爱的小老鼠，最亲爱的妈妈，我们很快就会又在一起了。这

together again. Is not that good news? And it is true; they all say it is true."

The mother mourned, saying:

"Poor child, how will she bear it when she knows? I shall never see her again in life. It is hard, so hard. She does not suspect? You guard her from that?"

"She thinks you will soon be well."

"How good you are, and careful, dear Aunt Hester! None goes near her who could carry the infection?"

"It would be a crime."

"But you see her?"

"With a distance between—yes."

"That is so good. Others one could not trust; but you two guardian angels—steel is not so true as you. Others would be unfaithful; and many would deceive, and lie."

Hester's eyes fell, and her poor old lips trembled.

"Let me kiss you for her, Aunt Hester; and when I am gone, and the danger is past, place the kiss upon her dear lips some day, and say her mother sent it, and all her mother's broken heart is in it."

Within the hour, Hester, raining tears upon the dead face, performed her pathetic mission.

8

Another day dawned, and grew, and spread its sunshine in the earth. Aunt Hannah brought comforting news to the failing

不是好消息吗？这是真的，她们都说这是真的。”

母亲感到痛苦，说：

“可怜的孩子，她知道时怎么能受得了？我活着再也见不到她了。这很残忍，太残忍了。她没起疑心吗？你们没让她知道吗？”

“她认为你很快就会好起来。”

“你们太好了，太细心了，亲爱的海丝特姑妈！没有任何带传染病的人靠近她吧？”

“那简直就是犯罪。”

“但是你们会见她。”

“隔了很远——是的。”

“这太好了。别人靠不住，但是你们这两位守护天使——钢铁也没有你们那样真诚。别人可能会不忠，并且很多人会欺骗、撒谎。”

海丝特垂下眼，她那可怜的、衰老的嘴唇颤抖着。

“让我为她亲亲你，海丝特姑妈。等我死了，危险过去的时候，有一天把这个吻印在她可爱的嘴唇上，就说这是她妈妈给的，里面有她妈妈那颗破碎的心。”

不到一小时，海丝特对着死者的脸庞泪如雨下，完成了这个悲伤的使命。

八

又是一个黎明到来，天渐渐亮了，阳光普照大地。汉娜姑妈将令人欣慰的消息带给虚弱的母亲，还有一封快乐的短笺，上面又说：

mother, and a happy note, which said again, "We have but a little time to wait, darling mother, then we shall be together."

The deep note of a bell came moaning down the wind.

"Aunt Hannah, it is tolling. Some poor soul is at rest. As I shall be soon. You will not let her forget me?"

"Oh, God knows she never will!"

"Do not you hear strange noises, Aunt Hannah? It sounds like the shuffling of many feet."

"We hoped you would not hear it, dear. It is a little company gathering, for—for Helen's sake, poor little prisoner. There will be music—and she loves it so. We thought you would not mind."

"Mind? Oh no, no—oh, give her everything her dear heart can desire. How good you two are to her, and how good to me! God bless you both always!"

After a listening pause:

"How lovely! It is her organ. Is she playing it herself, do you think?" Faint and rich and inspiring the chords floating to her ears on the still air. "Yes, it is her touch, dear heart, I recognize it. They are singing. Why—it is a hymn! and the sacredest of all, the most touching, the most consoling. ... It seems to open the gates of paradise to me. ... If I could die now. ..."

Faint and far the words rose out of the stillness:

Nearer, my God, to Thee,
Nearer to Thee,

"我们只需要再等一小会儿，亲爱的妈妈，然后就可以在一起了。"

深沉的钟声从呻吟着的风中传来。

"汉娜姑妈，这是钟声，一个可怜的灵魂安息了。不久我也会的。你不会让她忘了我吧？"

"噢，上帝知道她永远都不会！"

"你有没有听到一些奇怪的声音，汉娜姑妈？听起来好像有许多忙乱的脚步声。"

"亲爱的，我们希望你不会听到。这是一个小聚会，为了——为了海伦的缘故。可怜的小囚徒。还会有音乐演奏——她喜欢这样，我们以为你不会介意。"

"介意？噢，不会的——啊，她那颗可爱的心想要什么就给她什么吧。你们俩对她多好啊，对我多好啊！上帝永远保佑你们！"

听了一会儿后又说：

"多么美妙的声音！这是她的风琴，是她自己在演奏吧，你说呢？"微弱、深沉、鼓舞人心的合唱通过寂静的空气飘进她耳中。"是的，是她在演奏，我的心肝宝贝，我听出来了。她们在唱，啊——这是颂歌[①]！所有歌声中最神圣、最感人、最安慰人的……就像天堂的大门向我敞开一样……如果现在我能死去……"

寂静之中升起这样的歌词，既遥远又缥缈：

愿我主与我相亲，

靠近我主，

① 圣歌，颂歌，赞美诗。基督教徒用于崇敬上帝的歌曲，通常由会众咏唱。源自希腊语 hymnos（意为"赞美之歌"）。

E'en though it be a cross
That raiseth me.

With the closing of the hymn another soul passed to its rest, and they that had been one in life were not sundered in death. The sisters, mourning and rejoicing, said:

"How blessed it was that she never knew!"

9

At midnight they sat together, grieving, and the angel of the Lord appeared in the midst transfigured with a radiance not of earth; and speaking, said:

"For liars a place is appointed. There they burn in the fires of hell from everlasting unto everlasting. Repent!"

The bereaved fell upon their knees before him and clasped their hands and bowed their gray heads, adoring. But their tongues clove to the roof of their mouths, and they were dumb.

"Speak! that I may bear the message to the chancery of heaven and bring again the decree from which there is no appeal."

Then they bowed their heads yet lower, and one said:

"Our sin is great, and we suffer shame; but only perfect and final repentance can make us whole; and we are poor creatures who have learned our human weakness, and we know that if we were in those hard straits again our hearts would fail again,

尽管那是个十字架
将我托起。[1]

颂歌结束时，另外一个灵魂也安息了。她们生前就是一体，死后也不会分开，姐妹俩悲喜交加地说：

“真庆幸她从不知道！”

九

半夜时，她们悲伤地坐在一起，上帝的使者[2]出现了，笼罩在一片人间没有的光彩中，光芒四射。他说：

“撒谎者有一个指定的地方。他们将在地狱之火中忍受永远的煎熬。忏悔吧！”

丧亲者在他面前跪了下来，紧合双手，低下那灰白色的头，祈祷着。但是她们的舌头紧贴住上颚，哑口无言。

“说吧！我可以把消息带给天庭的法官，然后再从他那儿带回不可上诉的天命。”

她们把头压得更低了，其中一个说：

“我们的罪孽深重，我们忍受着耻辱，只有最终、最完美的忏悔才能保持灵魂的完整。我们这些可怜的人，了解到自己人性的软弱，如果再次处在那种艰难的困境下，我们的内心还会无能为力，我们还会像以前那样犯罪。强者可以获胜，然后被拯救，但是我们已

---

① 《更近我主》，作者莎拉•F.亚当斯(Sarah Flower Adams, 1805—1848)，英国女诗人。
② 耶和华的使者，是服役的灵，奉差遣为那将要承受救恩的人效力。

and we should sin as before. The strong could prevail, and so be saved, but we are lost."

They lifted their heads in supplication. The angel was gone. While they marveled and wept he came again; and bending low, he whispered the decree.

10

Was it Heaven? Or Hell?

经迷失了。”

她们抬起头来，想要乞求。但天使已经走了。她们正在为此惊奇、伤心流泪时，天使又来了；他深深弯下腰，低声传达了上天的旨意。

十

上天堂？还是下地狱[1]？

① 地狱，遭厌弃、受诅咒的地方。基督教则称不信仰耶稣的恶人于末日审判后在地狱受永罚。